Queer Visibilities

RGS-IBG Book Series

Queer Visibilities

Space, Identity and Interaction in Cape Town

Andrew Tucker

WILEY-BLACKWELL

A John Wiley & Sons, Ltd., Publication

Blackwell Publishing was acquired by John Wiley & Sons in February 2007. Blackwell's publishing program has been merged with Wiley's global Scientific, Technical, and Medical business to form Wiley-Blackwell.

Registered Office
John Wiley & Sons Ltd, The Atrium, Southern Gate, Chichester, West Sussex, PO19 8SQ, United Kingdom

Editorial Offices
350 Main Street, Malden, MA 02148-5020, USA
9600 Garsington Road, Oxford, OX4 2DQ, UK
The Atrium, Southern Gate, Chichester, West Sussex, PO19 8SQ, UK

For details of our global editorial offices, for customer services, and for information about how to apply for permission to reuse the copyright material in this book please see our website at www.wiley.com/wiley-blackwell.

The right of Andrew Tucker to be identified as the author of this work has been asserted in accordance with the Copyright, Designs and Patents Act 1988.

Library of Congress Cataloging-in-Publication Data

Tucker, Andrew, 1980–
    Queer visibilities : space, identity, and interaction in Cape Town / Andrew Tucker.
        p.   cm.—(RGS-IBG book series)
    Includes bibliographical references and index.
    ISBN 978-1-4051-8303-1 (hardcover : alk. paper)—ISBN 978-1-4051-8302-4 (pbk. : alk. paper) 1. Gay men—South Africa—Cape Town—Social conditions. 2. Sexual orientation—South Africa—Cape Town. 3. Sex discrimination—South Africa—Cape Town. 4. Gay men—Identity. 5. Cape Town (South Africa)—Social conditions. I. Title.
    HQ76.2.S6T83 2009
    306.76′6209687355—dc22

                                                                                                2008024001

A catalogue record for this book is available from the British Library.

Set in 10 on 12pt Plantin by SNP Best-set Typesetter Ltd., Hong Kong

1   2009

Contents

Figures and Tables

Figures

Unless otherwise stated all photographs taken by and © the author.

Tables

Series Editors' Preface

The RGS-IBG Book Series only publishes work of the highest international standing. Its emphasis is on distinctive new developments in human and physical geography, although it is also open to contributions from cognate disciplines whose interests overlap with those of geographers. The Series places strong emphasis on theoretically-informed and empirically-strong texts. Reflecting the vibrant and diverse theoretical and empirical agendas that characterize the contemporary discipline, contributions are expected to inform, challenge and stimulate the reader. Overall, the RGS-IBG Book Series seeks to promote scholarly publications that leave an intellectual mark and change the way readers think about particular issues, methods or theories.

For details on how to submit a proposal please visit:
www.rgsbookseries.com

Kevin Ward
University of Manchester, UK

Joanna Bullard
Loughborough University, UK

RGS–IBG Book Series Editors

Acknowledgements

E·S·R·C
ECONOMIC
& SOCIAL
RESEARCH
COUNCIL
This book was made possible with the assistance of the Economic & Social Research Council of the UK.
    I say with absolute certainty that had it not been for the continual support of my PhD supervisor, Gerry Kearns, this book would not have come about. It is with equal certainty that I say Gerry is one of the most kind, thoughtful and intelligent people I have ever met. My time at Cambridge has been immeasurably enriched by knowing Gerry and being able to explore and think about the world with him in ways that I had never thought possible. It is therefore with great thanks that I dedicate this book to him. Cheers, mate.

In South Africa I could not have survived without the help of so many individuals. I would especially like to thank Marina Griebenow for always being there to pick me up and dust me off whenever life in the city became a bit too *hectic*. As a continual source of kindness and information about the Mother City she helped set me on the course that concluded with this book. Cape Town is a better place with her living in it.

I would also like to give a big thank you to the staff of Triangle Project, the Gay and Lesbian Archives of South Africa (GALA) and all the other organisations I met and got to know. Thanks therefore go to Dawn Betteridge, Anthony Manion, Toni Sylvester, Mabhuti Mkangeli, Funeka Soldaat and Vista Kalipa. In particular, I'd like to acknowledge and thank Glenn de Swardt for showing me not only the breadth and depth of the city of Cape Town, but also how to cope with its extremes. Over the years that I have known him, Glenn has worked tirelessly to achieve a better world for all queer individuals in the city. It is perhaps an indicator of both his humility and effort that today so many queer men and women in the city do not even know how he has helped them. South Africa is a country that, despite its problems, has achieved so much good for so many in such a short period of time. To continue astounding the world, it will need more individuals like Glenn.

A special word of thanks also needs to be extended to Paul Wise for battling through countless hours of tape and transcribing the most muffled comments into comprehensible prose. Thanks also need to be extended to Leon Kruger (for all those chats, coffees and nights out) and to Sharad Chari, Ismail Jazbhay, Vasu Reddy, Graeme Reid, Teresa Dirsuweit, Peter van der Walt; David Stoch, Nathan Romburgh, Alex Hivoltze-Jimenez and Jean Mearing for their friendship and assistance. And lastly on that note, a big thank you to David Stockwell, my *consiglieri* on the Cape (and then later in London). As a sounding board and as a friend, David made the whole process of researching and then writing just that much more enjoyable.

In Cambridge a big shout-out also needs to go to Jane Robinson, Jane Hampshire and Robert Carter for helping me source so much information. Further thanks to Philip Stickler for applying his prodigious skills to help create the maps in this book. Thanks also to Simon Reid-Henry, Steve Legg, Karen Till, Richard Smith, Phil Howell, Jim Duncan, Liz Watson, David Nally, Steve Trudgill, Stu Basten, Hannah Weston, Tom Welsh, Andrew Rudd, Marco Wan, Andrew Ferguson, David Beckingham, Fran Moore, Rory Gallagher and Jacob Levy for their friendship through thick and thin.

In a similar yet also unique vein, a big thank you to Fran Sainsbury for always bringing with her a moment of calm, fun and friendship. From 'spiders making gravy' to the RCSA to life as adults you've stayed a person I know I'll always love and respect.

A big thank you also to Kevin Ward, editor at the RGS-IBG Book Series, for his encouragement and support. At Wiley-Blackwell a huge debt of gratitude needs to be paid to Jacqueline Scott and Hannah Morrell for their highly professional help in guiding my book through the process towards publication. And a further shout-out to Kit Scorah for applying her truly excellent and tireless copy-editing skills to this book.

Thank you also to Jon Binnie and Jennifer Robinson for their constructive comments on earlier drafts of this work.

A special thank you also to Mum and Dad and my sister, Ronnie. To each of you in different and yet equally important ways I say how grateful I am, knowing that you have always been there for me along the way. And I state with the deepest love how proud I am to be related to you.

And lastly, to Richard Nkulikiyinka for keeping me sane and filled with happiness.

Chapter One

Queer Visibilities in Cape Town

Introduction

At the end of 2006 South Africa joined a very small, yet very special club. Indeed, this club was so special that, since its creation at the beginning of the new millennium, it had lead to incessant discussion among many other nations. While very few other countries seemed particularly enthusiastic about joining its membership, several spent a remarkably large amount of time explaining why those who had joined were mistaken in doing so. Commentators in nations stretching from the Middle East to Eastern Europe to Africa all appeared to believe that membership must never be sanctioned and, if possible, should be actively legislated against.[1] The President of the United States even went so far as to suggest subscribing to the club's ideas might imperil the 'most fundamental institution of civilisation'.[2] This was therefore, in some ways, not only a special, but also apparently a rather dangerous club.

South Africa had decided to grant same-sex couples the right to marry. It joined the Netherlands, Belgium, Spain and Canada. The legalisation of same-sex marriage has helped position South Africa as the most progressive country on the entire continent. Nationally, same-sex marriage has been held up as one of the strongest examples of the country's move away from an intolerant past – a past now more associated with the opponents of same-sex marriage than with the current South African government. Some might fairly argue that such achievements have been well worth the hyperbole from 'less progressive' countries.

And indeed, the achievement of South Africa in this regard should not be underestimated. In just one and a half decades the country has gone from persecuting and arresting individuals with same-sex desire, to allowing them to adopt children and marry. No other country has so radically changed its position towards queer individuals or the world's perception of itself in such a short period of time.

Yet while such achievements have indeed been admirable, the legal rights attained do not necessarily equate to daily improvements in the lives of many queer South Africans. While, *de jure*, queer citizens in South Africa now have the ability to marry, *de facto*, many still cannot. And while cities such as Cape Town are able to boast about their liberal and accepting stance towards queer individuals, the reality on the ground for many, even in Cape Town, may be considerably different. This book explores this gap between liberal law and the more dangerous reality for groups of queer men in Cape Town.

To understand this gap requires first an acknowledgement of the diversity of queer experiences in the country and, as this book will show, the diversity across urban space in one particular city.[3] As researchers in other locations have shown, the variety of community experiences that make up queer existence across the globe is truly staggering (Cruz-Malavé and Manalansan 2002; Hayes 2000; Jackson and Sullivan 1999; Parker 1999; Patton and Sánchez-Eppler 2000; Reid-Pharr 2002). An attempt to understand any local queer community therefore requires a detailed exploration of the many issues that have affected, and continue to affect, it. Yet in a country such as South Africa, queer experiences are further complicated by the extraordinary way in which communities have historically been spatially regulated by the state. The use of 'race' as the basis of a system of discrimination has left the country with deep social, economic and political scars. Queer communities today have therefore also remained strongly influenced by the way colonial and later apartheid mechanisms compartmentalised, regulated and manipulated groups.

Indeed, while the regulation of difference based on 'race' has been well documented in South Africa, the direct effect it had on different queer communities has yet to be systematically explored. In large part this stems from barriers in gaining access to different communities. The legacy of apartheid makes it difficult to gain entrance and acceptance within communities historically segregated in the urban environment. Yet the lack of detailed cross-community research also perhaps signifies a greater problem, namely that of being able to explore the numerous nuanced ways different communities dealt with ideas of same-sex desire. By taking a geographical approach, this book will show how individuals from the three main historically and racially defined population groups in the city of Cape Town have come to understand and represent queer sexuality in remarkably different yet also related ways. It will be shown that in large part this is due to the different ways the apartheid state attempted to categorise and spatially contain them.

Only once this is achieved will it be possible to begin to understand why changes in South African law, while clearly laudable, remain marginal to the vast majority of queer individuals in the country. As many commentators have noted, the ending of apartheid in South Africa has not meant an ending to inequality or discrimination (Bollens 1998a; Lodge 2002; Saff 1994; Turok 2001). To truly begin to explore different queer communities in South Africa today is therefore also to set out on a journey that examines the social and political interactions of these groups. So much of South Africa's past is based on different communities' perceptions of themselves in relation to other, often neighbouring communities. The same is true for queer communities.

This is therefore a book that will examine the way different, specifically male, queer communities have been able to lead open and free lives, the problems and possibilities of cross-community interaction and the way these subjects and events have been shaped by the unique history of the country. The remainder of this chapter reviews a number of studies of queer groups and argues that a different approach is needed for Cape Town queer communities if their lives are ever to be adequately understood.

A Question of Visibility

The approach used by this book can be summed up by the notion of queer visibility. At its core, this is a geographical concept that examines how queer groups are able to overcome the heteronormativity of particular urban spaces; the options that are available for them to do so; the perception of the decision to undertake certain visibilities by different members of their own community and those of others; and the problems and possibilities of groups interacting based in large part on these very divergent visibilities. It is therefore more than simply an exploration of queer public performances. Neither is it a study which presupposes that visibility by itself is a positive outcome.[4] Rather, it is a study of how groups perceive themselves and each other in relation to their own community structures, the structures of others and the problems of social and political exchange.

In a city such as Cape Town, such visibilities will also be directly tied to the way communities were defined by artificial and arbitrary classifications of 'race'. As will be explored below, apartheid was at its core a spatial strategy, and as such, resulted in different 'racially-defined' communities being located at different points within the urban environment. If heteronormativity is viewed not as a monolithic entity, but as a type of regulative power dependent on other structures in society, then the options to overcome it must also depend on the factors that initially affect it. In Cape Town this means that queer visibilities will be strongly affected by the way apartheid's racial classifications impacted on different communities in different ways. What can be made visible to the wider community, and why it can, depends in large part on the racial history of the country and of this one city. Equally, to understand how groups are able to interact with each other requires understanding how they view each other and how they view each other's interactions with heteronormativity. These interactions will also be directly affected by the very factors that led to the development of different visibilities in the first place. In this way, the successes different queer communities have in becoming visible within their own communities can also be tempered by their ability or inability to stay visible when interacting with other communities. As this book will show, the problems faced by some queer communities in Cape Town mean it becomes very easy for them to remain invisible when attempting group interaction. Such invisibility can have dire consequences.

An approach such as this one will hopefully also help move scholars beyond an impasse of either looking at 'global'/'Western' forms of queer expression or looking at 'local homosexualities'. As William Spurlin (2001) correctly argues, there is as much danger for scholars from the West in inadvertently homogenising sexualities elsewhere within an almost imperialist Western framework as there is for European or North American cultural modes of production to usurp those found elsewhere. A process whereby the global is understood through the local, where agency remains central, and where difference is seen to be relational will help limit the dangers correctly highlighted by scholars such as Spurlin.

It will also help limit the problems encountered by scholars such as Natalie Oswin (2005) who argue that it remains difficult and dubious to analytically prise apart 'Western' identities and identities found in Africa. While Oswin is correct to highlight the fallacy of assuming a monolithic 'Western' gay identity or a wholly knowable and separate 'African homosexual culture', it becomes decidedly problematic to argue, as she does, that there is no imposing Western queerness or resistant African homosexual culture in the construction of the very successful international marketing initiative of 'gay Cape Town'.[5] As will be explored in more detail in the following sections, Oswin perhaps arrives at her conclusion as a result of the way she attempts to explore what exactly might be included within a category such as 'African homosexuality' or 'gay Cape Town'. A study of visibility initially shifts the focus of debate away from broader concerns over subjectivity or catch-all identity labels and their relationship to at times equally nebulous 'global flows', and instead first moves back to the core concern as to *how* groups have over time been able to position themselves in relation to their local heteronormative communities in particular locations in the urban environment. An attempt to find a direct comparison between Western queerness and African specificity amongst even a particular elite subset of a wider dynamic community without first excavating such histories runs the conceptual risk of sidelining the multifaceted, contradictory and at times exploitative interactions queer groups can subsequently have with other queers in the city. This in turn runs the risk of marginalising the dramatically divergent effects that the representation of 'gay Cape Town' has had on diverse groups of queers and the way such a representation is worked with, contested or confronted. Overlooking such complexity therefore also runs the risk of being unable to see where exactly each community may find repeated tension (or solidarity) with any other.

As the following sections will discuss, queer visibility is therefore an attempt to explore why difference may or may not exist within and between communities and how visibility and appreciation of difference depends on the way groups have developed elsewhere. It therefore also initially shifts the argument away from 'the global' or 'the local' and instead focuses on how difference becomes possible when communities interact internally. It then becomes possible to see how within different areas of a city like Cape Town difference is represented *by the communities themselves* through an appreciation of their own history – linked to apartheid and their own understanding of communities elsewhere. There is, therefore, an 'imposing Western queerness', but one that is filtered through a local lens. There is also without any doubt whatsoever a 'resistant homosexual culture', but one defined by a centuries-old history, that was shaped by pre-colonial, colonial, apartheid and post-apartheid ideologies. Today, as this study will show, it represents itself as a set of distinct visibilities precisely because it sees what is made visible in different spaces in the city (for example, among those who frequent the city's gay village). There are no simple binaries of 'the West and the rest' but instead communities with remarkably different histories that partly depend on each other today to exist at all. These groups can draw inspiration from 'the West' *and* from communities in Africa (or South East Asia). They are, however, to follow the schema taken up by Natalie Oswin, resistant to each other precisely because of their histories and the at times antagonistic relationships due to those histories. To argue otherwise would be to ignore not only the history of these communities but also the importance of acknowledging and safeguarding the needs of diverse queer individuals in Cape Town.

Yet a book that sets itself on such a trajectory immediately runs into some serious epistemological, methodological and ethical dilemmas. One of the most pressing is the issue of definition. Who, in other words, is this book meant to be exploring? And closely tied to that, how is the choice of subject justified? To put it another way, who is queer and how are they made visible? How can such terms be used for divergent groups in the urban environment? And how is a 'group' defined? To explore these issues, the next four sections will question and examine both the pertinent developments in queer studies and the formation of race-based discrimination in South Africa. The next section will briefly examine the trajectory of queer geography over the past thirty years. This discussion will lead directly into some questions in the next two sections concerning what we actually mean when we talk about sexual identities, ideas of 'the closet' and the relevance of 'queer' in post-colonial environments when seen in relation to visibility. The last two sections will examine how issues of race and questions of visibility remain tied to each other in Cape Town and wider South Africa.

Questioning the Sites and Categories of Study

For much of the past two to three decades, sexuality studies, queer studies and particularly queer geography have been concerned with understanding and explaining the lives of individuals with same-sex desire in ways that illuminate both the reasons for particular types of classification, regulation and discrimination and the strategies to end concealment of particular desires due to such discrimination (Brown et al. 2007). As one of the founders of what came to be known as queer theory, Michel Foucault, famously explained, the development of nineteenth-century Western discursive power, tied intrinsically to regulative techniques, brought into being 'the homosexual' and along with it its medicalisation and methods of control.[6] From this standpoint, scholars have been interested in unpacking how such control has evolved and how to confront or manipulate it. Historical studies such as Chauncey (1994), Houlbrook (2005) and Peniston (2004) on same-sex communities in major urban environments and more recent work on the evolution of Western forms of gay identity and rights-based political action tied to critiques of its essentialism (strategic, for example Armstrong (2002), Seidman (1993) and Wilchins (2004) or otherwise Nast (2002) and Schulmann (1998)) have all greatly enhanced our understanding.

Specifically from within geography, interest in 'gay spaces' has focused on a nexus of territory, transgression and identity (Binnie and Valentine 1999). In other words, what geographers have brought to the party is a foregrounding of the very spatiality of sexuality, its (re)production and regulation. For example, geographers have researched the politicisation, representation and contestation of sexual identity across different urban spaces and the transgression of nominally heterosexualised public and private spaces at a variety of scales (Aldrich 2004; Bell et al. 1994; Bell and Valentine 1995a; Phillips 2004). Manuel Castells was one of the first to bring together some of these ideas through his work on San Francisco (1983), where he explored the links between residential districts, voting patterns and social movements. By so doing, he created an early blueprint for examining the spatial and political dynamics of sexuality that has remained important (see for example Ingram et al. 1997). Geographers have therefore also gone on to explore how gay men have been viewed as an important element in urban regeneration, the gentrification of the city and as an element that could recreate parts of the city as new spaces of consumption and liberation (Bell and Binnie 2004; Binnie 1995; Chisholm 2005; Forest 1995; Knopp 1992 and 1998; Quilley 1997). In political terms, geographers have studied urban responses to AIDS (Brown 1997) and political transgressions 'outside' gay spaces, such as Pride marches and other interventions (Bell 1994; Brickell 2000; Davis 1995; Luongo 2002; Pourtavaf 2004). On a wider scale, sexual citizenship has been developed as a dynamic arena for relating issues of sexuality to the nation, state and globe (Altman 2001; Bell and Binnie 2000 and 2004; Waitt 2005). For Mitchell (2000) a central issue in this work concerns the sort of spaces where different sexual identities can develop and negotiate with others. Drawing here on Chauncey (1994), Mitchell explains a central theme running through much work on queer geography: 'like any social relationship, sexuality is inherently spatial – it depends on particular spaces for its construction and in turn produces and reproduces the spaces in which sexuality can be, and was, forged' (Mitchell 2000: 175).

But such studies have also been cast into relief by a growing body of work that examines the problems of relying on 'Westernised' gay communities and spaces as sites of study. While the importance of urban territories for gay-identified men has proven an important area of work, it does tend to ignore other groups who have not located themselves in such spaces (Brown and Staeheli 2003). Some of the earliest work in this field dealt with lesbian spaces through the city (Adler and Brenner 1992; Rothenberg 1995; Valentine 1993 and 1995). Other work has focused on individuals who live away from major urban areas, where attention has been paid to issues of rural lives and sexual identity (Bell and Valentine 1995b; Kramer 1995; Phillips et al. 2000; White 1980) and how the mythic space of the city acts as an important draw for individuals wanting to 'come out' (Brown 2000; Weston 1995).

Taking this a step further, increasing numbers of researchers are now exploring entirely non-Western and non-urban spaces in relation to same-sex desire. For example Byrne (2005), Hoad (2000), Moodie (1988 and 2001), Murray (2000), Spurlin (2001) and Patton and Sánchez-Eppler (2000) have helped destabilise many of the norms upon which 'traditional' gay and lesbian studies have been posited, shifting the focus away from 'metropolitan' environments towards the 'periphery' (Sinfield 1998). In these locations different configurations of sexuality and space start to materialise. Such configurations therefore also call into question the very way in which commentators have tried to categorise and rationalise the communities they study and the power that enacts on them. While the studies outlined earlier in this section have helped develop an important roadmap for understanding sexualities of difference, they can also be seen to be guided by certain assumptions that may not be applicable elsewhere. Consequently, for a study such as this one that includes numerous communities who understand sexuality in divergent ways, it becomes imperative to see how they may wish to subscribe to beliefs in ways both familiar and different to those traditionally found in queer studies and queer geographies. By remaining focused on a geographical approach to sexuality, it therefore becomes vital to unpack quite what we mean when we talk about identities and the limits and opportunities of expression associated with them in different spaces. Specifically, we need to be acutely aware of the histories behind ideas such as 'the closet', 'heteronormativity' and 'the queer' and how they relate to different spaces in very different yet compelling ways.

Questioning 'the Closet'

The more recent studies outlined above in new locations have allowed a re-evaluation of some of the fundamental tenets of the queer academy. Specifically, commentators have had to re-evaluate how 'the closet' has been viewed as the defining structure of gay oppression during the twentieth century (Sedgwick 1990). For a series of queer scholars schooled in post-structural thought in the 1990s, 'the closet' became an exemplary way of understanding how power/knowledge operates in society to regulate sexuality (Latimer 2004). As many of the works cited above acknowledge, an exploration of 'the closet' allows for a discussion of how the concealment and denial of homosexuality as a discrete sexual identity in society works to reinforce the heterosexual/homosexual binary and hence (following Derrida's (1982) concerns as to the unequal power relationships between different parts of the binary) the dominance of heterosexuality in society. For example, 'the closet' itself is continually maintained, since being 'out' of 'the closet' also requires the pre-existence of somewhere and somehow being 'in' 'the closet' too. Hence, the binary and the mechanism around which the binary functions are seen to be mutually reinforced. This powerful critique of the way modern society is able to regulate the hetero/homo divide also goes to strengthen queer political projects. Specifically, 'the closet' and 'coming out' have remained powerful mechanisms through which to engage political rights-based movements, both in the West and elsewhere (Hoad 2000; Human Rights Campaign 2004; Weeks 1990).

Geographically as well, 'the closet' has proved a powerful conceptual tool. While not necessarily always explicitly mentioned, it still forms the basis of much work on 'gay space'. After all, the regulation of space generally as heteronormative allows for a study of spaces which are not. The most prominent study of this type is Michael Brown's (2000) *Closet Space*. The aim of this study was to explore how power/knowledge signified by 'the closet' must actually occur in particular places at particular scales. For Brown, it was therefore crucial to see how 'the closet' works as more than just a linguistic metaphor, but rather to examine how it has a geography. As Brown explains:

> By its spatiality the closet is a material strategy and tactic: one that conceals, erases and makes gay people invisible and unknown. Because it is such a common, central term in gay and lesbian life, it implies a ubiquity and multidimensionality that suggests an exploration across a wide variety of spatial scales and locations . . . It simultaneously presented itself at several spatial scales from the body, to the city, to the nation, and finally to the globe. (p. 141)

'The closet' therefore has helped frame an understanding of how queer sexuality has been oppressed by examining the way the heterosexual/homosexual binary has been operationalised. From within geography, a primary concern has been exploring exactly where this oppression occurs and to see how the spatiality of power/knowledge itself goes to bring 'the closet' into existence in the first place (see also Knopp 1994). These are clearly powerful and relevant pursuits. Indeed, the continued framing of 'the closet' in personal 'coming out' narratives and more broad-based queer political projects points to the centrality of the term in the lives of many queer individuals. Yet as other commentators have explored, 'the closet' may not necessarily be relevant to a great many other queer groups.

As Seidman (1998) explains, one of the central beliefs on which much early work on 'the closet' was based, when seen in relation to its interface with issues of identity and community action, argued that there must already exist a formed sexual self. 'The closet' in much contemporary literature has therefore come to represent a barrier that needs to be broken through. Despite queer theory's warnings concerning unitary and fixed identity categories, the subject and their identity are thus often already seen to exist prior to their 'coming out'. This means that there still can remain an assumption that a 'coming out' represents the end of inauthenticity and self-alienation for the individual and the wider community. In turn, those that have yet to 'come out' can therefore easily be viewed as suffering from some sort of 'false consciousness' whereby they are yet to be saved by gay politics (Binnie 2004). In this reading 'the closet' tends overwhelmingly to manifest itself around a belief that all those with queer desire should be honest about their (already in existence) identity.

Even more problematically, this leads to the conceptually dangerous (and indeed in some instances, neo-colonial, see below) argument that those who do not free themselves of 'the closet' – and who do not do so in *particular ways* – are, quite simply, in denial and suffering from an 'outdated', 'pre-modern' and possibly secretive mode of sexual identity (Hayes 2000). For example, men who engage in sex with other men, yet who view themselves – and are seen by others – as heterosexual and do not see their identity as inauthentic fail to fit within 'the closet' schema (ibid.). To take that argument a step further, those men who do view themselves as homosexual yet overwhelmingly seek out sexual relationships with men who view themselves as heterosexual to sustain their own sexual identity are also skirting the borders of what would be 'acceptable' given the liberationist ideal associated with 'the closet'.

The root cause of this problem is that within much contemporary thought, 'the closet' *itself* remains based on the existence and the history of a particular type of Western European and North American queer subject – and one that can only exist with a particular rigid heterosexual/homosexual binary relationship. This subject persists in a strongly oppositional relationship to heterosexuality, whereby its own identity can only gain authenticity when placed in somewhat public and open opposition to heterosexuality. Any discussion of 'the closet' is therefore in danger of reifying a relationship between 'normal' and 'other' – in effect bringing that relationship and parts of the binary into existence and ignoring all others.[7]

'The closet' as schema for study therefore can become problematic when applied to communities that do not place such prominence on proclaiming a particular 'authentic' sexual identity located around a particular Western European 'closet' binary (Howell 2007; Quiroga 2000; Reid-Pharr 2002; Ross 2005; Wallace 2002).[8] Different individuals will relate to heterosexual society/societies in different ways and therefore may chose to 'come out' but do so in ways that might not lead to unilateral ideals of sexual 'liberation' in direct antagonism to secrecy and oppression and a 'knowing by not knowing' commonly associated with 'the closet'. Relying solely on 'the closet' can cause conceptual harm to those who do not subscribe to its sometimes stringent effect on understanding identities, communities and political action and also cause harm to those who might relate to it in very different and at times conflicting ways.

Perhaps understandably therefore, scholars working in post-colonial contexts in particular have decided to err away from using 'the closet' as a way of exploring sexual identities of different communities. A great deal of this work has instead tended to focus on the uniqueness of particular forms of sexual identity in different racialised locations or on the way these identities are later affected by and in turn affect Western influences (see Jackson

2001). Works by commentators such as Moodie (1998 and 2001), Murray
and Roscoe (1998) and Epprecht (2004) have tried to historicize the experiences of groups in places such as sub-Saharan Africa, in part to explain
exactly why their understanding of sexual identity may be so different to
those mostly studied in key sites in the West. Other work, such as Herdt's
(1994), has explored effeminate gender identities and their relationships to
forms of non-heteronormativity. Some of this scholarship has also therefore
ended up calling into question whether it is even possible to call some of
these groups 'homosexual'. Indeed, it again becomes increasingly apparent
that 'the closet' and much of Western society's understanding of 'the homosexual' only work when played out in relation to each other. To refer back
to Foucault, the creation of 'the species' of 'the homosexual' perhaps only
works within a rather narrow epistemological framework. And that framework requires 'the closet'.

This, of course, is not to argue that in these new locations there is an
absence of same-sex desire. Neither is it to argue that there is no naming
of difference. In any community where same-sex desire is seen, as Halperin
(2002) might term it, as 'a means of personal identification', then some
reason must exist as to why identification should occur because of it. In
other words, there must be some understanding of dissimilarity. What these
new studies point out, however, are the remarkably different ways in which
some variant of a heterosexual/homosexual binary formation plays out. This
is not to assume that the 'creation' of a Foucauldian conception of 'the
homosexual' exists. Rather it is to acknowledge that a binary of some sort
must exist. In this light, 'the closet' becomes just one way of conceptualising
this how this difference is manifest – and hence a Foucauldian concept of
'the homosexual' as a medicalised entity becomes just one way of naming
that difference. (As described below, 'homosexuality' and 'homosexual' are
therefore used in the following chapters only when discussing this particular way of naming sexual difference and not in other instances.)[9]

What can therefore be taken from 'the closet' is the way it initially forces
us to examine how a particular heterosexual/homosexual binary has actually worked and is reproduced within a Western culture. 'The closet' is by
definition directly caught up in the concept of personal identification. It
therefore forces us to see how that identification is applied to individuals,
by examining the power enacted on individuals to bring a subject position
into being (and how subjects themselves can discursively reiterate such
power). As described above, it can however tend to remain fixed into a
particular narrative defined through a particular historically regulated interpretation of concealment and then a particular interpretation of openness.
As such it has perhaps also narrowed the way in which researchers attempt
to understand sexualised communities and cross-community interaction,
normalising certain life stories, social structures and methods of openness

to the detriment of others. Consequently, this fixity can then result in an easy teleological developmentalist (and at times, neo-colonial) progression towards 'modern' gay identities and more lately 'queer' identities (Binnie 2004) (see below). These identities often remain knowingly or unknowingly anchored to ideas of 'the closet' and lead into particular ideas of sexual identity liberation, 'gay spaces', political representation in opposition to 'traditional values' and the development of civil society rights and legal rights such as 'gay marriage' without much appreciation for how they affect diverse communities in diverse locations. For researchers, it therefore can become easy to only look at the end result of such developments, and fail to see the historical specificity that allowed those developments to emerge. Once this step has occurred it becomes hard to fully conceptualise or appreciate how other groups located within different political histories in different places with different variations on the heterosexual/homosexual binary relate to this narrative.

What emerges, as a result, are three options. The first, as already mentioned, is an important acknowledgement that there are indeed different ways in which communities have appreciated sexual diversity and the naming of difference. As the studies highlighted above have explored, this has led to an appreciation that there is indeed difference 'out there'. At a foundational and key level, these studies repositioned Western studies of sexuality within a wider set of practices and discourses. Yet second, there has also been a concerted effort to understand how difference itself must relate to what is increasingly being referred to as the 'global gay' – the supposed exportation of a particular sexualised culture that originated mostly in North American 'gay spaces' to locations elsewhere in the world. For some, this has meant exploring how issues of commodification and its association with neo-liberal forms of citizenship work in new locations, creating sometimes hybrid forms (Altman 2001). Yet understandably, a variant of this body of work has questioned quite why such cultural, social and economic flows must always be only from the West to the rest of the world (Oswin 2006). Indeed, a focus solely on unidirectional cultural flows is in danger of reifying a neo-colonial gaze onto communities elsewhere. It is also in danger of reinforcing the supposed hegemony of sexualised identities located around a Western 'closet' structure. Therefore, third, there has also developed a growing body of work that has tried to be more self-reflexive about the relationships between different communities (see, for example, Bacchetta 2002; Jackson 2001; Manalansan 1995; Parker 1999; Puar 2002). At its best, this work has successfully shown the strategic ways in which local communities have selectively appropriated, re-imagined or reconstructed specific Western influences while rejecting others. This work highlights an egalitarian strand within work on cultural diffusion, showing us the ways in which knowledge is reproduced and re-articulated through diverse social structures and human agents at a variety of scales. Yet while this work is important and vital, there are also two distinct dangers that at other times can emerge, both of which relate to a broader problem of failing to explore the geographical specificity of communities and taking as read the existence of a Western 'closet'.

The first danger comes, quite simply, by focusing at the level of representation and limiting an understanding as to how materialities that surround, limit and give opportunity to different communities can go to affect such representations.[10] Looking only for hybridity or capitulation to particular Western global flows as an 'end point' is to completely miss out an understanding of the 'building blocks' that go to inform the idea of identities founded upon attraction to one's own sex in different locations in the first instance. Issues of concern here must surely include historical race-based discrimination and segregation, long-standing gross economic inequalities, spatial dislocation, the constant threat of HIV/AIDS tied to inequitable access to education and health care services, the effects of violent crime and contemporary racism. These factors must certainly be seen to work both in affecting material constraints and in offering specific avenues of change and development. For example, as Marlon B. Ross (2005) has explored, 'the closet' as an epistemological guide towards understanding identity and interaction fails to work in some inner-city African American and Latino communities precisely because of some of these factors.[11] Some men who engage in same-sex sexual relationships within such spaces have very little in common with those traditionally researched in studies of 'Western gay spaces'. Their identities are known about amongst themselves and some elements of wider heteronormative society and their anxiety or pride in their own identity function around a variant of the heterosexual/homosexual binary. And yet concerns to seek some form of 'authenticity' are far from their primary concern. Groups such as those highlighted by Ross (2005) have traditionally received relatively little research attention. This issue in turn leads to the second problem, which is an inability to focus down on the actual spaces in which different identities emerge and relate to each other. When conducting cross-community research, it is surely vital to explore the relational effect that spaces and the groups that live within those spaces have on each other in the same city. Therefore, it is also vital to understand and unpack how different communities with very different histories might have remarkably different variants of the heterosexual/homosexual binary (and hence readings related to, or very dissimilar from 'the closet') which go to inform their views of others and their position and understanding of themselves in relation to others. At an extreme, a limited acknowledgement of these issues can lead to the false assumption, even when only looking at a particular commodified subset of a wider dynamic community, that there is no direct 'resistance' to global or particular cultural flows to begin with – or that too great acknowledgement of such local resistance on the part of researchers is to compartmentalise and 'romanticise' local cultures and their own agency (see, for example, Oswin 2005).

In other words, the local specificity as to how some variant of the heterosexual/homosexual binary – and hence heteronormativity – located around issues such as race and class and the spaces in which these issues play out may not always be sufficiently explored. This is strongly conditioned by an overzealous attention towards issues of representation without exploring the materiality that wraps around such identities. Concurrently, it seems that sometimes hidden behind a concern for acknowledging sexualised difference are the remnants of a very Western 'closet' schema – one that is looking towards, or searching first for, particular sexualised identities, without appreciating the diversity of histories that could lead to the development of different identities associated with different challenges to begin with. This in turn limits the view of researchers attempting to understand difference.

This book therefore suggests that a key step that must be taken when attempting to undertake cross-community research in a city such as Cape Town is to understand first the ways in which different queer groups relate to wider heteronormative groups within their own communities in particular historically racially-segregated spaces. Then it is to understand how such relationships are understood by, and go towards affecting, others. This is not to reify local difference and set it in stone. It is also therefore not to assume that a category such as 'white gay man' is neatly bounded. Rather, it is to understand how an appreciation of such differences by different communities *themselves* must be understood to contribute to and help render the ways each develops. In effect, this book is therefore calling for a greater geographical appreciation as to the options different communities have in overcoming the heteronormativity of particular spaces – to become visible in space – so as to better understand how they subsequently interact across space – and only then, how each might relate to, for example, global or transcultural flows. It is calling for a greater awareness of how queers have been able to relate to very different manifestations of the heterosexual/homosexual binary tied to different variants of heteronormative regulation in different spaces some of which are a far cry from Western ideas of 'the closet'. When, for example, only gay commodification as an 'end point' is set to be explored, researchers may miss how the links that lead to the development of a unique commodity culture in particular Western spaces might come from a particular history of Western gay rights movements that themselves are based around only one interpretation of the heterosexual/homosexual binary focused most prominently on 'the closet' (chapters 2 and 3). Such a reading might ignore why some sexualised groups in a city such as Cape Town might not overtly desire such a particular spatialisation of commodity culture to begin with, having formulated their relationships to wider heteronormative society and space in remarkably different ways – which are themselves located around particular racial, class-based and spatial challenges (see chapters 2, 3, 4 and 5). Failing to see resistance to a globalised gay commodity culture in Cape Town is therefore not to suggest there is no resistance at all, but rather to suggest that perhaps the wrong questions are being asked of a community in the first instance. Equally, failing to see the problems of very Westerncentric legal rights – themselves located powerfully within ideas of Western sexual liberation tied to a 'closet' binary of openness/equality and secretiveness/inequality – enshrined into South Africa law is perhaps to fail to see the specificity of local communities and the struggles that they themselves face (chapter 6).

As such, in a city such as Cape Town, the geography of the city must remain key. As later sections explore, it becomes vital to understand how a history of race-based spatial segregation has given different communities different opportunities with which to relate to wider heteronormative society. Consequently any exploration of a city such as Cape Town must also take into account the different ways such divergent relationships have been understood by and affected different communities. As will be described in the next section, such appreciation of difference by different communities makes for a decidedly queer reading of the city.

Recasting what is 'Queerly Visible'

This book therefore proposes that the idea of queer visibility might be productively used to help position a lens through which different communities are studied. Both 'queer' and 'visibility/visible' here are used in very specific ways that draw on particular readings as to what can be made 'queerly visible'.

First, returning briefly to issues surrounding 'the closet': As the above section argued, there is much danger of conceptual damage occurring when 'the closet' in a very Western sense is applied to communities elsewhere. This damage can also cause severe harm to communities located in Western centres. For example, Riki Wilchins (2004) has spoken eloquently about the problems transgendered and intersexed individuals have had in relating their lives within a broader 'gay and lesbian' political project. As such, queer theory has argued against the instigation of monolithic identity terms, looking instead at ways that categories of existence can be problematised and the power that is enacted to create them can be destabilised. As Donald E. Hall (2003) has explained, to be queer is 'to abrade classification, to sit athwart conventional categories or traverse several . . . [it] means that there is no *easy* answer' (p. 13). The term can therefore imply the action of disrupting, destabilising and problematising 'facts' held dear by hetero-normative societies. To 'be queer' therefore is often framed as an endeavour to consciously and continually question regulative agendas that normalise within society and offer ruptures in discourse so as to allow power to coalesce in new and liberating forms.

Yet running parallel to such concerns is also a particular class-based reading of what queer is capable of achieving. As Cathy Cohen (2005) has argued, to 'be queer' often leaves unspoken the class- and race-based privilege that allows for such projects. At a very basic level, this can mean that queer only functions for those with the time, money, resources and community that allow for it. This is clearly a valid point. Not everyone can be queer or even wants to be queer. And even those that do perhaps cannot do so all the time. There is therefore perhaps rightful concern about over-laying a term such as 'queer' onto communities located outside of Western centres of privilege. For example, if being queer is often to be 'knowingly queer', then how can communities that are simply striving for basic survival against homophobia find the opportunity to playfully destabilise those structures that threaten their lives? Taking this issue further, despite the liberationist dimension of 'queer' in relation to 'gay', there is also rightful concern when exporting the idea of queer along with some form of teleo-logical assumption as to the creation first of 'the homosexual', followed by 'the gay' leading eventually to 'the queer' (Hayes 2000). Again, the legacy of one particular reading of 'the closet' should not automatically be read into other communities elsewhere. Indeed, in post-colonial contexts there are hugely important political, ethical and moral issues both in using Western terms and in deciding how those terms relate to wider problems associated with modernist scales of 'development' (Robinson 2006).[12]

Yet it is also worth realising that positioning communities elsewhere as 'not queer' or unable to 'be queer' because of their different history to the West is also to assume that 'queer' can only emerge from communities that have a particular history and a particular reading of 'the closet'. It is also problematic to unilaterally assume that only the privileged can be queer. While the mechanisms for queer pursuits may be remarkably different in different locations, it would be unfair for researchers simply to assume that those elsewhere cannot be queer. One reason for deploying the term queer in this study when describing many different groups of men is therefore to frame these communities in a way that gives back to them the possibility of knowing subversion. As researchers we should not see these other com-munities as too poor, too uneducated or too constrained to be queer. The emancipatory dimension of queer beliefs should not be denied to commu-nities simply because they have yet to fully engage with or have chosen not to follow a particular path towards subverting power. Indeed, as the following chapters will show, the divergent strategies deployed by different communities show remarkably different attempts at confronting and questioning heteronormative regulation, all of which could be seen to retain some element of 'queerness' as a confrontation and anxiety for wider society. Further, not only do these methods highlight the contingent nature (and hence at times, fragility) of heteronormativity (and distance this discussion from simplistic ideas of a monolithic and intractable heteronormativity), they also highlight how Western notions of 'the closet' become decidedly 'queered' and questioned in a country such as South Africa. Indeed, Cathy Cohen's (2005) points about the class-based nature of queer are well taken and it is therefore precisely because this study does try to take into account issues of class- and race-based privilege that it chooses to focus on the diverse ways in which communities can be queer in sites away from Western centres. Yet to take this discussion further, it is also necessary to step back and explore this study's focus on visibility.

As Eric O. Clarke (2000) points out, visibility in terms of sexual identity and sexual politics is anything but a neutral term. Discussing communities in the West, he observes:

> Over the past thirty years, lesbian and gay political and intellectual struggle has focused an enormous amount of time, energy, and resources on the politics of visibility, a politics that strives for greater access to and presence within diverse cultural, economic and political forms of representation . . . [The intention has been to] diminish the debilitating effects of homophobia . . . The quest for visibility, however, has raised important concerns about the terms on which this visibility will be offered and in terms of which lesbian and gay men attempt to achieve it. (Clarke 2000: 29)

A frequent debate among commentators interested in understanding sexualised groups is therefore one that centres around who exactly is being studied and who is gaining most representation. Indeed, the quest to understand group visibility is in some ways a very old one for scholars. It is after all a quest that has its roots in the original founding of the gay and lesbian 'movement' in the 1960s (Armstrong 2002; D'Emilio 2002; Seidman 1993). Today it often centres on the term 'homonormative', and the problems that emerge through normalisation (quite often linked to an assimilationist agenda) of a social, cultural and political identity. Much recent geographical work on sexual citizenship has moved this debate forward, specifically Bell and Binnie (2006), Duggan (2002) and Stychin (2006). For many, the issue nonetheless remains one centred fundamentally between those who seek out 'inclusion' into heteronormative regimes such as 'marriage' and those who eschew any 'regimes of the normal'. As Eric O. Clarke expertly points out in his work, visibility, and the achievement of it, is not an abstract term wholly separate from wider structures in society. On the contrary, in one interpretation to be visible is to have enmeshed oneself at some point within wider systems of control that allow for visibility and invisibility.

Yet in this study, the focus on visibility is also driven by a desire to understand the opportunities for group acceptance and, to follow Clarke's point, diminish the destabilising effects of homophobia. It does this by looking at the different ways queer groups have positioned themselves in relation to heteronormative regulation within their own community before looking at issues of, for example, homonormalisation. As such, it aims to bring back into focus the way different individuals with same-sex desire can make themselves known as such to the wider community – can become 'visible' – and the problems that such knowingness has for other queer men and the wider community. Therefore, it focuses down initially onto one particular element of same-sex identity – the way individuals relate to and become publicly known to heterosexual society. It is therefore concerned most strongly in understanding how variants of the heterosexual/homosexual binary work in communities with different racialised histories. It is also therefore heavily focused on the way space itself works and is made to work in the production of different sexual identities. Here, the concern becomes how groups are able to appropriate divergent heteronormative spaces to become visible across the urban environment. Issues here include how heteronormative space is itself conceptualised by different groups and the remarkably different ways they see spaces as safe or not. Such issues themselves can only be understood by appreciating the wider complex racial and spatial history of South Africa.

This stance, however, is not to argue that all sexuality takes place in the public realm. Nor is it to argue that visibility in the face of entrenched and deadly homophobia is automatically a 'good thing'. It is however a way of opening up and 'queering' an exploration as to how differences within broad identity labels (which Western researchers are already nervous about applying to other communities) function and how they relate to heteronormative spaces in very different ways. It is therefore a study that focuses on initial identity formation: it explores the 'whys' and the 'hows' that go to inform particular sexual identities.

Such an approach is also presupposed on the relational nature of different identities. So being, a focus on and use of the term visibility is also to draw attention to the way different communities view each other and how such knowledge goes to inform the production of their own visibilities. The use of the concept of visibility is therefore also to offer sexuality researchers a way of understanding how in any multi-community space, a production of a particular identity will be directly driven by the way a community's awareness of difference elsewhere is understood.[13] (Again, it is not arguing that the only way such communities understand each other is through public spaces – issues surrounding private erotics are not discussed directly here). In Cape Town research interest has focused heavily on studying 'white gay space' and, importantly, ways to deconstruct its meaning (Elder 2005; Oswin 2005; Visser 2002; 2003a; 2003b). Such work could perhaps be further enriched not only by spending more time understanding how the representation and bounded nature of 'gay Cape Town' can only exist because of the way those who represent that space see difference elsewhere in the city – and subsequently how they try and relate to and engage that difference in relation to their beliefs. Such work could also be enriched by exploring how those elsewhere in the city need to be understood in relation to the way they perceive both the discursive dimension and the materiality of spaces of privilege and those groups that represent those spaces.

Only once this is understood does it become possible to more fully appreciate the way communities may fight over the very issue of visibility. As the quotation by Clarke (2000) above [p. 17] helps us understand, since the 1960s, sexuality studies have been concerned with who is represented and by whom. As Riki Wilchins (2000), in the previous section pointed out, some sexual minority groups can easily become sidelined within essentialist rights-based agendas. In the post-colonial city, such issues need to be explored in light of the remarkably divergent ways same-sex groups may have come to reach points of safety within their own communities by appropriating heteronormative spaces in different ways. It then becomes important to see how different visibilities, together with the mechanisms that led to those different visibilities, may themselves keep some groups invisible when they attempt interaction. Such invisibility can have dire consequences in terms of political representation. They can also have severe consequences in terms of understanding and servicing health needs.

Visibilities can therefore remain constantly in tension with each other. As the following sections and the rest of this book will examine, the ending of apartheid has helped bring groups together and relate to each other in ways previously impossible. They have also caused communities to question and in some cases to re-evaluate the basis of their own identities, ideas and prejudices, shifting and enriching the debate about homonormalisation to take account of wider diversity. When, as later chapters will explore, the appreciation of such differences – in terms of, for example, appropriating space, relating to wider society, constructing gendered and raced binaries, developing spaces of consumption, promoting national discourses of rights – is so stark, the effect may be to cause an anxiety and possibility of self-reflexivity (or not) on the part of the different communities in question. Diversity promotes appreciation or anxiety. The power of these different visibilities in relation to each other is therefore the ability of them to question the perceptions of other communities or keep exclusionary perceptions rigidly enforced. The very visibility of different communities in relation to each other in the post-apartheid (and to a lesser extent, the apartheid) city is what gives them the opportunity of being queer. Queer visibilities among different groups of men therefore exist in a space where such diversity of sexual identity expression is possible and where such diversity is increasingly understood to exist (and then quite possibly strategically ignored) by different groups.

In the following chapters, different identity labels will at times be deployed at specific points to highlight the specificity of the group being discussed. However, for the reasons described above, each group in light of its at times contentious and controversial relationships with others – and in light of the need to 'level the playing field' so that no one community gains prominence over any other (academically, in terms of research focus and theoretical perspective or practically, in terms of community development) – is also designated to be most certainly a queer visibility. To explore this issue in more detail, the following section will examine how race has been constructed in South Africa and how it has directly affected the options of queer groups.

Yet lastly on this section, it must be stressed that this book is not claiming to have explored *all* factors that go to shape particular variants of the heterosexual/homosexual binary in different locations and hence *all* factors that condition different queer visibilities. For example, the issue of religion and the contrast between Christian Calvinism and Islam in the city, while woven into the following chapters, is not explicitly explored directly in relation to the perceptions each has of the other. Further, and as will be discussed briefly in the final section of this chapter, this study's focus on gender is bounded to representing how masculinity and femininity play out among men – rather than looking more holistically at the way the gender binary and issues of racial patriarchy play out between men and women and go to affect same-sex communities. There is clearly a pressing need for further researchers to explore these issues – therefore the end of this chapter briefly examines the work that has already been conducted on gendered and queer sexualities in sub-Saharan Africa and offers a possible future direction for research.

The Construction of 'Race' in South African Urban Space

Geographers and anti-essentialists have a very long history exploring the social construction of race and racism (Barlett 1994; Delanty 1995; Mudimbe 1988; Wolff 1994). Through critical race theory, Stuart Hall (1993) has explored how binaries, be they around black/white or geographically around for example West/East essentialise the complexities of cultural identity. Yet as with sexual identity, it remains the case that there is no essence to a race-based identity; instead identity is continually being produced within vectors of similarity and difference. Such a position allows scholars such as Stuart Hall to remove from discussion the simplistic notion of the 'black' subject. Indeed, Stuart Hall's work on articulation is useful here. The apparent unity of identity is really the articulation of different elements which under different historical and cultural circumstances could have been re-articulated in quite other ways. There is therefore no essentialistic or automatic connection between a race and a class or gender identity. As Butler (1993) would argue through her study of performativity in relation to sexuality and gender, iterativeness is a process that creates the effect of fixity over time. Those iteratives through performance are conditioned around discourses and materialities of power, which, as Hall would argue, are not primordial but rather occurred because of specific historical junctures in specific places.

Nevertheless, it would also be foolhardy to dismiss 'race' as nothing more than a social construction. Indeed, 'race' can also be seen as a necessary fiction for the way groups see themselves in the world (Appiah's (1995) and Hall's (1993) application of strategic essentialism is relevant here. See also Spivak (1990)). As with sexuality, constructions of race and racism are real concerns for many groups and go to condition the way different individuals and groups view their own place in the world. Bodies become raced by the way power acts on them. Geographically, races are therefore made 'real' by a series of spatial strategies designed to make race a 'fact'. Therefore, both from within urban geography and outside the discipline, much work has been carried out into understanding the way spatial segregation and geographies of minority groups have developed (Anderson 1991 and 1998; Cohen 1993; Davis 1990; Gilroy 1987; Jones 1996). Indeed as Bonnett and Nayak (2003) and Kobayashi (2004) make plain, race is often made 'real' precisely by being fixed in space. Because of this, work has also focused on the way the conflicting representational strategies that surround particular spaces can be deconstructed (Jackson 1988; Jacobs 1996; Smith 1989). For these commentators there is (as with sexuality) no fixed or immutable meaning to any one space or the groups who inhabit it. Further, as Kay Anderson, in her path-defining studies of Vancouver's Chinatown (1987 and 1991) points out, the processes of racial spatialisations are inherently historical and caught up in other webs of meaning.

It therefore also remains important to see how a race-based identity also relies at times on a sex- and class-based identity (and vice versa) to exist (Saad and Carter 2005). As both Ann Stoler (1995) and Anne McClintock (1995) have described in epic fashion, the creation and deployment of historical race-based, sexuality-based and class-based discriminations often

rely on the existence of each other for justification. To look at race is therefore also to look at sex and class. And further, to understand the power
that is deployed to bring into being a sexed identity is also to look at the
power that was used to bring into being a raced identity. With specific focus
on queer sexuality, Siobhan Somerville's (2000) work has looked at how
the very 'creation' of race was deeply implicated in the 'creation' of homosexuality in America. From a geographical perspective, such studies must
subsequently point towards a need to see how the creation of particular
spaces as sexed, raced or classed can help reinforce each other today.

Many of the above analytical frameworks can and have also been applied
to South Africa and its history of racial designation, segregation and intolerance (Lester 2003). While the following chapters will outline in more detail
the salient attributes of apartheid and earlier colonial regulation which go
to inform queer visibilities, it is important here to first stress the enormous
effect colonial and later apartheid policies have had on the citizens of the
country in general. Many researchers in geography and from further afield
have grappled with this issue, exploring, amongst other spatial topics, urban
reconstruction and development post-apartheid in the face of apartheid
segregation (Ashforth 1997; Bollens 1998a and 1998b; Christopher 1995;
Robinson 1996 and 2004; Visser 2001), the great importance of the mining
industry generally and the massive impact mining migration had on gender,
capitalism, resistance and race (Campbell 2003; Crush 1994; Elder 2003;
Hartwick 1998) and the strategies communities deploy in relating social
memory and forgetting in light of draconian discrimination, violence and
in some cases torture (Coombes 2004; Minty 2006; Nuttall and Coetzee
1998; Popke 2000; Till 2004). For many of these studies, the power of
apartheid and its effect on people's lives was, and remains, its ability not
only to define and name groups on social scales that placed fairer-skinned
above darker-skinned individuals but also its ability to keep groups separated spatially, socially and culturally from each other. Clearly, there is
nothing inherent about different individuals' places on such social scales.
Instead, these categories were created through power and spatial regulation
(Western 1981). Such power has continued to affect communities in South
Africa today. In the South African case, space and spatiality therefore
helped to make 'race' in the country, to the degree that race requires the
separation of peoples into groups which in the process only went to reinforce ideological notions about race in the first place (Anderson 1987 and
1991; Mitchell 2000). As with different groups of queer individuals and
their links to variants of heteronormativity, the creation of racialised difference has occurred through its very perception as distinct from the 'norm'.
And as with queer individuals, communities today continue to feel the
effect of the monumental lengths the state went to in attempts to legitimise
itself and its race-based classifications and urban compartmentalisations.

Apartheid also operated at a number of scales. At the individual scale there was the regulation of (amongst others) buses, toilets and building entrances. At the wider urban scale, apartheid divided cities into different residential areas for different race groups (chapters 3 and 4). At the state level, 'homelands' were created for black Africans groups, which, together with the 'pass laws', helped regulate the settlement and movement of different racial groups around the country (chapter 4) (Bickford-Smith et al. 1999; Christopher 1994 and 2001; Western 1981). It was therefore this ability of apartheid planners to employ different spatial strategies at different scales that allowed the state to maintain formidable control over the different 'races' for such a long time. Indeed, as Jennifer Robinson (1990 and 1996) makes clear, apartheid was in large part able to exist because of its ability to spatially regulate its domination over different groups. Apartheid in this sense is an excellent example of how race and space work together. The hierarchy imposed by the state could only be maintained by its application through space. As Robinson points outs:

> The racial South African state survived for decades at least partly as a result of its ability to implement routine governance by means of what I have called the 'location strategy' . . . The power of apartheid, of the setting apart of racial groups, was therefore rooted in the spatial practices referenced in its very name: much more than simply an expression of a political order, the spaces of apartheid constituted and sustained that order. (Robinson 1996: 2)

Yet it is also telling that the South African state was very selective in the way it went about defining race. As chapter 2 will explore in more detail, 'English' and 'Afrikaners' were not always classified as different 'races'. Black African communities were however separated into different groups. This was part of a policy of 'divide and rule', separating black African communities into smaller groups to help maintain power with the white minority. Again, the artificiality of race, and Hall's attempts to deconstruct racial categories are highlighted. While there are linguistic and cultural differences between black African groupings, they were no more 'eligible' for different racial classifications than white groupings. Indeed, one need only look at the different political, colonial, economic, linguistic (and indeed spatial) histories of the English and Afrikaners in South Africa to see the grouping of 'white' as a highly artificial racial category (Deegan 1999; Douwes-Dekker et al. 1995; Dubow 1992; Giliomee 2003; Le May 1995; Welsh 1998).

Yet a debate about the construction of race as a category should not detract from the fact that it had real-world effects on groups in South Africa. As the following chapters will show, race has remained a defining element in South African society, even after the end of apartheid. Yet in South Africa race itself has also always historically been strongly related to class (Elphick and Giliomee 1989; Worden 1985). And as Boraine et al. (2006) and Saff (1994 and 1998) point out today, political apartheid in South African cities in many cases has now been replaced with economic apartheid. This is apparent in cities such as Cape Town, where large numbers of individuals continue to live in the same environments they did during National Party rule. Some individuals, of course, have been able to move away from township locations and move into historically white-segregated areas of the city.[14] These movements are indicative of a growing black African middle class in the major cities (Burgess 2002; Saff 1998; Southall 2004). Yet in Cape Town, the vast majority of black African and coloured individuals continue to live in the townships and certain areas of the Cape Flats (Bickford-Smith et al. 1999; Turok 2001; Western 2001).[15] This study will therefore focus its attention on the overwhelming majority of black Africans and coloured queer men in Cape Town, who continue to live in the same spaces designated to them by the apartheid state. This is not to deny the real possibility of social change in South Africa – a change that would de-link (in Hall's terms, remove an articulation between) class and race in South Africa. Rather, it reflects that at present, the majority of black African communities in Cape Town are economically disadvantaged in relation to white communities, and spatially separate from the rest of the city (Spinks 2001).

Today in South Africa much emphasis is therefore rightly paid to attempts to address the social and economic imbalance between communities. Yet while conditions have slowly improved for many since the early 1990s, many others remain critical of the government's economic and social redistribution policies. In particular, concern has emerged over the lack of support for working-aged people trapped outside the formal labour market. Meanwhile white groups have continued to benefit from a massive human capital advantage (Seekings and Nattrass 2005). The legacy of apartheid means that great effort will have to be applied for many decades if different communities are ever going to be able to interface with each other on anything approaching an equal footing. Indeed, even with continued attempts on the part of the ANC to bridge the economic and social gap between communities, concern and apprehension continue to linger (Lodge 1999 and 2002).[16]

The importance of queer visibilities therefore hopefully again becomes apparent. The quest to explore these visibilities is not merely one of queers' relationships to heteronormativity, but also of their relationships to each other. Race and sexuality combine here to offer two ways of examining these intra-group relationships. The first is an examination of the way different visibilities strongly associated with different racially-designated communities were able to develop due to the way apartheid was able to compartmentalise and spatially contain groups. The second is an exploration of how these visibilities interface with each other and, at certain times and in certain spaces, come into conflict with each other. As already mentioned above, the quest for visibility is also affected by the way other groups have become visible. Some groups may inadvertently be kept politically or socially invisible while others gain visibility among heteronormative society. In a country such as South Africa, the legacy of racial classification and race-based discrimination, tied today to class-based discrimination, will directly affect the way group interactions augment or hinder particular visibilities.

Queer Visibilities in Cape Town

The complexities of such issues are well represented in a city such as Cape Town. As the nation's oldest city, Cape Town has come to represent a particular yet very important take on wider concerns within the country. A mixture of Khoi and San peoples, Dutch and then British settlers, black African labour and south east Asian labour have helped mould the area around Table Mountain and the surrounding aeolian sand flats into one of the most cosmopolitan and culturally diverse locations on the subcontinent. It is also an area strongly shaped by apartheid spatial planning. Even before the onset of formal apartheid after 1948, Cape Town had become concerned with housing and the locations that different communities could reside within the city (Bickford-Smith 1995a).[17] After 1948, National Party legislation such as the Group Areas Act, the Immorality Act and the Separate Amenities Act started to shape the layout of the city and the options 'white', 'coloured' and 'black African' communities had within it.[18] While this was occurring throughout the country, Cape Town in particular was affected due to its large coloured population (chapter 3) and the pressing need of apartheid planners to attempt a reversal of black African urbanisation in the area of the country furthest away from any African 'reserve' (chapter 4). It was further conditioned by its historical image as the location of early European settlement and its strong ties to the British when compared to cities further north and east (issues that continue to uniquely define it in the present – chapter 2). Post-apartheid, the city has been tremendously successful at re-branding itself as one of the continent's premier tourist destinations – and as a city fully embracing its new image as a liberal and accepting paradise.

For many queers, Cape Town has therefore come to symbolise the most liberated and inviting location not only within South Africa but on the entire continent (chapter 2). But such imagery only goes to mask the reality for the majority of those who live there. While Cape Town has pushed forward with new elite leisure and tourist developments such as the Victoria and Alfred Waterfront and the International Convention Centre, it also remains a fact that racial tensions and gross and enduring social, cultural and economic inequalities continue to define the city. A key justification for focusing on Cape Town rather than any other South African city is therefore the sheer disparity between popular representation of the city in relation to its liberated 'gay community' and the shocking reality for most of the queers who call it their home.

Indeed, it is also perhaps surprising that while detailed sexuality-based ethnographic studies have been conducted in other cities in the country, including some excellent work in Johannesburg (Donham 1998; McLean and Ngcobo 1995) and Durban (Louw 2001; Reddy and Louw 2002; see also the following chapters), no work has yet attempted to examine the complex and nuanced relationships between communities in one urban area. Further, while South African queer studies as a field has grown tremendously within the past several years, producing some excellent historical and political accounts of queer experiences of the lead-up to the political transition and its aftermath (De Waal and Manion 2006; Gevisser and Cameron 1995; Hoad et al. 2005; Krouse and Berman 1993; van Zyl and Steyn 2005) an attempt to read such experiences simultaneously through communities in one city has yet to occur. In Cape Town this is doubly troubling due to its continued representation as liberal and accepting towards diversity. Further, within Cape Town, besides the endeavours of William Leap (2003 and 2005), hardly any work has been conducted on the fastest growing group of queer men in the former black African townships. No research has attempted to examine black African queer intra-group dynamics in the city. The city's historical and geographical scars and contemporary dilemmas therefore represent fertile ground to see how communities understand each other because of apartheid and how they now try and relate to each other post-apartheid.

A study of queer visibility in Cape Town must consequently be seen both as a project that draws on geographical concepts of sexuality and race and also an attempt to offer a new perspective on work dealing with cross-cultural queer communities in post-colonial environments. It is an approach that draws inspiration from geographical studies that focuses on issues of transgression and appropriation of different environments. Yet it is also a study that moves away from some sometimes implicit assumptions about sexual identity, 'the closet' and somewhat unilateral ideas of development. At its core, it is a study focused most strongly on understanding how different groups have been able to overcome regulative ideas of sexuality associated strongly with variants of heteronormativity. Yet it is a study that does so by embracing the many different ways heteronormative regulation manifests itself and the many different ways it can be overcome. In South Africa, this therefore also becomes a study of how racial classification affected different queer communities. It is of course not a study that attempts to reify these categories or to assume they are fixed. It is however a study willing to examine how communities themselves perceive the issue of race in the city and how they are willing to perceive each other. By taking visibility as a starting point, the project is therefore able to move in two different directions, both of which allow for broad appreciations of the factors that affect different communities. These directions are explored in the first and second parts of this book.

The first part of this book 'Visibilities', offers an opening up of ways of understanding different queer groups within the urban environment. Looking at visibility, and specifically the way visibilities are related directly to particular spaces, foregrounds the possibility of variation. In particular, it helps us to explore how racial classifications in the South African context may have helped these variations to develop. Further, visibility, as described above, includes an exploration of the way 'the closet' may or may not be implemented, but crucially, also allows for a broad contrast with identities that may relate to spaces in different ways than those traditionally posited on 'the closet'.

Each chapter in this first section will examine one of the three major 'race-based' communities in Cape Town today. As described in the last full South African Census, these communities are designated through the self-identifying terms 'white', 'coloured' and 'black African'. While, as discussed above, these terms carry with them a history of racial discrimination, they are nonetheless the most commonly used terms in South Africa and within Cape Town at present.[19] Further, the (attempted) standardisation of these terms during apartheid directly affected the opportunities these queer communities had to develop both during and even after apartheid.

Chapter 2 focuses on white queer men in the city, examining in particular the important links between apartheid ideology towards 'non-whites' and discrimination against those implicated in the 'queer conspiracy' within the white community. It argues that this situation placed many white queer men in a uniquely handicapped position, both socially and politically. The inability, in particular, to develop a coherent political movement has helped keep many within the white queer community fractured in the years after the fall of apartheid. While Cape Town has been remarkably successful at developing its own urban 'gay space' in the 1990s, this space, in an apartheid-era white designated area of the city, has helped polarise white queer men. In particular, historical ethnic and spatial divides between 'English' and 'Afrikaners' have been augmented by the importation of a particular commodified form of queer expression with roots initially in urban spaces in Western cities which is itself directly related to issues of class. In such a way, the visibility in urban space attained through the development of the De Waterkant gay village has gone to hide deep-rooted division amongst white queers. These divisions help call into question the popular representation of Cape Town as a liberated and accepting queer space – an issue that is returned to throughout this book.

Chapter 3 begins by exploring the historical development of the coloured community in Cape Town, travelling from the heart of the historically segregated white city to outlying areas of the Cape Flats – areas that are traditionally associated with apartheid forced relocation. It shows how the coloured racial category came to exist and how colonial and apartheid ideology positioned it between the 'civilised' and the 'uncivilised'. It goes on to expose how these racist ideologies inadvertently gave working-class coloured queer men the opportunity to become visible within their communities through sustained and overt cross-dressing. The chapter also examines how gendered performances affect the construction of queer identities and compares cross-dressing queer men with the heterosexually-identified men that many of them have sexual relationships with. The precarious social position of coloured identity within South African society due to apartheid is further discussed in relation to the strongly enforced divide between middle-class and working-class coloured queer men. The historic aim of the middle class to 'appear civilised' and therefore remove themselves from a metaphorical and material space of ambivalence has led to a distancing from coloured cross-dressers. For many middle-class queer coloured men, cross-dressers were and continue to be a sign both of premodern sexual identities associated with cross-dressing and racially inferior social identities. This chapter therefore exposes how and why many middle-class coloured men look towards what they perceive as an overtly visible and commodified white queer culture in Cape Town as a model they should strive to emulate. However, this chapter goes on to critique the assumption that the type of visibility associated with the gay village in the city is supposedly sexually and racially 'superior'. Both coloured cross-dressers and men who more readily frequent the gay village have achieved a 'coming out' within their respective communities. Yet the processes through which they have become visible represent different ways of appropriating heteronormative space. These strategies are directly related to the way racist policies socially, politically and spatially positioned these two communities.

Chapter 4 explores the development of queer visibilities within the rapidly growing black African former townships in Cape Town. Focusing mainly on Xhosa communities, this chapter travels in a different direction out from the historically segregated white city, uncovering for the first time the unique strategies black African queer men have deployed to become visible and gain acceptance in sometimes hostile and dangerous environments. It begins by tackling current debates surrounding the 'un-Africanness of homosexuality' currently being propagated by black nationalist leaders. As supporters of Winnie Mandela have infamously stated: 'Homosex is not in black culture'. This chapter adds its voice to a growing body of work that argues that while a discrete heterosexual/homosexual binary (and certainly one located around 'the closet') cannot be uniformly mapped onto diverse African communities, visible displays of same-sex desire most certainly are and always have been in black African culture. Yet it also takes this argument further, by showing how apartheid ideology and spatial control not only limited the degree to which some black African communities could maintain a history of same-sex desire but also how the ending of apartheid has only increased homophobia within Cape Town's former townships. It therefore argues that the sudden ending of race- and sexuality-based discrimination in 1994 gave space for Xhosa queer men not only to become visible in particular ways but also that those visibilities, in turn, created widespread confrontations with the wider community.

This chapter then goes on to explore how current visible manifestations of queer sexuality in the townships have been influenced not only by continued homophobia but also by other communities in Cape Town. These visibilities are strongly geographically demarcated around 'social-nodal' structures, where individuals feel able to express themselves separately from a homophobic community. When combined with sustained homophobia (which itself is often related to apartheid spatial and ideological controls) this chapter articulates in yet another way how race and sexuality are inextricably linked and how queer visibility interacts with diverse power relations in specific places.

The second part of this book, 'Interactions', focuses on the problems different queer communities might have in interacting with each other due to the different forms of visibility they deploy, or the underlying reasons why such visibilities may have developed. Concerns over social justice therefore now come more into focus. In some instances, these problems (and also queer possibilities) remain closely tied to issues of race-based classifications in the country and also to problems in the way some groups continue to view particular visibilities as the most progressive and 'enlightened' to the detriment of others.

Chapter 5 returns to the space of the gay village in Cape Town, first discussed in chapter 2, to see how other communities interface with it. While the space today is rightly represented as a relatively liberated space in comparison to, for example, some areas of the former townships, it also takes with it a history of race-based exclusion. These exclusions function both as a result of the way different communities have understood queer sexuality and been able to position themselves in ways that mark them out as visible and distinct from heteronormative societies, and as a result of the factors that allowed different visibilities to develop in the first instance. These exclusions therefore help keep the diversity of queer life in Cape Town partially invisible. Further, the forcefulness with which these invisibilities are felt by some has led to calls of racism within the space of the gay village. This chapter therefore attempts to unpack the multitude of cross-cutting reasons that lead some to assume a racist undertone to this space. While this chapter does not attempt to deny the possibility of discrimination solely on the basis of skin colour, it also demonstrates how the situation is also a great deal more complex.

Chapter 6 moves away from purely social interaction and focuses both on political invisibilities and the possibility of queering the agendas of events and organisations because of increasing visibility of different communities. Taking the three examples of the local sexual health non-governmental organisation 'Triangle Project', Cape Town Pride and the recent same-sex marriage campaign, this chapter explores first the issue of community participation by laying out the different and sometimes conflicting needs various queer groups bring to Triangle Project and Cape Town Pride. Both the model of service provision traditionally offered by Triangle Project and the ideological history of Pride are shown not to mesh well with the needs of the vast majority of queers in the city. Questions as to how visibility itself has developed in the former townships – and how that visibility is understood by others – become central in understanding why this problem has occurred and how people are trying to solve it. As such, rather than simply ignore this issue, both Triangle Project and the organisers of Cape Town Pride have gone to great lengths to acknowledge not only diversity among queer groups but also wider unity. The unique methods deployed by both organisations over the past few years point towards broader solidarity and self-reflexivity among queer groups in service provision and Pride events than would appear to be the case socially in the gay village.

Yet while recent successes are indeed very encouraging, especially in light of the social isolation experienced just two decades previously, there are still distinct problems. The last part of this chapter therefore explores the issues faced by queer groups during the same-sex marriage debate – a debate that neatly epitomises many of the themes that run throughout this book. While successful, the marriage campaign also highlighted the deepseated negative feelings among large sectors of South Africa's population not just about same-sex marriage, but also queer lives in general. While many queer individuals are now permitted to marry, large numbers remain unable to, in no small part due to the very heightening of public feeling *against* queer life because of the marriage campaign. This chapter and this book therefore serve to point out not only the sheer diversity of queer lives and the sheer diversity of problems queers face – and the need for researchers to take account of such diversity – but also the ease with which such diversity can become masked by the apparent freedoms queer South Africans are now meant to be able to enjoy.

Chapter 7 draws together the major findings of this book and attempts to show how many of them feed into a pressing need to examine these communities in relation to HIV prevention programmes. This final chapter therefore sets itself the task of exploring how an understanding of the diversity of queer visibilities in the city is vital to provide targeted HIV educational materials. The paucity of information specifically about the problems queer men face compounded with an inability to see how their identities are directly affected by the ways they have become visible in heteronormative spaces means that any education campaign is hampered in being able to directly address different groups' divergent needs. This is the ultimate cost of queer invisibility.

Some Notes on Methods

This book is the culmination of ethnographic and archive research begun in 2003 and completed in 2007.[20] It involved concentrated periods living amongst and getting to know different groups of queer men in the former townships, traditionally coloured areas of the Cape Flats and affluent areas of the historically white city. Over the course of several years I became known within these different worlds and found it possible to slowly come to understand how each community views itself and others. The description of the lives of individuals in the rest of this book are therefore the result of a long struggle to be accepted and trusted within different groups of men. The majority of interviews were conducted in English. However, where necessary, I was also assisted by a series of culturally attuned translators.

The choice of these communities and the choice to focus solely on male queer sexuality were not however arbitrary ones. The communities themselves were chosen due to the decision to focus on three 'typologies' of visibility, which are largely distinctive of developments within the three racially defined communities and the history of spatial location within the city. As the following chapters will explore, these three visibilities are conditioned around different appropriations of heteronormative space. It must however be stressed that these visibilities are not demarcated simply or neatly into different 'racially-defined' communities. Neither is this study claiming to have explored all forms of queer visibility among all groups of men in Cape Town. For example, I have not included men who self-identify as bisexual or transsexual men, among other possible topics. Instead, this study was driven by the desire to explore how difference is understood in the different communities. Therefore, as Valentine (2005) would argue, the research findings in this study are *illustrative* of the way different groups understand male queer visibility, rather than *representative* of all types of visibility in all population groups.

Further, as numerous studies have shown, women's same-sex desires encompass a wide range of identities in different spaces and have been represented in different ways (Inness 1997; Rothenberg 1995; Valentine 1993). As mentioned above, work has focused on the sometimes different ways in which lesbians in the West have appropriated space and become visible. Other work has focused on the social, economic and political relationships between lesbians and gay men and HIV/AIDS (Gorna 1996; Patton 1994; Treichler 1999). All this work points to a complex set of intersections between the identities of queer men and women. In South Africa as elsewhere, such intersections remain strongly regulated through perceptions of patriarchy (Nast 2002). As described above, I did not have the time or opportunity to do justice to this topic and hope that others can take up this important issue. There have indeed been some very intriguing and exciting developments within both queer and feminist scholarly work on women in South Africa (see Beffon 1995; Dirsuweit 1999; McClintock 1990; McEwan 2000 and 2005; Muthien 2005; Sam 1995; Swarr and Nagar 2003; Vimbela and Olivier 1995). There is therefore also a pressing need for future researchers to attempt a very important and indeed exciting study that explores the links between queer men and women in South Africa, both historically and in the present.

Notes on Form

The chapters in this study employ the following terms of definition:

• 'white', 'coloured', 'black African'

These terms are used to denote the different racially defined population groups in South Africa. They represent the terms used in the current South African Census.

• 'historically white city/CBD/City Bowl', 'coloured Cape Flats/outlying areas of the Cape Flats', 'black African townships/former townships'

These terms relate to the geographical areas under study in this book. As each chapter explains, these areas are not 'exclusively' the domain of one particular racially defined population group – and neither are they neatly bounded spatial regions. They further are not meant to imply a re-inscription of binary oppositions between communities. Instead, they simply reflect the contemporary layout of the city, as illustrated in current census data. For simplification, these terms have been used to denote different groups and the communities they predominantly live in.

• 'homosexual', 'gay', queer'

As highlighted in this chapter, 'homosexual' functions directly as a very Western term in tandem with ideas of 'the closet'. In this book it is therefore limited in use and referred to most often in terms of its application as a form of anachronistic identification – for example when discussing state, legal or nationalist sanctioned discrimination against a 'medicalised' condition or state 'threat' or when exploring the argument that 'homosexuality is unAfrican'. 'Gay' can be seen to work in a developmentalist framework as a 'progression' from 'homosexual' (see also chapters 2 and 3). As the following chapters explore, while originating within particular Western spaces (and still finding most purchase there) it also functions as a common (and sometimes ideologically un-tethered) word for broadly defined same-sex groups or projects. However its deeper ideological roots limit its application in this study among those with less overt links to the historical development of gay rights movements that emerged in certain sites in the West during the latter part of the twentieth century. As such, 'gay' will only be used when discussing such self-labelled entities as 'gay villages', 'gay movements', 'gay rights' or 'gay pride' – places, events or activities that clearly draw on this history (or when quoting individuals who use the term themselves as a shorthand for same-sex groups). As explained above 'queer' is used overwhelmingly to describe the same-sex groupings under study in this work.

• 'heterosexual/homosexual binary'

The term is used to illustrate the creation and marking of sexual difference. This term should not be confused with the use of 'homosexual', above. It does not only refer to a Western construction of 'homosexuality', but rather the way different varieties of the binary can function and work to help regulate and reproduce variants of heteronormativity.

Interview extracts are indented in the following text, as are quotations and extracts from secondary data. For anonymous interviewees, a fictitious first name is given along with their real age at time of first interview. For example, 'CRAIG/31'. This format, along with information about quotations provided in the following chapters, is intended to make it easy for the reader to distinguish between different respondents. For interviewees representing organisations or businesses, a full and correct name is given. A small number of anonymous interviewees representing particular bars, clubs or events in Cape Town are listed with just a fictitious first name, for example 'MICHAEL'. My own questions, where deemed appropriate (for example, during focus group discussions as the conversation evolves), are labelled with my name, 'ANDREW'.

Lastly, where interview quotations have been truncated three full stops indicate the point of break in the conversation (. . .). Where a natural pause in the conversation occurred, either because the interviewee paused for thought or changed the direction of the conversation half way through a sentence, then a dash is used (–).

Part I

Visibilities

Chapter Two

Legacies and Visibilities among White Queer Men

Introduction

Sitting outside Cafe Manhattan on a late morning in February generates the uncanny feeling of having found a temporary oasis from the barrage of heat already besieging the city. Perched on the balcony that runs parallel to Dixon Street, one hardly needs to lift the head to feel the cooling air rushing up from the sea. From this spot in the sun, it is possible to see inside to the restaurant and across to the bar. Even on a weekday, the place is already filling up. Waiters are already taking orders as locals make an early escape indoors, away from the sun's fierce rays. Unlike the seasoned locals, any one of the thousands of queer tourists who holiday in the city during the summer months will probably have chosen to sit outside, where they can more fully appreciate the beauty of the surrounding colonial buildings – and soak up the sun.

The ear that whiles time away on this balcony soon becomes attuned to the picking out of American, British, Dutch, Australian, German and South African accents in the midst of the growing cacophony. Amongst the clamour, it is very likely to hear people talking about one of the numerous gay bars, clubs or restaurants they visited the night before. This is, after all, the very heart of Cape Town's internationally famous De Waterkant gay village. A few steps town the hill towards the sea are several nightclubs including the old stalwart, The Bronx 'action bar', while the new Cape Quarter leisure development with its many fashionable catering and entertainment addresses is just around the block.

As the morning comes to a close, a time-honoured Cape Town tradition provides a moment that never fails to entertain the onlooker: At twelve noon on the dot an ear-piercing crash will be heard as the cannon on Signal Hill just behind the village lets everyone in a five kilometre radius know it's midday. Caught unawares by the sheer loudness of the bang, those new to the city will recoil in momentary terror. Quite a few will give an involuntary duck. But just as soon as it has happened, the momentary silence is quickly replaced with talking and laughing. Overhead, the fluttering of birds in search of a new place to rest from the heat is the only sign it has happened at all.

For some, the midday gun is but one example of what marks out Cape Town as unique on the list of international queer tourist destinations. The gun itself, a remnant of colonial times, was once used by nearby ships (some carrying slaves) to check the accuracy of their chronometers. Yet for others today, the cannon blast is just a quaint reminder of a past quickly drifting away on the breeze. Throughout the City Bowl there are of course many other reminders of a past defined by systematic discrimination and racial intolerance. But for many tourists this past is but a setting for the vibrant queer community taking shape close to the shore. As this chapter will show, this community has spatially become overtly visible through the development of the gay village. By so doing, this community has come to be defined by an openness and visibility unique to sub-Saharan Africa. Today it inhabits an economic and political position that does not require, and in some cases actively eschews, any link to South Africa's intolerant past. For many therefore, Cape Town is represented both nationally and internationally as a 'gay Mecca' on par with San Francisco, New York, London, Vancouver, Amsterdam or Sydney. A popular representation of Cape Town is consequently one of a city now fully immersed within the networks of what some commentators have termed a 'global gay' culture (Altman 1996 and 2001); a culture embedded spatially in the built environment of the gay village (Visser 2003a, 2003b and 2004). For commentators such as Altman, this representation is a clear indication of the way a particular element of Western, and specifically North American and Western European, forms of economic, cultural and political expression is finding global dominance in places as far flung as Manila or Cape Town.

Yet as Harvey (1989) and Massey (1995) have pointed out, albeit in very different contexts, globalisation does not mean a total erasing of the local. And as described in Chapter 1, global cultural flows do not simply generate carbon copies of queer identities in new locations. While Cape Town has indeed been successful at appropriating what men who live there themselves see as a particular element of a queer culture initially formed in certain Western spaces, such an appropriation will still only always be selective. (Further, as chapters 5 and 6 explore in more detail, such appropriations are also directly affected by identities and practices among other queer groups closer to home.) Local cultures and ideas will be affected by globalisation in different ways (Binnie 2004). Beneath the relaxed façade of the gay village, white queer men in Cape Town continue to be defined by a history conditioned by apartheid. To understand how and why white queer men in Cape Town developed a visibility spatially embodied in the De Waterkant, it will therefore be necessary to explore the history of sexuality based discrimination within the white community along with perceptions of difference between white groups. This history will illuminate how rather than reflecting a unified and liberated community as popular representations wish to inform us, white queer men in Cape Town remain in many ways trapped within their past, unable to fully break free of a history defined by sexual intolerance. The spatial 'coming out' of white queer men through the development of the gay village, in addition to popular representation as a site of openness, therefore serves two further purposes. The gay village both goes to hide local differences between groups of white men, and further accentuates those differences.[1]

To begin therefore, this chapter will uncover a saga of homophobic discrimination dating back to the middle of the twentieth century, exploring how the ideological justifications for apartheid racial control were easily transplanted to justify control over other groups. The forcefulness and effectiveness of such control meant that, unlike their contemporaries in Western Europe and North America, white queer men in Cape Town were unable, for the majority of the century, to begin confronting the binds of state and societal homophobia. This legacy means that many white queer men today, while remarkably successful at becoming visible within the city, and freeing themselves spatially of decades of direct heteronormative oppression, have not been able or willing to see beyond superficial renderings of a particular Western commodified queer culture towards wider social and political unity.

The Intertwining of Racial and Sexuality-Based Discrimination

As discussed in chapter 1, the segregation of black African from white, European from African, is without doubt the single most defining characteristic of twentieth-century South Africa. While not officially implemented until the ascendance to power of the National Party in 1948, apartheid or 'separateness' had existed in various forms since the arrival of the first Dutch settlers at the Cape of Good Hope in 1652. Yet it would be during the second half of the twentieth century that some of the most draconian methods ever witnessed to separate and regulate the lives of individuals on the basis of their skin colour would be put into practice.

Historical research has provided many explanations as to why some white groups where able to rationalise and intellectualise apartheid. The impact of the Boer War along with the concurrent need to foster an

Afrikaner nationalism in opposition to the British settlers and black African communities has proven a well documented phenomenon as has the economic imperative of creating a massive yet separate and low-paid black African workforce (Clarke and Worger 2004; de Villiers 1971; Giliomee 1987; Norval 1996; Welsh 1998). Equally however, apartheid also gained credence within white society through recourse to Christian Calvinist fundamentalism and early twentieth-century theories of race (Dubow 1995; Furlong 1991). As Chistopher (1994 and 2001) explains, the National Party came to power in 1948 with the intention of creating a white Christian national state, spatially and ideologically separate from black African peoples. Indeed, Christian nationalism from the 1940s, through the mainly Afrikaner Dutch Reformed Church, had provided a nicely self-referential discourse and convenient blueprint for apartheid (Huddleston 1956).[2] In particular, Christian principals of welfare were juxtaposed with a separatist nationalism created and justified by reference to white superiority and protectionism. At an extreme this manifested itself as a fear that white Christians would be overrun – spatially and ideologically – by the black African 'masses' that, at the same time, still needed some form of white Christian assistance.[3]

The philosophical power of these Christian, nationalist and conservative views was not, however, solely limited to discrimination on the basis of race. The same justifications used to impose control over black African and coloured groups were also employed to regulate discourses of white gender and sexuality. Indeed, as Robinson (1996) has shown, the ideological foundations of racial segregation were equally used to justify discrimination against white women. In part these justifications stemmed from a fundamental belief that white Afrikaner women (and their primary function as mothers and wives), were a key embodiment of the Afrikaner nation. Burgeoning Afrikaner nationalism needed to be nourished, and that nourishment would come primarily from the home. White women who, in the 1930s, started to find employment in the expanding industrial sector, were therefore perceived by some nationalists as a threat to the stability of the white nation. These concerns were also furthered by the additional anxiety that young white women would be working alongside black African men in these jobs (Ross 1999). Discourses of the over-sexed black African male had long been in existence.[4] The employment of women in the industrial sector therefore went not only to increase fears as to the survival of white nationhood, they also added to the perceived need for that nationhood in the first place – by raising the spectre of intimate contact between black African men and white women.[5] As McClintock (1990) documents, in a move similar to that which occurred in Victorian Britain, a revamped and more powerful ideology of motherhood was deployed by nationalists in the 1930s to firmly position white women within the private sphere. 'A gendered division of national creation prevailed, whereby men were seen to embody the political and economic agency of the *volk* [people], while women were the (unpaid) keepers of tradition and the volk's moral and spiritual mission' (p. 108). While exclusions against women in the workplace were not legislated, powerful ideas as to the place of white women in relation to black African men and wider white society clearly helped to limit the career opportunities of this group. For the nation's survival, isolation from other race groups bred concern over those, including professional women, who did not fit neatly into ideas of what white society should be. Their employment opportunities were dictated first by their role as housewives and supporters of their husbands. Those that attempted to move outside the remit of respectable white society fell foul of an ideology based largely on systematic discrimination (Gaitskell and Unterhalter 1989; Viljoen 1994).[6] It therefore perhaps comes as little surprise that such a society would also hold negative views of queer sexuality within the white nation.

From the 1960s onwards the South African state found itself caught in a moral panic concerning white men who were seen as going against Christian nationalistic beliefs. Two interlinked explanations can be seen to account for the rise in moral panic concerning homosexuality during the 1960s.[7] First, the heightened prominence of queer men in the certain sites in West, and the possibility of the decriminalisation of homosexuality in the UK and US, had raised the profile of male homosexuality, shifting it from the position of unspoken-about vice to an increasingly tolerated aspect of all modern societies. Second was a belief within South Africa that the white nation cut off from the West on the tip of Africa was facing an ever-growing array of insidious forces. As Mark Gevisser's detailed work (1995 and 2000) concerning same-sex desire during the period highlights, the Afrikaner-led National Party was becoming increasingly consumed by paranoia and conspiracy rhetoric. To the growing list that already included black African, communist, Jewish and English conspiracies could now also be added the queer conspiracy. This fear ran so deep within the National Party that the South African police recommended that, as with suspected communist groups, informers should be used to infiltrate and report on homosexual gatherings (see also Retief 1995).

The prospect of a secret and seditious queer underworld within white society was further advanced by sensational reports within the media. Beginning in 1966, with a raid on a house party in the Forest Town suburb of Johannesburg, an image started to be constructed of a new and perilous group that threatened the white nation.[8] The day after the raid in Forest Town *The Star* reported under the front page headline 'Vice Squad finds 350 men in one house' that 'A large number [of men] . . . [were] in various stages of undress and behaving in a "grossly obscene" manner' (1966). And as the article on the front page of the *Rand Daily Mail* the following week commented: 'The party's guest list is believed to have included doctors, lawyers and company directors, many of whom had travelled a long way to attend the gathering' (*Rand Daily Mail* 1966). The fears ignited by the Forest Town raid continued to be felt within white South Africa for over a year. For example, articles in the *Sunday Express* in 1967, under headlines 'Spotlight on S.A.'s Growing Social Problem: One in ten may be deviant' (Wallace 1967) and 'They often meet in bars' (*Sunday Express* 1967) repeatedly stressed the 'problem' for South Africa's white community.[9]

By 1967 the paranoia associated with this new conspiracy found its way to parliament when the Minister for Justice, Peet Pelser, made a speech decrying homosexuality. In that speech he stated: 'It is a proven fact that sooner or later homosexual instincts make their effects felt on a community if they are permitted to run riot . . . Therefore we should be on alert and do what there is to do lest we be saddled later with a problem which will be the utter ruin of our spiritual and moral fibre.' The following year a Select Committee was set the task of investigating the perceived new threat and making recommendations as to the best ways to combat it. Of specific concern for the security services were the limited powers available to them to arrest queer men. Despite attempts by some white queer men to prevent the implementation of new legislation, amendments were made to the Immorality Act in 1969. As the now Constitutional Court Judge, Edwin Cameron has explained, this amendment made it illegal for any man at a party to commit 'any act which is calculated to stimulate sexual passion or to give sexual gratification' (Cameron 1995: 92). A party was defined as 'any occasion where more than two persons are present' (ibid.). As an illustration both of the newly enhanced powers of the police and the extreme lengths to which the South African state had gone in its attempts to root out any instance that could 'provoke' queer sexuality, it was now technically within the remit of the law to arrest three men shaking hands with each other in an office.[10]

By the late 1960s, social hysteria, sensational media reports and new laws had firmly implicated queer men as both a menace and jeopardy to the white nation. As Retief (1995) has documented, now police found it far easier to conduct random raids on many different clubs and private parties. Police would freely arrest any men they found at such events. The police would even take note of the registration plates of cars parked nearby suspected queer clubs or bars. Such actions only added to the constant fear queer men who socialised at these venues had that their identities, along with their pictures, would be published in newspapers (van der Merwe 2006).[11]

So ingrained had this fear become that it was now also, in some cases, possible to discredit and dismiss opponents of the state by associating them with homosexuality. The high profile End Conscription Campaign (ECC), fighting for the disbandment of compulsory military service in the South African Defence Force (SADF), suffered heavily because one of its prominent members, Ivan Toms, was openly queer. Between 1983 and 1988 (when Toms was sentenced to eighteen months in prison for refusing to complete his military service), the SADF implemented a smear campaign against Toms and the ECC based on Toms' sexuality. Posters and graffiti suspected to have been sanctioned by the SADF appeared around Cape Town proclaiming that 'Ivan Toms fucks young boys', the 'ECC does it from behind' and 'The ECC believes in fairy tales'. The vehemence with which these attacks were realised led the ECC to try hard to distance itself from any mention of Tom's sexuality (Toms 1995). Yet as Conway (2004) has shown, this attempt by the ECC proved relatively unsuccessful. Individuals who refused military service were, in white nationalistic terms, portrayed by the state and the SADF as effeminate, weak willed, impotent, untrustworthy and complicit in the black African threat – in other words, the stereotypes of what many queer men in South Africa were by that point already perceived to be (see also Phillips 2005).[12]

For many white queer men, the period from the 1960s to the early 1980s was one of severe state censure and social stigmatisation (although such censure was not necessarily uniform throughout the entire period – see below). The apartheid state had developed, at least in part, as a result of a perceived need to protect white Christian society and its (supposed) moral values. While defined most strongly in relation to black African communities, the ideological justifications of apartheid could easily be used to validate control over other groups. The social world inhabited by white individuals was therefore characterised by a need to identify, isolate and confront all those who threatened it. Women suffered if they came into conflict with an ideology that positioned them as guardians and nurturers of the white family. Queer men suffered when they were identified as another group conspiring against the values and principles of white (and largely Afrikaner) nationalism.

Yet by the mid-1970s, white queer men were beginning to create social networks that withstood potential harassment. By the late 1980s, at the same time that apartheid rule began irrevocably to falter, white queer men were surfacing, publicly, from decades of state intolerance. By the early 1990s, queer men had emerged as one group that seemed likely to greatly benefit from the hoped-for new dispensation. As the following section will explore, in the space of only fifteen years, white queer men went from inhabiting a social and political position based on secrecy and the real threat of persecution, to existing in a society where they could slowly begin publicly and visibly expressing their identities. While the above discussion has highlighted the unique character of sexuality-based discrimination in South Africa, the next section will therefore underscore how it was the very nature of this intolerance – rather than the actions of large numbers of white queers themselves – that allowed for such a dramatic shift in the fortunes of queer men.

A Developing Culture and the Dying Days of Apartheid

As Edwin Cameron, then a human rights advocate, stated to a group of individuals in 1986:

> The shocking truth is that many gays in South Africa have to a great extent been living a dream that is in fact a legal nightmare. The simple fact is that male gays in South Africa have no legal rights to practice their gayness. Almost every gay here this afternoon, is according to South African law, a criminal. (quoted in Gevisser 1995: 60)

A lot had happened in the years leading up to the late 1980s to justify this claim by Cameron. Despite the Immorality Act, more and more gay bars and clubs had opened in Johannesburg and Cape Town. A burgeoning queer subculture, still in some parts secretive and all but invisible to wider society, was now slowly being granted limited acceptance by the faltering apartheid state. Ironically, it was the investigation by the Parliamentary Select Committee and the amendments to the Immorality Act that had allowed these first nascent attempts at wider community development. Simply put, the apartheid state had slowly come to realise that despite its best efforts it was impossible to totally eliminate what it saw as the 'homosexual threat' from the white population. As with a growing admission that black African communities could never be fully placated, it became clear that white homosexuality needed to be contained. At the same time, white queer men came to understand that as long as they remained unobtrusive to the state they would be able to limit any potential harassment (Gevisser 1995; Retief 1995). There would always be the fear of arrest but, for many men, it was that very fear, heightened after the national panic, which helped strengthen them in a way not possible before the state clampdown. As this interviewee explained when asked what he enjoyed about gay bars in Cape Town in the 1980s:

> I think there was something more childish about it. You know in the eighties the police could just walk into those places, and they could just arrest people. So it was something like being naughty at school about it. You know, doing something naughty and expecting to be caught out any moment. GARATH/38

And as this interviewee describes, while the threat of police raids against gay bars was an ever-present danger, it was that threat that helped heighten the excitement of going to such establishments to begin with:

> There were always fears that the club would be raided. These fears were very real, the police did raid clubs and I heard frightful stories of the police coming in and searching everyone and herding guys out onto the pavement. The assumption was that the raids were an expression of the rampant state homophobia at the time, which for many guys added a kind of adrenalin-rush to [the] whole experience of going to a gay club in the first place. GRAEME/44

Therefore, rather than curtail the existence of homosexuality within the white community, the policies of the apartheid state towards queer groups only helped further them. Similarly, the 'exposure' of homosexuality had shown the apartheid state that it could never control it. The very conditions that had made queer lives so difficult were now also helping to give the community a limited space of acceptance within the state.

As the 1980s drew to a close, it was also becoming obvious to the National Party that the very logic of white separatism that had helped justify and maintain apartheid during the previous half-century, would itself be one of the ultimate causes of the National Party's undoing. So it was that during the same period that white queer men were beginning to experience limited acceptance, the apartheid state began to accept that their position on racial segregation was no longer tenable. Increasing insurrection among black African groups forced to live in spatially separate and economically impoverished locations to white communities, internationally choking economic sanctions and recession at home had forced the government into secret negotiations with Nelson Mandela, at the time a political prisoner on Robben Island (Thompson 2001; Worden 2000). On the 2 February 1990 the new President, F.W. De Klerk, announced at the opening session of Parliament that he was un-banning the black African-led African National Congress (ANC), the South African Communist Party (SACP) and the Pan African Congress (PAC) along with 31 other organisations previously seen as threats to the state. For many South Africans however, there would be little time to truly rejoice for another four years. In the space of just over four years between De Klerk's speech in Parliament and the election of Nelson Mandela and his ANC party to power on 9 May 1994, there would be fourteen thousand politically related killings. This became the highest death rate in South Africa during the twentieth century (Clarke and Worger 2004). As negotiations for the political transition took place, South Africa found itself witness to groups on all sides of the political spectrum engaging in bloody attacks on each other as they sought to consolidate their power and weaken the position of their opponents.

But for white queer men, there were signs that the New South Africa would be a far more tolerant place than the world they were currently living in. Rather than be satisfied with a tacit truce between the queer community and the apartheid state, queer groups could now look forward to full legal, political and social rights within the country. In part this was due to an embryonic legal movement in South Africa, which was proving successful at lobbying for the inclusion of a sexuality equality clause in the Interim Constitution (Cock 2005 and chapter 6). At the same time, however, the *de facto* party elect, the ANC, was becoming increasingly aware of the importance of gender and sexuality rights. The actions of individual members of the ANC such as the late Simon Nkoli[13] and authority acquired initially from outside the party (Tatchell 2005), had sensitised them to the need to reject all forms of discrimination – not simply those based on race. When the Constitution was finally ratified in 1996, South Africa became the first country in the world to make it unconstitutional to discriminate on the basis of an individual's sexuality (Croucher 2002). Throughout the 1990s and into the twenty-first century, laws discriminating against homosexuality would slowly be repealed. Laws against sodomy were removed in 1999. By the beginning of the new century, queer men and women would enjoy the freedom of adoption rights, pension support rights and foreign partner immigration and citizenship rights. By December 2006, the state would also acknowledge the rights of same-sex couples to marry (see also chapter 6). In the space of fifteen years South Africa went from one of the most repressed societies towards homosexuality to one of the most politically liberated.

Yet to return to the statement by Cameron above, it is debatable how far white queer men themselves were actually responsible for such a shift. Unlike Western groups during the period, it was relatively impossible for white queers in South Africa to work together to change civil society's opinion of them, or the state's laws against them. While allowing a degree of tolerance towards white queer men, the South African state was unwilling to allow any claim to group minority 'rights'. As Mikki van Zyl (2005) has discussed about Cape Town queer groups during the period, political identification, had it been implicit or explicit with broader rights movements in South Africa, would have proved suicidal in the face of authoritarian state oppression (see also Rydström 2005). Many early activists realised that they were never going to be given the political space to fight for rights at a time when the government had announced a state of emergency and was deploying increasingly violent methods against black African groups in a last ditch attempt to regain control over the country. In other words, in a country bordering on civil war, they accepted that the state would never allow the propagation of any opinion publicly opposed to it.

And as recent work documenting the work of sexuality-based organisations in South Africa in the 1980s is now revealing, several groups also failed or refused to see the links between homophobia and racism and how both were perpetuated by the state. The aim, it seemed, was to create within white society a safe and accepting space for others. Yet such a mission failed to acknowledge its race-based bias. As Ann Smith, a founding member of the largest such organisation in the country during the period, the Gay Association of South Africa (GASA), has stated:

> Of course we knew that GASA had far, far more white members than black, but we did not see any way out of this except to make the GASA premises a racially integrated space . . . it is true that we were afraid, in our white liberal safety, to rock the boat too much: it was dangerous enough in those days to defy the tenets of apartheid by having an association open to people regardless of their colour. (2005: 61)[14]

Concurrently, unlike their contemporaries in the UK or US, white queers in South Africa did not have sufficient political strength or momentum to confront homophobia by the state or civil society. The development of a gay rights based movement in the West had rested upon a long history of small political gains being made by groups since the end of the Second World War. The momentum needed to create a gay rights movement had been building slowly for forty years before the Stonewall riot in 1969 in New York, which effectively helped usher in an era of gay identity politics (Altman 1972; D'Emilo 1983 and 2002; Warner 1993 and 2000). South African white queer groups were in no position to attempt such a transformation of their own political landscape. In such a way, sexuality rights only came into being in South Africa as an adjunct to wider needs to create a truly free South African nation. Civil society was not called upon to debate and then force a change in state oppression towards queer groups. But to return to the quotation at the beginning of this section once more, it is questionable how far this paucity of public political engagement among white queer men was actually felt by them.

Comparatively, white queers had not suffered discrimination nearly as harsh as black African or coloured communities in South Africa. They did not have to carry passbooks allowing them to walk the city centres where they lived, not were they forcibly relocated away from their homes. Police, while by no means friendly to white queers, had, at least, limited the degree to which they were systematically targeting them. Nor were many able or willing to risk engagement with broader rights based struggles. Throughout the 1980s a queer subculture continued to develop, fostered by news of a burgeoning set of lifestyles and communities in sites in the West. In a state where political gains by any minority were virtually impossible to achieve, many white queers were content with the fact that they were no longer being rounded up and arrested on a regular basis (Luirink 2000). As one journalist in Cape Town pointed out:

> *It's almost as though the focus was on the political struggle for [black African] enfranchisement and gay men didn't go through [that] . . . you know there was no real politicisation of the gay struggle, other than through individuals, intellectuals in the late seventies and eighties. But that was very, very small compared to New York or London. And I just don't think there is anywhere near that level of politicisation that you'd expect. [There's a] surprising sense of not being in touch with the issues.* CHRISTIAN/31

And as one activist noted about gay rights movements generally in South Africa:

> *I think it is a very difficult time in South Africa for gay issues. There are a number of reasons for that. One is, there has never been a strong integrated gay movement.* PIETER/28

The ideological power of Christian national beliefs tied to a separate white nationalism, and the creation of a massive low-paid black African workforce, were powerful justifications for apartheid. For nearly half a century, the Afrikaner-led National Party attempted to maintain control over all groups it saw as threats to its own prosperity and security. Early on, white queer men were singled out as a group requiring specific attention by the state. However, it was soon realised that control over white queers could never be total. Instead, despite the continued possibility of arrest, this group was given limited acceptance by the state. State policies also inadvertently helped white queers to begin forming social networks that could start withstanding police harassment. While never able to overtly become visible and open either to the state, or spatially through, for example, the creation of visible spaces, queer men were still taking the first steps towards wider social and political acknowledgement and acceptance. This group were therefore in a strong position to benefit from political change in the 1990s. Yet unlike black African groups, white queer men did not have the opportunity, or necessarily the inclination, to effect political change themselves. As such, it becomes increasingly apparent that apartheid policies set white queers on a trajectory that not only helped give them a social space not possible before the state crackdown, but also meant they never were able to form a coherent or unified political consciousness – as, it can be argued, happened for a short time among some similar groups in the West (see below).

As the rest of this chapter will explore, a legacy of the social taking prominence over the political has continued today in Cape Town among the most visible group of white queer men who inhabit or pass through the De Waterkant gay village. For many, the local history of political intolerance towards white queers has been overshadowed by new freedoms and connections with particular elements of a culture located in Western spaces. For some, it appears that any undeclared or partially buried feelings of political apathy within the white queer community can easily be set aside as many white queers take advantage of the seemingly exhilarating and internationally influenced opportunities that Cape Town – and the overtly visible gay village – now offers them.

The West as Destination: Visibility on the Cape

> The music was changing its rhythmic flavour, from frenetic hip-hop to utterly frenetic hip-hop, and Terry was saying, 'rather a lot of tat here tonight, don't you think?' That was exactly the same thing Terry always said in the club, mused Howard, before he left with the most desirable boy in the room on his arm . . . Howard squeezed towards the bar . . . The bare-chested bar boys, chosen clearly for their svelte pecs and general muscle tone . . . smirked and hit 'ting' on the bell overhead with the small change. It was an ordinary night in the early promise-of-summer season in Cape Town's famed Pink Triangle, and the night was stripped for action. (Willoughby 2002: 17)

Only a few years after the end of apartheid Cape Town has successfully re-branded itself as a liberal and accepting city towards queers not only within South Africa, but also internationally (Oswin 2005). In a little over a decade, Cape Town has eclipsed Johannesburg or any other South African city to become, as Cape Town Tourism calls it, South Africa's 'Reigning Queen'[15] (Bath 2004; Mock and Rattan 2006). One recent travel guide referred to the city as 'Africa's self proclaimed gay capital . . . Cape Town has everything a gay traveller could want' (Verlang and Bedford 2006: 784). Others, including local business owners, have represented it as the 'San Francisco of Africa' (Thomasson 1998).[16] Today, Cape Town represents for many white men a 'gay Mecca' on par with San Francisco in the US or London in the UK (Castells 1983; Kelley et al. 1996). With a growing Gay Pride Festival (chapter 6) and a nationally renowned costume party, the 'Mother City Queer Project', Cape Town has developed a reputation as the most liberal and accepting city in the country (Visser 2002). Indeed, nationally Cape Town succeeded in positioning itself in opposition to other South African cities with 'less progressive' views of queer tourism.[17] Much in the same way that West Hollywood succeeded in recreating itself as a queer safe haven in the 1990s (Forest 1995), so too has Cape Town developed an image as a location where queer sexuality is not only accepted but also celebrated.[18]

This image acts as an important draw for queer men from across the country. As work on queer mobilities has highlighted, specific sites in key urban areas remain fundamental in understanding how queer groups wish to represent themselves.[19] And as Weston (1995) has discussed in other contexts, migration (both temporary and permanent) to Cape Town by white queer individuals in South Africa has been fostered by the idea of the city as an almost mythic space of freedom, inhabited by many other like-minded individuals. As these two white queer men, originally from Durban in Kwa-Zulu Natal province and Pretoria in Gauteng province, explain:

> I'd been to Cape Town for work and I then made it sort of my mission to go again . . . I came from Durban [and] I never had hundreds of friends . . . So part of the reason I went to [the gay village in Cape Town] was to get into the gay community . . . living it out to the absolute, trying to merge myself into this whole community. JOHN/41

> I think it's akin to the relationship between San Francisco, New York and the Midwest in the [United] States. There's this common perception that Cape Town is liberal, just like there's a common perception that Jo'burg [Johannesburg] is dangerous and money driven. Everything between is a bit of a cultural wasteland . . . Most of my friends in Cape Town were not born here. It's something of [a] vacuum cleaner sucking up the people that have outgrown their home town, and being gay is one sure way to outgrow a small town or even a city like Pretoria. LEWIS/26

At the heart of this newly formed centre, like The Castro in San Francisco, Greenwich Village in New York or Soho in London, is a 'gay village', De Waterkant, located in the affluent Green Point district of the city, on the outskirts of the Central Business District (CBD)/City Bowl (Figure 2.1). As Visser (2003a, 2003b and 2004) has explained, between 1996 and the present, the De Waterkant area of the city has ballooned in size, becoming the most visible expression of queer life on the African continent.[20] Today, the area covers several city blocks, between Somerset Road close to the ocean and Waterkant Street further inland and from Hudson Street close to the centre of the City Bowl to De Smit Street in the direction of Sea Point (Figure 2.1).

The central function of the gay village is clearly that of leisure. Like similar urban spaces in the West, the De Waterkant area of the city is filled with locations where individuals can socialise, shop, eat and enjoy a vibrant nightlife (Figures 2.2 and 2.3). A gay sauna, the Hot House, is also located in the village and offers the opportunity of anonymous sexual encounters. The gay village therefore has particular appeal to a certain group who are able to afford to visit it on a regular basis and who find enjoyment in the

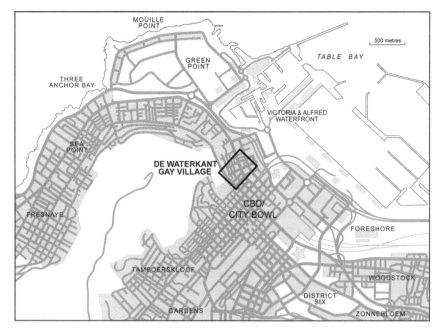

Figure 2.1   The location of the De Waterkant gay village in the centre of Cape Town.

Figure 2.2   A view up Dixon Street in the gay village.

different leisure activities it offers. For this group, the gay village represents the physical embodiment of a lifestyle new to South Africa. As these men explain:

> *There aren't many faults. It's a new, it's a new culture . . . It's sort of post-religion, post-issues and conservative edges, and it's very forward-thinking, it's very open, it's very sophisticated, and it is better than what we had before . . . All the people that I come into contact with are lawyers, journalists, doctors, all the classic professions . . . They are all high achievers, the work-hard-play-hard set . . . So it's sort of your club-going, professional, gym-going . . . buying into gay culture, very much so, the gay people that live in Green Point . . . Friday night, let's just say it's drinks, it's dinner-party culture, it's, you know, big houses, swish cars. [Then] they go to the clubs, they go to the pavement at [The] Bronx, the pavement at Café Manhattan outside. You just sit and you talk to people, have drinks. That is the culture. [Saturday,] during the day, you go with about six or eight people to a trendy spot. Everybody's wearing sunglasses, tank tops, and you're always in a big party and you're sitting and you're lounging.   MICHAEL/21*

> *[The gay village] is just one huge jungle gym.   LEWIS/26*

> *[Café] Manhattan would be social, Bronx would be dancing, and there are one or two other little coffee bars where you can go and you sit. And you go there, and you might score, you might pick up somebody, and you might finish up at the end of the day having sex, but the other – as I see it, the initial intention of going to the place is either you want somewhere where you can dance and get rid of some energy, or you want to go to a place where you can sit and chat and chill, or you want to go to a place where you can have a fuck.   PATRICK/53*

As the above quotations illustrate, there are many similarities between perceptions of the De Waterkant and a particular popular espousal of an element of contemporary Western queer culture.[21] Indeed, the excerpt at the beginning of this section from Guy Willoughby's novel *Archangels* describing a night out in the Cape Town gay village could easily be mistaken for descriptions of similar spaces elsewhere. North American authors including Augusten Burrows (2004), Jameson Currier (2000), Armistead Maupin (1980) and Edmund White (1997) along with British authors such as Alan Hollinghurst (2004) have described similar scenes of sexual desire, developed physiques and excitement in corresponding queer spaces. Specifically, many commentators have explored how leisure, recreation and conspicuous consumption make up a significant and highly visible element of this queer culture (Binnie 1995; Binnie and Skeggs 2004; Nast 2002; Schulmann 1998; Simpson 1996; Sinfield 1998; Tucker 1997; Weir 1996). While increasingly critiqued for only presenting an essentialistic interpretation of a wider dynamic community (Elder 2002; see also below), this representation still has found purchase among particular groups of men in Cape Town and helps frame how they perceive and enact difference.

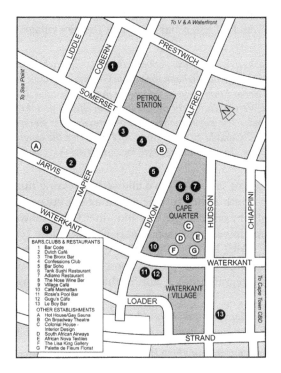

Figure 2.3   The location of various leisure and consumer venues in the gay village.

There are several historical and more recent factors that can go towards explaining why Cape Town would be receptive to implementing this lifestyle and to have visibly embodied it in the space of the gay village. First, for many white queer men in Cape Town, knowledge of queer life in London or New York or Amsterdam has become an important element that goes to define how they view their own lives. In part, this has clearly driven by the Dutch and British ancestry of the white community in the city. Even before the end of apartheid, increasing numbers of white queer men had been travelling to Europe and North America and bringing back stories of the promising new lifestyles found there (Gevisser 1995; Luirink 2000). The creation of a burgeoning queer sub-culture in South Africa during the 1970s and 1980s was therefore augmented by news of similar developments abroad. As several commentators have since documented, by the beginning of the 1990s, the creation of a queer lifestyle in part influenced by images of conspicuous consumption and the styles and fashions that existed in urban centres in the West was becoming firmly entrenched in the centre of Cape Town (Elder 2005; Gevisser 1995; Visser 2003a). This process only accelerated through the 1990s with the full initiation of South Africa onto the world stage. As DYLAN, a bar owner in the gay village, commented:

> *I mean, if one looks at it, the whole notion of the gay village which we have in Cape Town is an offshoot of perhaps what happened in Greenwich Village in certain places, in London, like Soho, I think – ja . . . And you must understand that the dominant culture here is a Western European culture in South Africa, and the gay culture too follows those trends. The publications you buy here are from Europe and from the United States and Canada as well. So – And of course the languages which we speak are, of course, European languages too.*   DYLAN

Further, the lifting of sanctions have allowed increasing numbers of young white men from South Africa to take advantage of greater travel and work opportunities to, for example, the UK and other Commonwealth countries. Having spent time in various queer spaces abroad, these young queer men return to South Africa looking for similar experiences at home. For many of these men, exposure to Europe and also North America drives their wish to emulate, and integrate into, a culture that many view as 'superior'.[22]

> *England and all of Europe is culturally older. This is a fact. And age has its advantages. Europe is more stable, more wealthy, better integrated.*   LEWIS/26

> *We are all insecure towards anything British. Just because English culture is very – centre of the world, from where the light comes.*   CRAIG/25

The emulation of a particular element of Western queer culture has also been strongly augmented by the growing tourist industry in Cape Town. The re-branding of the city since the end of apartheid as a cosmopolitan city for foreign tourists has resulted in it being represented internationally as one of the most 'gay-friendly' destinations for tourists in the world (Elder 2005; Visser 2003a). With an estimated 70,000 queer men and women visiting Cape Town each year (Seymour 2003), it is considered important enough for Cape Town Tourism to view it as a niche market that requires specific attention.[23] As the former head of Cape Town Tourism, Sheryl Ozinski, describes, there has been a concerted attempt to render the city as a favourable location for a particular (in no small part, essentialistic) queer (Western) tourist:

> *It's about Cape Town being a hip and happening city. One wants to create the impression, which I think is real as well, that there are lots of things that are happening . . . If you come to Cape Town you will experience a lifestyle [that] is much perhaps like your own, in terms of the night life and the ability to meet people . . . [queer tourists] like to do other things that most people like to do, but they also like to enjoy clubs. We have plenty of those. They enjoy meeting people and I*

think we can offer that opportunity in the clubs for example. We have great music here . . . So it is really about Cape Town as a lifestyle choice . . . Cape Town as a lifestyle destination. SHERYL OZINSKI

The branding of Cape Town for foreign tourists with a lifestyle centred on nightclubs and leisure has naturally had an effect on the composition of people who visit the gay village and the city. Increased numbers of foreign tourists will visit. These men therefore also disseminate knowledge of particular gay spaces and particular renderings of queer experience in the West into Cape Town.

Yet this image of Cape Town as a liberal city with a well-defined queer community – that draws inspiration from elements of queer culture located initially in some Western cities – has also helped hide large differences and inequalities among groups of white queer men. As the following section will explore, the recent visibility of white queer men as a result of the development of the gay village, has helped create a lifestyle that while seemingly open and accepting, is strongly biased towards middle-class men who subscribe to a narrow interpretation of queer lifestyles. The development of Cape Town as a 'gay Mecca' and the parallel urban development in De Waterkant gay village can have the same criticisms lobbied at it as similar developments elsewhere (Nast 2002). Just as Schulmann (1998) has argued, cities that queer men migrate to have, over the past 20 years, tended to promote a lifestyle centred on parties and leisure, only going to hide the diversity that exists among such men. While the idea of what Nast (2002) has termed the 'white queer patriarch' has itself been criticised for only framing queer men in a narrow (and sometimes essentialistic) framework (Elder 2002),[24] it must nonetheless be realised that an aspiration towards (or association with) such a rendering can itself lead to exclusions and the perpetuation of difference. At the same time therefore, the images used to promote a space such as the gay village can also go to further difference between groups of white queer men. As the following section will explore, popular representations of the De Waterkant through the way it has become seen as an overtly visible queer space overshadow locally defined difference between groups in the city and at the same time go to further those differences. Such a situation has also been created and is now furthered by a failure to develop a politically aware queer community.

Cracks in the Façade

Class has long been viewed as a divisive factor within many contemporary queer cultures. Yet in Cape Town, class divisions between white queer groups have been perpetuated by uniquely South African (and unique to

Cape Town) historical factors. Two complementary components are important here. First, is the perceived historically bounded ethnic divide between English speakers and Afrikaans speakers in Cape Town. This distinction has existed in South Africa since the nineteenth century and locates representations of English and Afrikaner individuals into different social groups based around oppositional histories to each other. Historically, those with English ancestry in the city have been viewed as more wealthy and urbanised than Afrikaner 'Boer' farmers (Bickford-Smith et al. 1999).[25] For many queer men in Cape Town, these differences – while not as nearly as stark as they once were – have helped maintain distinctions between English and Afrikaner.[26] As these quotations describing the classed nature of the English and Afrikaner divide illustrate:

> *They'll have a barbeque in the afternoon. They do what their parents do, their Afrikaans parents. And many of them will go to church as well, they'll be churchgoing. Or they'll watch rugby. And they'll decorate their homes so that you can identify the Afrikaans look, as I like to call it . . . usually quite kitsch. You just get that sense of the Afrikaans look. Its difficult to explain but I'll show you a photograph. The décor is a certain look, which [has] a definite attitude and look than [with] the English . . . The English are far more gentle and the Afrikaners are aggressive, bombastic, loud and they get very drunk.   GARATH/38*

> *I think that many Afrikaans families buy into the concept of patriarchy, more so than English-speaking families. My perception, as an English-speaking white gay man, is that more Afrikaans families absorb Calvinist-type crap into their sense of reality. This makes them less tolerant of diversity and warier of anything that could possibly threaten their reality and sense of equilibrium . . . I think more Afrikaners live in quite small social worlds . . . I often think Afrikaners are more likely to be hypocritical and less congruent than English-speaking white South Africans.   GRAEME/44*

And from a viewpoint that contrasts representations of Afrikaner culture more favourably to that of the English:

> *It's interesting in that perhaps, there is a greater sense of community among Afrikaner gay men. Sort of older guys, younger guys, there being an obvious form of jollity and sort of friendliness towards each other that I don't always see among English speakers in Cape Town.   CHRISTIAN/31*

> *English people [have] thought, 'Well, we're not Afrikaans. We're English-speaking and that's why we are better than the rest.'   GERHARD/46*

> *[When growing up] Ja, that Afrikaans people thought that English people were shallow.   ROBERT/39*

These views are clearly based on stereotypes of each group. And as such, it would undoubtedly be wrong to assume that all English regard all

Afrikaners as being of lower status, lower class or not as cosmopolitan as them. Equally it would be a gross misconception to assume that all Afrikaners associate English speakers with conceitedness or pettiness. Further, it is increasingly difficult to find families that are entirely English or entirely Afrikaans.[27]

These distinctions, while clearly voiced by interviewees, therefore need to be placed in a wider context. Here, the second class component, that of spatial differences among groups of white queer men requires attention. The deployment of English and Afrikaner as distinctions among queer men is deeply tied to the location of these groups within the city. Historically, Afrikaners inhabited the Northern Suburbs of the city, while English speakers lived in the Southern Suburbs. The dividing line in the city between these groups is refereed to (by both) as the 'Boerewors Curtain' – named after a popular type of 'farmer's sausage' in South Africa, implying its rural (and hence Afrikaner) extraction. While this line of demarcation is not exact, it is understood as roughly bisecting the city. Places on the peninsula close to the City Bowl such as Pinelands, Rosebank, Newlands and Claremont are viewed as being part of the Southern Suburbs. Places towards the north east of the city such as Bellville, Durbanville, Parow, Goodwood and Milnerton are recognised as being part of the Northern Suburbs (Figure 2.4).

For some queer men located in the City Bowl or the Atlantic Seaboard (made up of areas such as Sea Point, Bantry Bay and Camps Bay), the suburbs generally, and the Northern Suburbs in particular, are viewed as less favourable areas of residence. For these men (who are a mix of both English and Afrikaners), their area of the city is understood as being located close to the very heart of the city and hence is believed to be more expensive, exclusive and cosmopolitan to live in than the suburbs. As this interviewee from the Atlantic Seaboard explained:

> *You see it around you, you see the interactions between different people. You see what people say about other people, and for instance [a] Sea Point [Atlantic Seaboard] person is very disparaging about people living in Durbanville, [Northern Suburbs]. There is a division, in the Northern Suburbs. Whereas they are not as disparaging about living in the Southern Suburbs . . . They mix at the same parties. But they are not as accepted. The intelligence and social standing in terms of career, that definitely separates people. So at a party, you would be at a big party you would be together and you would talk because he is cute. But, and you might like him, but you are definitely not going to take him home on a regular basis. But, you'll fuck him because he is cute anyway. NEIL/28*

While this division is most acute for men in the Northern Suburbs, men in the traditionally English Southern Suburbs also noted it as well:

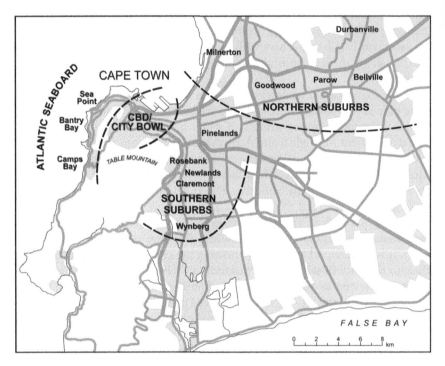

Figure 2.4   The location of suburban areas in relation to the CBD/City Bowl and Atlantic Seaboard.

It's sometimes common . . . There I was at a party, and another guy and I eyed each other, when it came to the crunch later, we were going home together – 'Your place or mine?' But when he heard I was not from the city centre, he looked me in the eyes and said, 'I'm sorry', and stalked off. Well, that comment threw some icy water on that budding night of pleasure. ALEXANDER/39

These distinctions based on ethnicity and spatial location are also observable through opinions of Gat parties, held in the Northern Suburb of Milnerton every two weeks. Called 'Gat' because they initially took place in an abandoned quarry (Gat is Afrikaans for 'hole'), these events have become an institution among some queer men, particularly for Afrikaner men who live in the Northern Suburbs. Each party takes place in a large hall with long tables facing length-wise into the space. While dancing occurs in the middle of the hall, the prominence and arrangement of tables make the events largely about conversation. Each table, which can seat up to twenty individuals, is often pre-booked weeks in advance.

While very popular among certain groups, there also exist strong negative discourses of Gat parties, which engage both spatial and ethnic justifications. For English-speaking queer men, there is an assumption held by some that because the parties are viewed as Afrikaans in origin and located spatially in a different area of the city, away from the more cosmopolitan City Bowl or Atlantic Seaboard, that they are not necessarily events they would like to visit. For these men, Gat parties are nothing more than a parochial Afrikaner indulgence. As these English queer men explained:

> [In response to 'what do you think of Gat parties'] I hate it . . . I hate it. It's not my style of music at all, and it's . . . the dancing. I mean, it's just not my scene at all. It's, like too damn conservative. GEORGE/39

> The Gat party, it's just simply that it's not quite my planet, not my culture. CRAIG/25

> People who live in Bellville [a Northern Suburb] are more like to go to the Gat parties, people who live in the City Bowl [CBD] are more likely to go to Sliver [a night club in the gay village]. GRAEME/44

For Afrikaners living on the Atlantic Seaboard, similar justifications were also used:

> I went once, but more as an anthropological exercise. LUC/42

> Hillbillies . . . I feared that they were going to get aggressive as well, that they'd start picking on our table because they were heading in that direction. GARATH/38

Again however, these views are based largely on stereotypical assumptions about different groups in the city. It would be wrong to assume that Gat parties are solely for suburban Afrikaner queer men. A significant minority of English men from both the suburbs and the City Bowl or Atlantic Seaboard areas of the city do visit them. As one current organiser of the Gat parties, CARL, explained, for him the difference between Gat parties and the lifestyle popular in the City Bowl or Atlantic Seaboard areas is fostered equally by the type of visibility that the gay village promotes:

> Well, I think the majority of people tended to be Afrikaans, though, I mean, there is a lot of English-speaking people . . . But I will say majority is Afrikaans . . . Well, unfortunately, some of my people, you know, the feedback I got from them is they don't like to go there [the gay village] because they don't [want] to be in the public. You know, unfortunately, a lot of people, gay people, are still like that. They don't want to be publicised, you know. [The Gat parties are more] a private function and that's why they want to be there. And that's why they don't like to take part in [Pride] marches [which occur in the City Bowl/Atlantic Seaboard (chapter 6)] or whatever. CARL

Gat parties therefore, despite the reservations based around class distinctions held by some groups, offer a space for white queer men to socialise in that is not structured around nightclubs and the leisure lifestyle found in the De Waterkant. They are also not as visible to the wider community. The Gat parties are far less expensive and less ostentatious than a night in the gay village and also offer a unique communal, almost family atmosphere:[28]

> And you can go out on a 'jol' [celebration/party], or on a social, for R20 [£1.67] an evening, and you can book a table. So you sit at a table. I mean, if you go to a club or any other place, you haven't got that facilities there. So you've got a nice table . . . I think everybody feels like one big family there. And, I mean, you can talk to anybody there. Everybody mix[es] with everybody.   CARL

> It's all very informal, you bring your own booze and book a table as a group. It all takes place in a gymnasium, and the music is a mix of pop and rock and the occasional traditional 'sakkie' [traditional Afrikaans dance]. It is a very different experience from the [gay] village. It's much more casual, less pretentious 'gesellig' [an environment where discussion and socialisation is possible] and down to earth . . . There's a frank, unfettered joy in simply 'jolling' [to celebrate/have a party] with your mates . . . No jacket required.   LEWIS/26

Clearly, it is possible to describe and articulate numerous distinctions between groups of white queer men in Cape Town, only some of which have been highlighted here. Yet the distinctions that have been explored in this chapter help us to see how the dominant image promoted of Cape Town as a 'gay Mecca' that has unabashedly drawn inspiration from a Westernised representation of queer culture – and particularly its most recent commodified and spatially demarcated form – can actively obscure, and also further, differences between groups of men in the city. Class distinctions located around ideas of historical ethnic divides and spatial divides have helped condition and perpetuate these differences. Further, the very visibility of the gay village in heteronormative space – which goes to define much of the city's queer imagery and the perception of Cape Town as a visible 'gay Mecca', is clearly not favourable to some queer men who live in the city. For some men, Gat parties offer a community atmosphere not available in the gay village.

Commentators such as Binnie (2004) and Tan (2001) are therefore correct to point out that it is simplistic to view queer groups as homogenous and equally affected by globalisation. To assume that a global queer culture is usurping all those it encounters around the world could be to deny the possibility of hybridisation and an appreciation of diversity. It would also be to sideline discussion of what elements of any particular queer culture are actually being transported to new locations. If an anti-essentialistic position is taken, it therefore becomes necessary to explore why groups choose at certain times and certain places to adopt outside influences, while at other times choose not to. It therefore must be understood that white queer men exist within both global and local arenas. The popular representation of Cape Town as a liberated space for queers, with a culture similar to that represented in spaces in the West, does not reflect the diversity that exists within the city. As the final section below will explore, to understand why this diversity has remained largely hidden, and why groups continue to delimit themselves along ethnic and spatial lines, it will be necessary not only to look again at the development of queer men's lives in Cape Town, but also at the roots of Western queer culture.

Locating the Visibility of White Queer Men

The development of a contemporary queer culture – and its latest commodified from – in sites in the West was directly affected by specific historical factors prevalent during the latter part of the twentieth century in the US and Western Europe. A period from the Second World War to the 1970s saw the slow mobilisation of men in the first steps to end centuries of discrimination against them. First with groups such as the Homophile Movement and the Mattachine Society in the 1950s and then later with the Gay Liberation Front (GLF) in the 1970s, these groups slowly formed the basis of a social movement centred on ending homophobia in society (D'Emilio 1983 and 2002).

Like other interest groups at the time, movements such as the GLF based themselves on the idea of a bounded group fighting for greater rights in society. This was decidedly different to earlier movements such as the Homophiles, who instead sought to assimilate into wider heteronormative society, rather than directly confront it. These earlier models aimed to limit the creation of, and even abolish, the term 'homosexual' as a distinct political (and in some cases, social) identity – in no small part due to its medicalised associations (Seidman 1993; Warner 2000; see also chapter 1).[29] By comparison, 'gay' identity politics, as pursued by the GLF and other similar groups, focused on the belief that social discrimination could only end by direct confrontation with wider society. Gay men therefore modelled their pattern of social and civil protest on that which was proving successful for African-American and feminist activists (Hall 2003). By attempting to affect social change in this way, gay men created for themselves an ethnic identity model, with an emphasis on cultural difference, community building and an identity-based interest group politics (Warner 1993) – which itself helped position contemporary liberationists' concerns with freeing oneself of 'the closet' based around a particular rigid heterosexual/homosexual binary relationship (chapter 1). Indeed, the very term 'gay' in part gained prominence through attempts to create a social and political identity where previously there had only been a medicalised perversion. Out of this movement, urban gay spaces or gay villages developed (chapter 1).

Over time, however, critics have pointed out that this model resulted in an increasingly essentialistic representation of gay culture gaining prominence. Two reasons exist for this. First, was the problem of exclusion. Unlike ethnic minorities or women, gay political leaders found it difficult to section off a distinct section of society. It proved far harder to use sexual identity as a call for greater rights in society, than it did with other socially constructed markers such as race and gender. As will be discussed more in the next chapter, these men were not as easily distinguishable a group needing special political attention. Further, gay men themselves appeared to limit the degree to which they wanted to associate with other groups of sexual minorities. As Blum (2002) and Seidman (1993) have argued, liberationist politics constructed simple binaries around 'straight' and 'gay' that they felt necessary if group rights were to be achieved. Because of this, bisexuals, for example, have only been partially included within the gay movement (Power 1996; Wilchins 2004; see also chapter 3). Over time, this artificial boundary created to justify a call for social and political rights meant that the focuses of several campaigns in the West were decided by an ever smaller group of men. These men, through access to financial and political resources, tended predominantly to be middle-class and white (Valocchi 1999).

Second, an increasingly visible gay community resulted in certain elements' increased commercialisation, leading today to calls that sectors of this community have reached a point of 'homonormalisation' (chapter 1). As Simpson (1996: xiv) has simply put: 'Nowadays, gay is goods'. Marketing targeted at an allegedly homogenous 'gay community' – who are perceived to have uniformly 'come out' of 'the closet' and associated with particular urban spaces – has perpetuated the conceptually damaging myth that all such men are wealthy. Today, this can help further the visibility of a certain group of queer individuals (predominantly middle-class men) who can actually afford to 'buy into' a culture centred increasingly on, for example, conspicuous consumption, while sidelining others. This has resulted in the image both to queer men and to wider society that the queer community is predominantly affluent. One need only look at the range of products aggressively targeted at this group, including designer furniture, boutique clothing, exclusive spirits and exotic holidays, to see how far this image has seeped into popular consciousness. As Weir (1996) discusses, by the 1990s, a particular segment of the queer community had come to represent the new class of urban professionals, further obscuring other queers. The homogenisation and essentialising of queer culture, begun with political projects in the 1970s based around gay identity politics and furthered by subsequent commercialisation, has helped make one of the most visible forms of queer culture today an exclusively white and middle-class phenomenon.

While clearly at best only reflecting the lives of a small number of queer men in the West, such a representation nonetheless still has great power to exclude and delineate communities (Nast 2002). And indeed, upon first reading there would appear to be some strong similarities between this history of homogenisation and what has emerged in Cape Town. Popular representations of a particular group of queer men in Cape Town would seem to indicate that they too are directly, consciously and purposefully attempting to follow a pattern set in place among some groups in certain spaces in the West. A group of middle-class men are able to enjoy a lifestyle that requires a certain level of disposable income and which they see as actively emulating a culture found in sites elsewhere. Nightclubs, bars and restaurants in the gay village cater to this group. Foreign tourists are also able to enjoy what the gay village has to offer. For these men, a particular Western form of queer culture has been created, focused on their needs and pleasures. This lifestyle is in contrast to that of semi-secrecy that pervaded the lives of white queers during apartheid.

Yet the appropriation of this culture, because of uniquely South Africa factors, has only been partial. These men were not able to engage in gay identity political struggles to nearly the same degree as groups in the West. The ideological justifications that the state used to rationalise and implement apartheid limited the ability of this group to form any kind of coherent political consciousness. At no point during the latter part of the twentieth century was there the possibility to politically unite around sexual identity politics in South Africa to the degree achieved in some sites in the West. Yet as Binnie (2004) has clearly argued, the developments of late twentieth-century queer cultures and identities, based on Western models, are intrinsically bound up in political struggle. White queer men in Cape Town and in wider South Africa did not have access to the necessary resources to create an identity that was as much as political tool as it was a form of social expression.

But equally, in a country that boasts the most liberal constitution in the world, it is arguable that many white queer men do not feel the need to engage in political struggles around sexual identity rights. These men, unlike those in the West and elsewhere in the world, found that the sudden ending of apartheid had easily concluded state discrimination against them. Even during apartheid, these men were largely unwilling to acknowledge or attempt political change based around sexual identity rights. As this chapter has shown, the majority of white queer groups during the period were content with what little gains they had been begrudgingly given by the state (see also Gevisser 1995).

In this way, the development of a lifestyle centred on the gay village in Cape Town, that only takes one of the latest incarnations of a particular Western queer culture – of commercialisation and exclusion – suits a segment of white queer men well. For some queer men who live in the City Bowl or Atlantic Seaboard, this incarnation is at its most visible. For these men, a leisure lifestyle is justified both by recourse to the gay village and by understanding how their identities are in stark contrast to those who live elsewhere in the city. For these men, who have the financial resources to support such a lifestyle, it therefore becomes possible to see that there is little need to assume their identity is anything but a 'truly' Westernised and globalised version of queer life. Yet these men also do not need to view their own past in the city as anything other than a distant history. Their current lifestyles would appear to be culturally severed from the past located in Cape Town or elsewhere. These men, as this chapter has shown, have instead actively sought out a lifestyle which they view as new, culturally 'superior', international and cosmopolitan. The large number of foreign tourists who visit the city further justifies and augments such as choice. Foreign tourists, drawn to the city by a tourist board activity promoting Cape Town as a global queer hub or 'Metropole', further enhance the image of the city to the men who live in the City Bowl or Atlantic Seaboard, as precisely that.

But history does continue to affect these men. For some men from the City Bowl or Atlantic Seaboard, Gat parties and the lives of men who inhabit the suburbs (and especially the Northern Suburbs) appear at times incongruent with their own lifestyles. In interviews, a significant number of men from the City Bowl or Atlantic Seaboard proved open in discussing how historical perceptions of class, ethnicity and space play key roles in justifying why they do not necessarily always wish to socialise with other groups of men. For men who visit Gat parties, the lifestyle associated with the gay village is sometimes seen as unattractive. The gay village is perceived as less friendly, more expensive and more pretentious than what they are able to experience at Gat parties. Further, the very visibility associated with the gay village limits the number of men who would want, or feel able, to visit it.

This point can also be taken further. In many sites in the West, despite explorations as to how a prominent element of contemporary queer culture is increasingly exclusive to the middle-classes, there is still an understanding that certain sites were important for the development of lifestyles that all men are now able to enjoy. Gay villages are therefore important because they provide a form of cultural and historical legacy to the recent freedoms associated with modern queer identities. As Castells (2004) has pointed out, gay villages grouped men together and allowed not only for the creation of a culture, but also the accumulation of individuals allowing a degree of visibility necessary for the promotion of an identity-based political movement (see also chapter 3). Cape Town does not posses such a site. Gay men in Cape Town, indeed in South Africa, were never able to achieve large-scale mobilisation around gay rights. They were instead strongly circumscribed by a separatist and conservative state in creating a coherent culture; relying instead on what little information they could glean from the West. It is ironic therefore that Cape Town should develop its own gay village – and one that looks towards the West for inspiration – *after* the enshrinement of sexuality rights in the new constitution. The gay village is a space that only superficially represents similar spaces overseas. Without a historical legacy, queer men who live in the Northern or Southern Suburbs have fewer reasons to associate with a space that does not hold much cultural meaning, as exists for some such spaces and such men in the West.

The processes that have led to the overt visibility of some queer men today, and the way that visibility is now achieved spatially through the development of the De Waterkant gay village, therefore can help keep groups of queer men separate from each other. In part, this has occurred due to an attempt by some men to import a particular representation of a culture that is dislocated both from local history and from the historical political struggles that helped form elements of that culture initially in the West. As this chapter has shown, there is also little reason to explore or critically examine how a lack of political engagement may have helped keep groups separate. Yet this separation is also driven by the type of visibility attained in the gay village. As the above discussion has pointed out, many men frequent Gat parties instead of the gay village precisely because they are less visible. While it is clearly not the aim of this book to morally chastise men who do not choose to become overtly visible (in part because there may be important strategic reasons to stay invisible), it must nonetheless be realised that the gay village in Cape Town has itself created new barriers to wider group solidarity. Any potential political power of a space such as the gay village is therefore muted.

Conclusion

The development of a particular queer lifestyle similar to that found in some spaces in the West has not simply helped homogenise groups of white queer men in Cape Town by cleanly bringing them in line with one version of what has been termed by some a Westernised and allegedly globalising queer life. Instead, the promotion of specific elements of a Western queer culture centred on a particular leisure lifestyle has gone to simultaneously highlight and hide local historical differences between groups of men. Some men have been made overtly visible in urban space, while others are kept partially invisible to wider society, tourists and other groups of queer men in the city. To sit outside Café Manhattan on a sunny February morning is therefore to exist in a space at once global and local. It is a space that at once has tried to distance itself from local history and embrace an abstracted interpretation of the global, yet it has also based itself in opposition to groups elsewhere in the city who came about precisely because of that history. Yet for many who visit the gay village in Cape Town on holiday, this history need not trouble them. For outsiders looking in, this history would seem irrelevant as Cape Town sells itself as a cousin to many of the other summer destinations on the global tourist trail.

Yet in a city such as Cape Town, the vast majority of queer men are not even to be found in the gay village or the surrounding suburbs. Instead, they live several kilometres away from the historically segregated white city, on distant parts of the Cape Flats or in the former townships. These men, as the following chapters will explore, have created for themselves different interpretations of queer culture and achieved sometimes different forms of queer visibility, drawing both on their past and their present and again calling into question the alleged benefits and freedoms of a lifestyle associated with the gay village.

Chapter Three

Coloured Visibilities and the Raced Nature of Heteronormative Space

Introduction

It is not hard to see why tourists think of Cape Town as a small city. The journey from the gay village to The Company Gardens, home to the Houses of Parliament, the South African National Gallery, the South African National Library and St George's Cathedral (made famous by Desmond Tutu) is 15 minutes on foot. If you fancy some shopping, it's just a short walk down into the harbour for a day at the Victoria and Alfred Waterfront, or a four-block stroll to Long Street. The journey from the gay village to Table Mountain by car takes about ten minutes. If you were feeling particularly energetic, and didn't mind the climb, you could probably walk that too. Even standing at the top of Table Mountain, one kilometre above sea level, you could be forgiven for thinking of Cape Town as nothing more than an undersized port. In front of you the City Bowl lies cradled by Lion's Head and Signal Hill in the north and Devil's Peak in the east. Out at sea you can spot Robben Island.

To get a glimpse of the rest of the city, you would have to walk east around the top of the mountain. On a clear day, having reached a point away from the cable car stop, you would be able to see beyond Devil's Peak the beginnings of an urban sprawl that stretches forty kilometres inland. The first of the black African townships, Langa, can be spotted in the distance by looking for the concrete towers of the Athlone power station. Behind it lie several others: Guguletu, Nyanga, Philippi and Khayelitsha. Yet to fully appreciate the enormity of the city you have to walk further, taking one of the long dirt paths that crisscross the top of the mountain. Once on the far side of the plateau you would be able to see to the south the true expanse of the Cape Flats. In the near distance are the Southern Suburbs, where neo-colonial architecture marks out homes in the wealthy suburbs of Pinelands, Newlands and Claremont. Look further however, out towards the horizon, and you might be lucky to see the tiny specks of outlying suburbs such as Retreat, Grassy Park and Lavender Hill.

It is in these latter, predominantly coloured locations, up to 28 kilometres from the gay village, that another form of queer visibility has its home. In these places, working-class cross-dressing and effeminate gendered behaviour have come to dominate aspects of queer life. Quite why these locations have become synonymous with cross-dressing is a story that stretches back to the beginnings of Cape Town itself. As this chapter will show, coloured cross-dressing men are uniquely tied to the progression of apartheid race-based logic among ruling whites and the evolution of spatial segregation. It is therefore perhaps not surprising that for many working-class coloured queer men who inhabit the outlying areas of the Cape Flats, visible expressions of queer sexuality are not only spatially but also racially distinct from those of white queer men. This supposed schism has led some middle-class coloured groups to distance themselves from queer cross-dressing, looking instead to allegedly globalised and 'racially superior' forms of sexual expression found in the gay village.

Yet despite the distance between the suburbs on the horizon and the gay village in the heart of the City Bowl, the actual histories of both coloured and white queer men are in many ways directly linked to each other. As this chapter will argue, both groups have been successful in freeing themselves from variations of heteronormative regulation – in the process becoming overtly visible within their own communities. Both have been directly influenced by apartheid ideology, shaping their understanding of their own racial and sexual position in the city. What distinguishes between some within these two communities is not simply their physical distance, nor their different racial classifications under apartheid. Rather, their current manifestations are marked by two radically different ways of appropriating heteronormative space.

To understand these different appropriations it will therefore be necessary in this chapter to travel away from the small port towards the horizon. It will also be vital to investigate the way gendered power dynamics within some coloured communities help condition the way queer and non-queer alike are able to interact. Yet to fully explore a unique queer spatial appropriation in the city, this chapter will begin a lot closer to Table Mountain, on the edge of the City Bowl, at what many now have come to see as the spiritual home of coloured groups in Cape Town.

The Creation and Destruction of a Coloured Community

Today the area of Cape Town called Zonnebloem, located to the eastern edge of the City Bowl, is visited largely by students of the Cape Technikon.

Figure 3.1   Zonnebloem today, close to the heart of the city.

For many residents of Cape Town, Zonnebloem is just one of several inner suburbs that you pass when coming into the city centre on the N2 highway or when driving along the edge of Table Mountain on De Waal Drive (Figure 3.1). Thirty years ago however, District Six, as it was called then, was home to a vibrant coloured community. It had come into being during the late nineteenth century as a racially mixed community of freed slaves, merchants, artists, labourers and new migrants (Bickford-Smith 1990; Bickford-Smith et al. 1999). A powerful and cohesive form of community solidarity developed for those living in the district. As Le Grange (1996) and Ahluwalia and Zegeye (2003) argue, the social fabric of the place was unique to Cape Town. Group identity was based not only on common socio-economic circumstances, but also on a shared sense of place. Hemmed in on all sides by white communities who were becoming increasingly disdainful of coloured residents in their midst, District Six acted as a galvanising and concentrating space. Ethnicity and religions were not simply used to exclude groups (as clearly happened among white groups in the city); instead that very diversity was used to promote the value of living within the District.[1] In such a way, District Six is today considered by many as the cultural home of the coloured working classes in Cape Town (Soudien 2001).[2] And as one of the coloured characters in Richard Rive's novel *Buckingham Palace, District Six* exclaims:

> You know, it's a funny thing, but it's only in the District that I feel safe. District Six is like an island, if you follow me, an island in the sea of apartheid. The whole of District Six is one big apartheid, so we can't see it. We only see

it when the white man comes and forces it on us, when he makes us see it –
when the police come and the council people and so on – or when we leave
the District, when we leave our island and go into Cape Town or to Sea Point.
(Rive 1986: 95–96)

But even such a strongly developed form of cohesion could not withstand
government racial planning. In 1966, under the Group Areas Act, the District was designated a white only area. Over the next twenty years more
and more coloured groups were moved away, to outlying suburbs such as
Lavender Hill, Mitchell's Plane and Retreat. But the residents of the District did not go easily. Over a period of twenty years, numerous attempts
were made to stall the relocations and bulldozing of homes.[3] While these
efforts were successful in slowing the rate of forced relocation, they only
succeeded in postponing the inevitable.[4] By the early 1980s a total of
55,000 people had been relocated.

The relocation of coloured groups to dwellings on underdeveloped and
undesirable sand flats was the culmination of state policies towards coloureds
in Cape Town. The spatial rezoning of the city centre and destruction of
District Six in effect went a long way to solving the long-standing problem
of where exactly to 'place' coloured groups within an evolving apartheid
policy (Western 1981). Since colonial times, mixed-race (or later 'coloured')
communities had caused significant problems for white rulers (Jeppie
2001). Who were coloureds? And how and why should they be treated differently to white or black African groups? To understand these issues, and
to fully explore why the destruction of District Six was so successful despite
decades of protest by residents, it is necessary to look back at the original
founding of Cape Town in the seventeenth century.

'The Vices of Both Parents and the Virtues of Neither'

Coloured communities are by far the largest racially defined group in Cape
Town. While nationally coloured individuals make up fewer than 9 percent
of the country, in Cape Town they account for over 48 percent of the city's
inhabitants (Tables 3.1 and 3.2). Yet for observers unfamiliar with the

Table 3.1 Size of racially defined population groups in South African, 2001.[6]

	Black African	Coloured	White	Indian and Asian
South Africa	35,416,131	3,994,349	4,293,624	1,115,205
Total as a percentage	79.0	8.9	9.6	2.5

Table 3.2   Size of racially defined population groups in Cape Town, 2001.[7]

	Black African	Coloured	White	Indian and Asian
Cape Town	916,520	1,392,658	542,581	41,492
Total as a percentage	31.7	48.1	18.8	1.4

history of South Africa, the term 'coloured' can easily cause confusion about a particular section of South African society. Similarities with the common Western European and North American term 'people of colour' can erroneously allow the inclusion of black African individuals within the coloured racial category. Yet 'coloured', as initially a colonial categorisation of ethnicity, is far more complex and does not include any black African grouping. On a purely etymological level, coloureds are the product of inter-racial sex between the first whites from Europe to land at the Cape, their slaves (brought from places such as the Indonesian Archipelago, Madagascar, Mozambique, Angola, Bengal, South India and Sri Lanka), and the original inhabitants of the Cape – the Khoisan (made up of Khoi-khoi pastoralists and San hunters, otherwise known as Hottentots and Bushmen, respectively).[5] As with Creole societies in the Americas and West Indies, a mixing of disparate groups at the Cape over time created a new and place-specific community. Due to influences from Dutch settlers and slaves from the Dutch East Indies, coloured individuals drew their history from European and Islamic countries. At the same time, they associated more with Afrikaner culture than with any other group. For example, the first coloured political organisation formed in 1883 was called the 'Afrikaner League (Coloured)' (Western 1981).

Yet from the very beginning, this community was marked by its precarious position 'between' black African and white groups. Unlike black African individuals, coloured individuals could not easily be grouped together as one 'race'. Neither could they be easily relegated to the status of black Africans within the country. After all, 'coloured' as both a burgeoning community and as a racial classification could not have come about without the actions of white individuals. No matter how socially inferior, in the eyes of white racist ideology, they would never and could never be classified with black African groups. There was, in other words, a begrudging responsibility to coloured communities that went beyond any form of pseudo-paternalism towards black African groups (chapter 4). As Olive Schreiner (quoted in Western 1981), the late nineteenth-century South African white feminist, explained: 'It is always asserted that he [sic] [the coloured individual] possesses the vices of both parent races and the virtues of neither . . . To his father he was the broken wineglass left from last night's feast or as a remembrance of last years' sin . . . He is here, our own; we have made him; we cannot wash our hands of him. When from under the beetling eyebrows in a dark face something of a white man's eye looks out at us, is not the curious shrinking and aversion we feel somewhat of a consciousness of a national disgrace and sin?' (Schreiner 1923: 124, 126 and 141).[8]

For the ruling British, coloured individuals were therefore quickly marked out as a problematic group in relation to their own social, political and moral existence on the Cape. While in general not as feared or belittled to the same degree as black African groups, coloured communities were still forced to exist in varying degrees of subordination to white communities. In some instances policies such as the Civilised Labour Policy of 1924 were intended to make sure that both black African and coloured workers could not be hired for a job unless all white workers in society were first employed. Frequently this meant coloured workers were reduced to taking employment as domestic servants or labourers. Yet some occupations, such as teaching, remained open to both coloured and white workers, although in such cases a white individual would earn approximately twice as much as a coloured individual (O'Toole 1973). Coloured communities were also granted greater political rights than black African groups, but these rights varied over time, as ruling whites tried different ways of regulating 'non-white' groups. While coloured groups gained emancipation in 1834, they would later be restricted in voting only for white representatives to parliament in the 1930s. Further, while coloured individuals were moved out of white-designated city areas, there was never an attempt to relocate them to politically 'independent homelands', as happened with black African groups (chapter 4). Instead, in 1983, coloured groups were given back limited political rights within the state in a tricameral parliament with white and Indian representatives (Meredith 2005).

With the ascendancy of the National Party, segregation became more pronounced, with spaces such as train carriages, post offices, graveyards, shop entrances, taxis, ambulances, parks and even park benches being sectioned between whites and 'non-whites'. It is of little wonder that following from this it also became necessary to know who was allowed to use different spaces. Legislation such as the Population Registration Act of 1950 was therefore introduced, requiring all people in the country to register their race. Yet for coloured individuals in particular, this classification was often arbitrary. 'Colour' could not easily be defined for a group that included individuals from many parts of the world made up of numerous 'mixes'. It therefore became necessary to carry out race tests on hair, nails, eyelids and babies' bottoms to discover if an individual who claimed to be coloured was 'actually' a black African individual – or perhaps of more concern to white nationalists, that someone who was suspected of being included within the coloured racial category was trying to 'pass' as white (Bickford-Smith et al. 1999; Clarke and Worger 2004; Worden 2004).[9]

The apartheid state, while acknowledging the unique position of coloured groups within their racial schemas, was now armed with the knowledge that would allow it to position the coloured racial category as a 'buffer' between white and black African groups.[10] As discussed in chapter 2, one of the major ideological factors that helped shape apartheid was the need for a separate white nationalism.[11] The use of coloured groups as a 'buffer' was essential to keep white groups distanced from all that was 'uncivilised' – morally, spiritually, socially and physically (Hendricks 2001; Reddy 2001; Western 1981).[12] Unlike the United States, which instigated a 'one drop rule', South African apartheid ideology required the maintenance of a separate social and political coloured category to limit the daily contact between white and black African individuals.[13]

The position of coloured groups within apartheid society was therefore strongly marked by their own diversity, racial 'superiority' to black African groups, state-imposed homogeneity and racial 'inferiority' to white groups. As would be expected, these conflicting discursive constructions called into question coloureds' own identity and sense of place within the country. As later sections will explore in more detail, the legacy of colonial migration and racist policies has perpetuated a deep sense of insecurity among some within the coloured race-based category about their own identity (Giliomee 1995; Jackson 2003). As Bickford-Smith et al. (1999) expressed:

> If [white] identity was complex, the notion of 'coloured' identity was still more fluid and ambiguous. Rejected by whites, coloured people were forced to redefine themselves. What were they: 'African' or 'European', 'Christian' or 'Muslim', 'English' or 'Afrikaans', 'Coloured' or 'Malay', working-class or middle-class, conservative or radical? (p. 80)

The importance of District Six as a spiritual home for coloured communities and the forcefulness with which they strove to protect it against white spatial segregation now comes more clearly into focus. As does the growing need for the apartheid state to relocate coloured groups away from the white segregated centre. For white rulers, the forced removals from District Six were often publicly couched in terms of poor hygiene and social corruption – issues of concern for white communities since the early twentieth century (ibid.). Yet in reality, coloured groups were simply not deemed suitable to live in the same racially designated areas as white communities. While coloured individuals were indeed perceived to be more 'civilised' than black African individuals, and would be looked after accordingly, they could never again be allowed to exist in the heart of the white city.

For coloured communities, the historical importance of District Six, tied to the brutality with which it was lost, has helped elevate the space to the level of mythic homeland (Rive 1990) and resulted in the creation of socially and politically vibrant memory projects such as the District Six Museum (Till 2004). District Six was therefore not simply another space that found itself the casualty of white racism. Rather, within Cape Town, it has become the defining example of how apartheid policies could use race-based logic to cripple an unwanted community. Church congregations, school classes and work colleagues found themselves living many kilometres away from each other on the Cape Flats. Families that had lived near to one another for decades now had to take long bus journeys to see each other. The story of dislocation caused by the destruction of the District has entered into legend not just for coloured communities, but also for white and black African communities in Cape Town. Less well understood has been the way such relocations affected the lives of coloured queer men who, alongside merchants, shop owners, labourers and mixed-race families, had also found an open and accepting space to express a very visible and unique culture.

Moffies!

If you walk along Keizersgracht Street in Zonnebloem today, you will find yourself flanked on one side by the imposing late modernist structures that make up the Cape Technikon. On the opposite side of the road you will see some empty lots. The removal of coloured groups from District Six not only involved the forced relocation of individuals; it also involved the wholesale removal of houses and in some cases entire streets from the area. Further south, all that is left of streets such as Clifton and Richmond are some paving stones hidden among overgrown shrubbery (Figure 3.2). The aim of apartheid planners was to entirely remove any indication of what the areas had once been. It therefore takes more than a little imagination to picture Keizersgracht Street, or Hanover Street as it was then known, as once the heart of a vibrant and very visible queer culture.

Detailed archive records dating back to the middle of the twentieth century give testimony to a coloured community based on effeminate gendered performances of queer sexuality.[14] Many of these men had their lodgings on Hanover Street but their community also stretched into the neighbouring suburbs such as Woodstock and Salt River (Chetty 1995; Gevisser 1995). For these men, cross-dressing would occur on a regular basis, with items such as women's suits, dresses, jewellery, wigs and lipstick being worn by men. Some men would cross-dress continually, while others would limit their cross-dressing to parties and when socialising with other

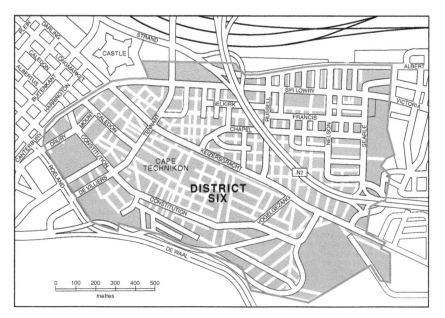

Figure 3.2   District Six prior to forced removals (in grey) and today.

men (figures 3.3 and 3.4). Parties at various clubs in and around the District, house parties and socialising in shebeens (taverns) became markers of this world. A further activity was to go on 'salon crawls' – visits to the many hairdressing salons owned or operated by queer cross-dressing men. Every year, these men would also lead the coloured New Year 'Coon Carnival' parade through District Six and Woodstock (Martin 1999). The ease and freedom with which queer life was able to flourish is well described by this coloured queer man who grew up in District Six in the 1960s:

> You would meet other people going to parties, dances and most of all at the age of fourteen, fifteen I used to go to often [*sic*] gay parties and meet up with different gays and different other people. But it was just to me a normal way of going to a function . . . They were loveable people. Gangsters here and there. Neighbours around, friends of mine. They were fantastic people. As a matter of fact those were District Six people which you can't degrade. They were loveable . . . (GALA, file AM 2709[15])

And when describing the fashions of the day:

> At that time it used to be jeans just started coming back into fashion and slacksuits started being worn around . . . some [queers] stood out by having longer hair and having makeup on. (GALA, file AM 2709)

Figure 3.3 Kewpie, a coloured queer hairdresser (image courtesy GALA South Africa, file AM 2886; Kewpie photographic collection).

Figure 3.4 Coloured cross-dressing 'moffies' circa 1960 (image courtesy GALA South Africa, file AM 2886; Kewpie photographic collection).

Ubiquitous in nature, this queer community became so well known that the term 'Moffie Drag' was used to denote their various activities. Today, the term 'moffie' has entered into common parlance in South Africa to mean any queer male. Yet while the exact root of the word has been lost, during the mid- to late-twentieth century, it was most closely associated with coloured queer effeminate men. Indeed, the secretive language spoken initially among this group during the period was termed 'Moffietaal' (later developing into 'Gayle') and many of its terms stemmed from female names (Cage 2003). For example, a 'Dora' was an alcoholic drink and to be 'Hilda' was to be unattractive.

At first glance, it seems strange that a community of queer men could develop and thrive within the apartheid city. As the previous chapter has explored, during the period, white queer men were suffering due to the effects of increased state attention. For many in South Africa, homosexuality was not something to be tolerated, but rather a medical affliction that should be rooted out, and if possible, cured.[16] Yet within District Six and neighbouring areas, queer life was able to prosper.

In many respects it was the fabric of District Six that allowed queer men to flourish. An eclectic mix of individuals with historical links from across Africa and across South East Asia, close-quarter living and a shared sense of struggle created an open and accepting social and physical space for queer men. As Gevisser (1995) has argued, the hybridity of coloured life in the District in particular may have helped protect the community from any one social or moral doctrine gaining prominence.[17] When compared to Afrikaner culture and its long association with Christian Dutch Reform ideology, coloured queers in places such as District Six were freer to experiment with a variety of social configurations. Sex-workers lived next door to families and young children. 'Skollies' or 'gangsters' were asked to contribute to neighbourhoods.[18] And queer men could walk freely along Hanover Street or any other. A form of social solidarity, tied to a developing cultural and social identity within the District gave queer men the opportunity to express their unique and very visible identity. As this interviewee who used to live in the District explained:

People used to live together. Your neighbours' mothers and fathers was like your mother and father. People . . . were together like families. You know what I mean? It's not like today. The people live so differently these days . . . There wasn't a day that you would go sleep without a piece of bread or a plate of food, because the neighbour would provide. If there wasn't in your house, the neighbour would always see that the neighbour's children will have food or whatever . . . That was also like the norm of the day, I should say . . . People didn't look at you askew when you came past with your netball short dress or your evening wear or whatever, wherever you went to . . . And it was the norm of the day. JERRY/57

Cross-dressing queer men were also an important political tool for coloured groups. As apartheid controls limited the movement of 'non-whites' throughout the latter part of the twentieth century, cross-dressing queer men came increasingly to represent a form of symbolic autonomy and freedom for coloured society. Defiant of wider (white) society – and exhibiting both seductiveness and pride in their own identity – moffies helped show to the world the unique nature and richness of coloured culture (Chetty 1995).[19] These displays were especially important at the New Year's Coon Carnival. This festival, dating back to 1907, became, by the middle of the century, the pre-eminent celebration of coloured culture (Martin 1999).[20] By celebrating queers, the carnival took from them a form of defiance towards the apartheid state and white power (Swarr 2004).

The unique history of coloured culture in Cape Town, combined with the social milieu of District Six, helped foster cross-dressing queer life. Cross-dressing men were not only accepted by large elements of coloured society, they were also used to promote it. Cross-dressing at the Coon Carnival became symbolic of wider freedom: to choose costume and appearance at a time when so much of coloured life was being regulated by the apartheid state. Yet in some respects this acceptance remained only partial. For some, coloured cross-dressers were viewed as objects of ridicule. While their spectacle exemplified the uniqueness of coloured culture, it also helped objectify and distance this visible form of queer sexuality from other sectors of the coloured community.

Respectability and the Ambivalence of Coloured Identity

Having seen how for many coloured individuals, cross-dressing was something to be celebrated, it is important to note that for others, it became an element of coloured life that, along with the Coon Carnival, was barely tolerated. For many, especially middle-class coloureds, a degree of unrespectability pervaded the Carnival and those that took part in it. As discussed above, coloured groups were located within apartheid policies as 'better' than black African groups, yet not good enough to be fully 'civilised' and granted the same rights as white groups. Coloured individuals themselves were naturally adverse to such an interpretation. Yet, while hostile to the racial classifications imposed on them, some were still aware that within apartheid social schemas there were distinct advantages in striving for what they understood as a white existence. This could be achieved literally by attempting to 'pass' for white. Or it could be achieved figuratively by showing wider society that coloured individuals could follow the same social norms and accept the social values of Europeans (Adhikari 1994;

Morse and Peele 1974).[21] As Sonn (1996) discusses: 'As [coloured] people, we have internalised the pervasive white racist message that "white is right" and "West is best". This has encouraged [coloured] communities to distance themselves from their African origins and seek greater identification with whites' (p. 62). And as this coloured interviewee explained when discussing growing up in Cape Town in the 1980s:

> ... *we always, always thought, thinking that the white way of living is the ideal and that's what we strived towards, so you, you live clean, you're clean on yourself and your body and your space that you live in, because you believe that white people are clean on themselves and the space that they live in. So, and wealthy as well, because white people are wealthy, so you, in your, in your, uhm, wanting to excel, in your wanting to improve your status in life, you are striving towards a white standard of living, away from a black [African] standard of living.* ZANDER/33

It is therefore hardly surprising that elements of the coloured middle-class would look unfavourably on cross-dressing queers that were associated with working-class areas such as District Six and events such as the Coon Carnival. The sight of coloured men and boys parading along streets with painted faces and wearing brightly coloured costumes was viewed by some coloured groups as only perpetuating white groups' assessment of coloured people as ignorant clowns (Western 1981). Cross-dressing queers were also a form of embarrassment to some middle-class coloureds. The carnival atmosphere was perceived by the middle classes to make permissible public displays that otherwise would not be acceptable (Jeppie 1990). The cross-dressing queer at the Coon Carnival in effect went to air what the middle classes saw as the 'dirty laundry' of the coloured community. Cross-dressers could be confined to areas such as District Six for most of the year. This would not be possible at the New Year's festivities.

These concerns were only heightened by the interest print media took in coloured cross-dressers. For a period of nearly 30 years beginning in the 1950s, publications such as *Drum* and *Golden City Post* contained numerous salacious headlines detailing the lives of 'coloured moffies' (Chetty 1995).[22] These publications were read widely by coloured and black African groups. To fuel their readership they often resorted to the scandalous, with cross-dressing coloured men easily and frequently fulfilling this need. For example, in 1959, under the headline: 'Oh, so this is what they call a Cape Moffie Drag':

> It was the most astonishing party you have ever seen ... There was whispering in corners, and smudged lipstick and high-pitched giggles. There was wine and song. But there were no women. Every one of the 40 or so people gathered ... was a man – or at any rate, male. This was a party given by Cape Town's famous 'moffies' ... Some of the older generation looked a little

grotesque. There were rouged pugilist faces peeping from underneath ginger wigs. And sometimes the shoulders above the strapless evening dresses had muscles that would have done credit to a weightlifter . . . Joey [the host] had insisted before the party began that it must end by 2am. Around 4am it did end. By that time the make-up was running down the faces of the older moffies, and their beards were beginning to show through. They looked tired and lonely and very pathetic. The younger ones were still having a gay time. (Berry 1959: 60–61)

Over the next two decades, cross-dressing queer men would continue to make regular appearances in these national publications. Stories concerning the new 'Queen of the moffies' – where disorganised 'elections' would decide a new 'leader' – were juxtaposed with others exploring in sometimes pathetic detail the downward spiral of life as a coloured moffie. For example, under the headline: 'Screaming "Doris Day" Sent to Jail':

'I only hope that tonight you will sleep in peace. Just remember, those who judge will be judged', Doris Day, alias Harold Blaauw, shouted shrilly at Magistrate, Mr G.J. Terblanche just after he jailed 'her' for theft. Doris, 32, one-time queen of Cape Town's moffie world was sentenced to two to four years. She pleaded not guilty to charges of theft and being in possession of suspected stolen goods. Dressed in blue trousers, black sweater, green jacket and brown suede shoes – minus socks, Doris flashed smiles at everybody in court (mostly the males) but after being found guilty 'she' glared at every policeman and even the prosecutor. (*Golden City Post* 1968: 8)

Coloured cross-dressing queers or moffies, like wider coloured society, existed in conflicting social and political positions. At once accepted and even celebrated by elements of coloured society, they also suffered as disrespected and sometimes comical figures. Wider coloured society, and especially sections of the coloured middle class, were caught in a racial schema that placed them in the fragile position between white and black African. For some white colonialists, coloured groups had begun as a community for whom embarrassment was the strongest emotion. Coloured cross-dressing queer men found that this racial schema also placed them in a fragile position, as both an important constituent of coloured culture and an embarrassing element that should hopefully one day be forgotten. But just as the destruction of District Six did not succeed in destroying the collective memory of coloured lives during apartheid, so it did not succeed in wiping from history the legacy of cross-dressing in Cape Town. Today, cross-dressing queer men are still prominent in some coloured communities. Their homes are now in places such as Lavender Hill, Mitchell's Plane, Steenburg and Retreat. As with coloured culture generally, cross-dressing queer men within these communities have continued to change. Yet as later sections will show, for some, class tied to race continues to instruct how these men are perceived.

A Legacy Continued: Gender and the Construction of Coloured Queer Communities

Many coloured communities today, as during apartheid, continue to strad-dle the divide between white and black African groups. As with all cities, some areas of Cape Town are visibly more affluent than others. Yet in Cape Town, it literally is the case that many apartheid-designated coloured areas act as the link between the wealthiest and the poorest of the city's inhabit-ants. While formal political apartheid ended in 1994, Cape Town like all other cities in South Africa continues to be defined spatially by racially demarcated zones. Politically, there is nothing to stop an inhabitant from Lavender Hill from moving to the City Bowl or to Sea Point. Economically however, this is almost an impossibility. In this way the forcefulness of political apartheid has been replaced by a far more intractable economic apartheid that will take significantly longer to remove (Bollens 1998a; Saff 1994; Turok 2001).[23]

To journey out towards distant parts of the Cape Flats from suburbs close to the port is to take an excursion from affluence to relative privation. In wealthy parts of the Southern Suburbs, the M4 or 'Main Road' begins near Groote Schuur Hospital – where Christiaan Barnard conducted the world's first heart transplant. Further along Main Road, lying nestled between the suburbs of Newlands and Claremont is the chic Cavendish Square shopping development. Yet when cutting across to Prince George's Drive, the road becomes wider with strips of open grassland on either side of the highway. Grassy Park is on the left, a predominantly coloured suburb almost indistinguishable from wealthy white suburbs. On the right up ahead are Steenburg and Retreat. On the left is Lavender Hill (Figure 3.5). As you journey closer to False Bay and the ocean, parts of these approaching suburbs begin to closely resemble developed areas of some black African townships.

Dotted within these suburbs are the homes of present day coloured cross-dressing men (Figure 3.6). Similar to the District Six era, some of these queer men cross-dress continually, while others limit their cross-dressing (or 'dragging') to special shows put on by moffies for the com-munity.[24] Yet all areas where dragging is common have remained some of the poorest in Cape Town.[25] For the men themselves, several explanations exist as to why they employ drag as a form of queer visibility. Most promi-nent, is an explicit understanding that their construction and implementa-tion of cross-dressing has its origins in District Six. Cross-dressing today

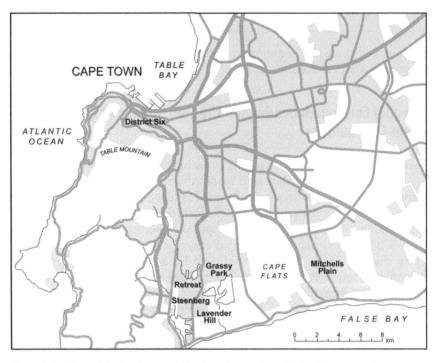

Figure 3.5 Some of the locations to which coloured groups from District Six were moved.

Figure 3.6 A coloured cross-dressing queer man today (note Beauty Pageant crowns in background).

is therefore seen as a continuation of a long legacy and normalisation of coloured queer expression:

> *Basically it was because of the District Six era. People thought, you know, that, I mean, gay guys were supposed to wear dresses, because that is how they were, with the Coon Carnivals and things and whatever . . . proper gay guys – would wear dresses.* PAUL/27

> *I think it's also the way the people in these communities see gay, that if you're gay you have to dress up, you must drag. That's part of the initiation to get to where you want to be. So it's just the way people perceive gay, you know. And it's also something that came all the way from District Six . . . and the moffies walking down Hanover Street. So that has come here, because a lot of the people were replaced here. So it's just still part of that whole development, that this is it, you know, you must parade, you must show who you are.* SAM/44

Closely tied to this rationalisation is the belief that, as with the men in District Six, cross-dressing allows a degree of overt visibility and freedom that they otherwise might not be able to achieve. As these two interviewees explain:

> *[In response to 'why do you drag?'] Attention, I mean, for attention, for starters. And to be pretty, sometimes to be beautiful and to feel loved and to just be yourself, to express yourself more.* STEVE/25

> *I do it [dragging]. I did it the past year . . . I basically do it for, it's just the experience and the fun and the excitement and everything that revolves around it. I do it for that purpose. And also just to throw it in somebody's face occasionally that I am gay and I enjoy flirting to extend something I am . . . and still being able to and comfortable in doing it.* SIMON/32

Additionally, there is a perception among many of these men that the history of the District Six moffies, while vital in justifying and explaining their current use of drag, also had its limitations. The criticisms lobbied at moffies of that era have clearly also been transplanted to outlaying parts of the Cape Flats, along with cross-dressing itself.

> *Being gay during that time [the District Six era], was to say that uhm, 'Oh come to a party, I'm invited to a party, we have a gay friend there', it looks like you as a gay person will still [think I'm] a freak basically because you provided the entertainment and you were supposed to keep the party going.* LUIS/39

> *There is even the gay person in the Coon Carnival, that person did the entertainment, on the stadium, whatever. The District Six people was uhm, 'okay we got a clown, come and see the clown here', you know.* TERRY/34

As such, cross-dressing queer men today, while acknowledging the possibility of heteronormative ridicule associated with overt effeminate spectacle, point also to the important place they inhabit within the wider community. Specifically, these men take great pride in the 'beauty pageants' or 'drag shows' where cross-dressing queer men compete for beauty pageant crowns. These shows are attended not only by other queer men, but also by heterosexually-identifying men and women. Often these shows will take place in order to raise funds for different community causes. It is believed that the high profile of these events helps strengthen solidarity between heterosexual and queer groups. As this interviewee discusses:

> *Someone comes to us and say they want to go, they need money to send a child or someone away, overseas, then immediately we jump into action, and we organise a pageant . . . and we raise funds for that person, . . . we click together by having a party . . . .the people will accept us even more and they will respect us for that, because we are there, we help them, and they in turn can help us as well, you know if we need them.   LUIS/39*

These shows are also taken very seriously by contestants. Winning a crown, or even finishing in the top three places, is viewed not only as an achievement, but also as a validation of an individual's ability to conform to effeminate gender norms. The shows also highlight the ease with which heterosexually-identified men socialise with cross-dressing queer men. At these shows it is quite common to see men who view themselves as heterosexual dancing with cross-dressing moffies (sometimes as female girlfriends or wives look on). Because importance is placed on cross-dressing queer men's ability to act and behave like females, the act of dancing with heterosexually-identified men goes to strengthen the gender binary they strive to associate with. This need to appeal to heterosexually-identified men can sometimes lead to competition between females and cross-dressing queer men:

> *When I enter beauty pageants or go to clubs . . . I want to be noticed [for] what your lifestyle really is . . . then we need to compete, really, sometimes with the other gender [females].   HARRY/37*

Association with heterosexually-identified men also goes further, with sexual relationships between coloured cross-dressing queer men and heterosexually-identified men held in high esteem by many queers. While sex with men who view themselves simply as queer and do not cross-dress also occurs (see below for more on this group), sex with a heterosexually-identified man is viewed as a particular achievement. As the first excerpt here from the sister of a cross-dressing queer man explained:

I would say the gays make it quite known that whatever straight guy they slept with, it will be world news tomorrow [among other queer men] . . . they make sure it gets around.   SARAH/34

And as one coloured queer man proudly exclaimed:

The wives [sometimes] come and fetch their husbands from the [cross-dressing moffie] person.   SAM/44

In the wider community, there is a degree of tolerance and even acceptance that heterosexually-identified men may have sex with queer men. Similar to findings in Latin America, South East Asia and the Middle East, the construction of gender within these communities helps to maintain discrete sexual identities (Herdt 1994 and 1999; Jackson and Sullivan 1999; Murray and Roscoe 1997; Parker 1999; Prieur 1998). In other words there is an acceptance that those men who maintain outward masculine appearance and mannerisms can continue to maintain a heterosexual identity despite having sex with moffies. Yet despite a degree of social acceptance towards this phenomenon, there is often an attempt on the part of the 'straight' man who is having sex with queer men to keep such information secret.

Heterosexual guys . . . [they have sex with cross-dressing moffies] each and everyone not knowing . . . They won't know about each other . . . they would give you the impression that 'no, no, I don't do that'.   PAUL/27

The ease with which sexual relationships between queer men and hetero-sexually-identified men are accepted is also furthered by the fact there are no exclusively queer bars or clubs within these communities. Unlike white queer men discussed in chapter 2, queer sexuality here is not socially or spatially demarcated within a specific place. Similar to District Six, overtly visible displays of same-sex desire take place in the same bars and clubs that are frequented by the wider community. There is no need to 'tone down' or make invisible displays of queer sexuality in nominally hetero-sexual spaces. It is also telling that there appear to be no bars or clubs that are viewed as too homophobic or hostile for queers to visit. Even the most tempestuous or riotous of venues (places where guns and knives are kept safely behind the bar until the patron leaves) hold drag shows for the whole community.

Queer men are therefore able to visit numerous socialising venues, even when drag shows are not taking place. Cross-dressing allows for an easy identification of an individual's sexual identity. For heterosexually-identified men who are attracted to cross-dressing queers, there is a clear understanding that they are propositioning another male. This knowledge, however, is mediated by two important rationalisations. First, the outward attempt at effeminacy of the man in drag goes some way to offset the idea that the heterosexually-identified man is publicly (or privately) propositioning another male. Second, is the belief that sex with another man is more likely to occur quickly after intentions are made clear than if the proposition had taken place with a female. These implicit understandings on the part of the heterosexually-identified men go to offset any risk of verbal or physical violence against the cross-dressing male. As this individual who cross-dresses regularly, but not exclusively, explained:

> *[Heterosexually-identified men or 'straight' men] are at a point that the majority of them, it's more open about having sex . . . and the reason why is it's more readily available. Because at the end of the day, being gay I'm still a guy, and I still have the same sexual tendencies as any other guy would have, where sex would be on my mind. [It's] basically the same as it would be on any other ['straight'] guy's mind. So that ['straight'] guy's not going to get sex from that [female] instantly, but me being a guy as well, and being sexually active as that guy is, that's what [makes it] more accessible to me, having sex with a [straight] guy . . . [In drag], yes, you do get more sex . . . more propositions, ja. Offers where, because the guy will know that you are gay . . . There would obviously be something appealing about you sexually as a female [too], because your tendency is more outlandish and outspoken when you are in drag. So that guy, knowing full well that you are gay, he will be more aroused by seeing a female figure that is available for sex. Obviously he would go for that and proposition you. SIMON/32*

The reinforcement of gender roles plays an important part in the social and sexual relationships that occur within these coloured communities. Similar to the cross-dressing men who lived in District Six, these men's attempts to emulate the social mannerisms and dress of women marks them out as a very visible and unique category of individual. Yet the positioning of coloured cross-dressing queer men within the community in this way also helps to 'make safe' their social standing.[26] Their work with the community through drag shows helps bind together queer men with wider heterosexual society. Further, sexual relationships with heterosexually-identified men are more easily facilitated by the use of queer feminine performances. The very 'obviousness' of many queer men in drag, tied to the femininity inherent in such acts, permits these men a degree of social safety when socialising with the 'straight' community. The long association coloured communities have with cross-dressing as a normalised expression of queer sexuality further limits the possibility of violence against them.

The importance of gender as a socially regulating power dynamic necessary for queer and wider groups to interact is also exemplified by the growing 'gangster' culture in Cape Town. Gang culture is now endemic in the Western Cape, and specifically in the coloured Cape Flats on the out-skirts of the city (Redpath 2001a and 2001b). While 'gangsters' or 'skollies' were documented during the District Six period, their numbers have grown considerably in the years following the end of apartheid (Haefele 1998). These gangs, commonly referred to as the '26s', '27s' and '28s' encompass a variety of illegal operations including shoplifting, residential house break-ins, drug dealing, protection rackets, car hijacking, armed robberies and murder.[27] As Epprecht (2004) has recognised, these gangs have strong associations with the prison system in South Africa dating back to at least the middle of the nineteenth century.[28] A uniquely South African phenom-enon, this gang culture has its roots in the high incarceration rates of 'non-whites' during the colonial era. For a long period, an individual could only become a gang member once they had been convicted of a crime and sen-tenced to prison (Kinnes 1995). Over time this rule was relaxed so that other individuals who had not spent time in prison could also become members.[29]

Within outlying coloured communities, two observable gang traits are important to understand their relationship to cross-dressing queer men. The first is the way these gangs operate through possession of certain spaces within the Cape Flats: their 'turf'. Here, groups of gang members will hold claim to different areas, usually demarcated by road intersections (with gangs operating on different 'blocks'). This configuration is ubiquitous in places such Lavender Hill and Mitchell's Plane. Crucially, many of these sub-groups each link up to the three dominant overarching gangs: the 26s, 27s and 28s. Some sub-gangs will be made up exclusively of members from the dominant gangs, others are a mixture. The second trait is the way they approach, and operate through, different conceptualisations of sexuality. Knowledge of the gangs is widespread in Cape Town – and especially on outlying parts of the Cape Flats. And so too is an understanding that while in prison, same-sex sexual activity may occur. Yet while it is known that members of all three gangs could well engage in situational same-sex sexual activity (Gear 2001), it is the 28s who are particularly renowned for this behaviour. Indeed, one of the defining characteristics of the 28s is not the type of crime they are involved in or their social standing in prisons (as with the 26s – accumulators of wealth through criminal but non-violent means – and 27s – 'thinkers', mediators or planners) but the fact that while in prison gang members will engage in sex with other men, making men into 'wives' (Steinberg 2004).[30] As this coloured man explains:

The 28s . . . they say they're straight, man, but they, you know, everybody knows what they're doing when they go to jail and they come out and they've been screwing each other . . . when they come out [of prison] they still have sex with men. CLINT/22

As the quotation above also suggests, none of these gang members consider themselves to be anything other than in possession of a heterosexual identity. The need for gang members to maintain an image of overt masculinity between each other and towards the wider community has been well documented (Pinnock 1997). They are therefore unable, and also do not see the need, to associate with any form of queer identity.[31] Queer identities, after all, are closely associated with effeminacy on the outlying Cape Flats. The forcefulness with which gender constructions limit any discussion that might question sexuality means that all gang members are simply 'straight'. As this interviewee explained, to suggest to a gang member that he might wish to associate with a sexual label such as queer, moffie or gay might well be to take your own life in your hands:

> *He will kill you. He will kill you. He will kill you just there. Because they are violent people . . . I wouldn't want to call any of them that. Because then I would be in a box [coffin]! . . . Not any of those terms would apply to him. Because he would go ballistic. No one's telling them they are gay while they're going through all these notions of going into prison and doing all those things and taking on an ideology. And no one's ever called them gay . . . They've never been termed that. They've been termed 28s. But the minute you term them gay it's a whole new thing you're opening up to them. And that's why they get so violent when you do. They've got an identity of an ideology, that's the way they live.*   BRADLEY/35

Both queer cross-dressing men and the heterosexually-identified men they have sex with are conditioned by the role gender plays in their lives. For cross-dressing men, effeminate gender performances allow a degree of social safety and acceptance tied to a form of overt visibility manifest throughout their community. This formulation also has recourse to a long historical legacy among coloured communities. Their effeminacy is also structured through a desire to have sex with overtly masculine men – an act that only goes to reinforce their desire to appear feminine. In turn, individuals who exhibit forms of overt masculinity need not view themselves as anything other than heterosexual, since to be queer would mean performing an effeminate visibility. Gender therefore reinforces the links between these two groups and at the same time keeps them distinct. While it would be a simplification to see all coloured queer men as effeminate or cross-dressers (see below) or to suggest all heterosexual men are closely tied to gang culture, it is important to accept that masculinity and femininity are used by both queer and heterosexually-identified men in their negotiation of sexual and social identities. Gangs on less affluent areas of the Cape Flats facilitate an archetype of masculinity that helps condition heterosexuality generally, in contrast to an effeminate queer visibility.

Yet this formulation of sexuality found on outlying suburbs of the Cape Flats does not suit all coloured queer men. For some, cross-dressing or over-effeminate behaviour are acts they wish not to associate with. It therefore becomes necessary to place coloured cross-dressers in a wider social context that acknowledges how race and class continue to shape the lives of coloured communities.

'It's actually quite scary . . . this effeminate dude that flaunts his fake-ass tits'

There is little question that coloured cross-dressing men are the most conspicuous and hence visible form of queer sexuality in places such as Mitchell's Plane, Lavender Hill, Retreat and Steenburg. For a growing number of men, however, cross-dressing is viewed both as a form of social disempowerment and as a culturally regressive act. For many coloured queer men who do not cross-dress, there is a perception that cross-dressing objectifies queer sexuality, shoring up heteropatriarchal norms and running the risk of turning queers into objects of derision. Despite attempts by cross-dressers to gain social standing within the community, negative perceptions of cross-dressing that came to prominence during the District Six era continue today. For queer men who do not cross-dress, this perception is often tied to a belief that cross-dressers are crudely treated by the heterosexually-identified men they have sex with. In other words it is thought that cross-dressers are simply used by heterosexually-identified men, and especially gangsters, for nothing more than sexual gratification. As these two interviewees explained:

> *[Straight] guys just come and knock for them [cross-dressing moffies] at all hours of the morning . . . then [later] they [straight guys] will pass terrible remarks about [them].* BRADLEY/35

> *Gangsters, to me, would . . . they would go for the feminine ones dressed up. It's mostly at night. They would get you . . . maybe, outside a club on the way home, and they'd made [sic] use of you. Sometimes they would come around to your house even, when they know where you live, and they'd bother you . . . But during the day they would stand on the corners [gang turf road intersections] and maybe mock you.* PAUL/27

These feelings are further strengthened by a belief that cross-dressing has only remained dominant within these communities because of its historical legacy. The poor treatment of coloured cross-dressing men by heterosexually-identified men would not today be occurring if drag had not already been normalised in these places. District Six is not simply a historical place to be immortalised, rather it is one of the root causes as to why cross-dressers continue to placed in a subordinate social and sexual position to the rest of society. Several coloured queer men who do not cross-dress therefore expressed discomfort at the idea they would be forced into cross-dressing by their peers even if they did not wish to undertake it.

> *Because actually it's part of the gay culture. If you come out, you have to drag.   ITIMAD/21*

> *You know, the only element of gayness that you are exposed to [on the outlying Cape Flats] are the drag queens, and you're thinking, 'What the use are all of this with drag queens?' What if you say now to your family you're gay, then the next thing you start wearing dresses and put on make-up? So I see a problem.   CLINT/22*

> *It's actually quite scary, because the majority of, like, within the coloured community, if you're gay, you're very effeminate . . . I think it's just that when they think gay, they think, you know, a flap, you know, flapping queens, whatever, you know, this effeminate dude that flaunts his fake-ass tits.   JAMIL/20*

In these areas of the Cape Flats, some queer men therefore have pertinent reasons not to express their sexuality by cross-dressing. Social disempowerment resulting from a wish to have sex with heterosexually-identified men is augmented by a belief that queer historical social norms limit the options not to cross-dress. Yet these criticisms also have a strong class dimension. Just as class led to negative views of cross-dressing queer men by the wider middle class in the District Six era, so now class remains an important contributing factor in these queer men's views of drag. As mentioned above, one of the reasons why cross-dressing has remained important for queer men has been the degree of social safety it permits. Cross-dressing moffies are easily identified within the wider community by their gender performances. However, an additional reason why such overt visibility has remained an important social marker stems from the living arrangements within less affluent areas. As with the configuration of homes in District Six, close-quarter living is more likely to occur in places that are economically disadvantaged. In these communities the possibility of privacy is diminished. Sharing of rooms and the close proximity of other dwellings means that the probability of being able to keep one's sexuality private is lessened. A solution to this problem is to become overtly visible. Yet in economically advantaged areas, this need to become overtly visible is not as pressing. Dwellings are more likely to be spaced further apart from one another, and living conditions will be less cramped.[32] Some coloured queer men are therefore able to explain their choice not to cross-dress as one closely tied to their more favourable economic position. As this queer man from Grassy Park explains:

In an area like Steenberg or Lavender Hill, they [cross-dressing queer men] live out of each other's houses . . . I don't go to my neighbours. I go to work in the morning. I come home in the evening. I won't go out now with them . . . They just 'rock up' [appear without invitation at each other's houses] . . . It's the economic environment. It's the norm for them. But for me it's totally unacceptable. BRADLEY/35

These class distinctions also go further. As already discussed, the social position of coloured groups within the apartheid racial schema was defined by their volatility between black African and white groups. For some coloured individuals, there were definite benefits in trying to emulate a white social existence. Post-apartheid, this need is of course lessened. Yet perceptions of race groups, tied to class, do still condition how far some coloured queers are willing to associate with cross-dressing. The end of apartheid has increased the likelihood of race group interaction. Awareness of, and comparison with, white queer men in Cape Town has therefore also increased. As would perhaps be expected, several coloured queer men expressed their dislike for cross-dressing by contrasting it directly with what they saw white queer men had created for themselves in places such as the central suburbs and City Bowl. In such a light, the same group of men who critiqued queer cross-dressers as being exploited by heterosexually-identified men understand white queer culture as one where men are not pressured into cross-dressing. For some coloured queer men, white queer men are in part defined by their lack of need to have sex with heterosexu-ally-identified men to complement an effeminate gender identity. As the quotations below demonstrate, white communities generally are subse-quently perceived as far more 'tolerant' and 'forward thinking' about queer sexuality than coloured communities. For some men it is the 'backward-ness' of coloured communities and associated cross-dressing in comparison to what they understand as goes towards comprising white communities that helps differentiate these two racially-defined groups.

I mean, the problem with being gay on the Cape Flats is that you are cast into spe-cific roles, so that you are either in 'the closet', in which case you aren't really gay and nobody knows about it [here referring to heterosexually-identified men who have sex with cross-dressing queers], or you are a hairdresser or a drag queen, in which case you are the stereotypical gay person, as projected by the sort of main-stream heterosexual press about these weirdo gay men who, you know, are – They really just want to be women, but – 'ah shame!' – they're men. Whereas, I think that there's nothing wrong with being a drag queen [cross-dressing queer man], but drag queens are necessitated by a particular – The more oppressive the space, the more likely it is that there are drag queens – Because it's kind of acceptable in a weird kind of way. In an oppressive society – and by 'oppressive' I mean heterosexual society – which has very strict gender roles, then the only way in which male homo-sexuality can be explained, really, is by men who – is that these people are men who want to be women. And so the only space available for people who are homosexual is that space – men who want to be women – and so gay men will take on that space so that they have some freedom at least . . . But – and maybe this is one of the reasons why there are fewer drag queens in [apartheid designated white centres] . . . because that harsh construction of gender identity is less in the city.   WILLIAM/27

White [queer] people generally feel more at ease with themselves and their sexuality.   CLINT/22

[In reference to heterosexual-identified men having sex with cross-dressing moffies and 'using' them] You know what it is; it's a cultural thinking. You don't get it in white areas in Cape Town.   BRADLEY/35

Without doubt it is possible to see some broad and at times distinct differences between particular groups of coloured and white queer men. But to argue that coloured cross-dressing is a culturally regressive act, or that white queer culture is not as structured by gender relations, would be misleading. Such statements tend to gloss over the way both racially defined communities have been affected by apartheid in different ways. And in turn, these statements would fail to see how queer men in each group have been remarkably successful in freeing themselves of heteronormative regulation and becoming visible within their own communities. These different appropriations of heteronormative space have led to two different ways of approaching the relationship between gender and sexual identities. It therefore becomes imperative to look again at the deeper ideological histories of some white and coloured queer visibilities, to more fully understand not only the differences but also the similarities between these two groups.

Queer Visibility in the City Bowl and on the Cape Flats

As discussed in chapter 2, a popular (although generalised) representation of white queer men in Cape Town and the associated gay village is that of a group of men able to behave as they wish without societal censure. Queer men from across the country travel to Cape Town in search of this newly discovered liberal paradise on the tip of Africa. As already discussed, this representation is a very recent one, and draws heavily upon particular Western European and North American queer influences, moulding such influences with local history into a unique Cape Townian form and subsequently affecting different groups of white queer men in remarkably divergent ways. Yet these representations are also inextricably tied to late twentieth-century gay liberation movements. These political movements in certain sites in the West were an attempt to confront homophobia in society by distancing their arguments from any discussion about the construction of effeminate gender identity. While, as already discussed, the development of white queer cultures in Cape Town must not be seen as wholesale appropriations of that which emerged in North America or Western Europe, it is also worth noting for this discussion the way gender, sexual identity and space affected each other in such locations.

As Chauncey (1994) has discussed, up until the early part of the twentieth century, cities such as New York had queer cultures defined by cross-dressing and effeminate men or 'fairies' and more masculine men (along with butch-femme lesbian couples). State crackdowns in the 1930s forced this culture underground, only for it to emerge again in the middle years of the century as something entirely different. As Chauncey explains about the period beginning in the 1940s: '[T]he ascendancy of *gay* as the primary self-referential term used by men within the gay world represented a subtle shift in the boundaries of the male sexual world. It reflected a reorganisation of male sexual categories and the transition from a world divided into "fairies" and "men" on the basis of gender persona into one divided into "homosexuals" and "heterosexuals" on the basis of sexual object-choice. The transformation in gay culture suggested by the ascendancy of *gay* was closely tied to the masculinization of that culture' (emphasis in original p. 358). A similar transformation has also been noted in London. Houlbrook (2005) has charted how working-class queer culture evolved over the middle of the twentieth century so as to sideline effeminate gender performances: 'The declining visibility of camp after the Second World War suggests that it was possible for workingmen to separate sexuality from gender as a component of personhood, to have sex with men while seeing themselves as masculine' (p. 163). A comparable justification to that found in New York is also evident to explain why this shift occurred: 'From the 1930s onwards, facing increasingly active policing, the proprietors of commercial venues – and, indeed, many other queer men – were less willing than ever to accept the risks attendant upon accepting the custom of flamboyantly camp men' (p. 164).

It was from within this culture, increasingly defined by masculine gender performances, that attempts were made to confront state and societal homophobia in the 1960s and 1970s. The gay liberation movement quickly found that it was easy for cultural conservatives to attack any political campaign by employing increasingly outdated queer gender stereotypes. Conservative groups deployed the idea of male homosexuality explicitly meaning 'a man wanting to be a woman' as an easy shorthand for all that was 'wrong' with gay liberation. Questions of equality for queers could be straightforwardly dismissed by the simplistic argument that men were 'inherently' masculine and women were 'inherently' feminine. Since queers 'obviously' did not conform to this most simple and universal assumption, they should never (or rather, could never) gain legal, political or social rights. For queer men, this meant an even more adamant disavowal of effeminacy as a part of the liberation ideal. As Wilchins (2004) succinctly explains: 'Rather than defend drag queens, fairies, and effeminate men, gay men responded by playing feverishly against type. "Macho gay" emerged as the new look, complete with the emphasis on the gym culture's hyper-muscularity that persists today' (p. 17). While, of course, it should be stressed that today in the West a significant proportion of queer men do not necessarily view themselves as overtly masculine, a large number no longer solely structure their objects of desire around the gender binary (see also Sedgwick 1990).

This reorganisation of queer sexual cultures in sites in the West also led to a reconfiguration of the spaces associated with queer desire. As numerous commentators have described, a growth in the number of men who understood their sexuality as more to do with sexual object-choice than gender identity led to a reduction in the number of socialising venues where queer men could meet heterosexually-identified men (or 'trade' in Chauncey's terms) for sex. Gay bars as they are known today were born, where men acting and behaving along masculine gender lines could meet similar men. The agglomeration of gay bars in the latter part of the twentieth century was also furthered by gay liberation's ideology that positioned queer individuals in oppositional spaces to heterosexual society. As D'Emilio (1983) explains, gay liberation movements in the US were distinct from earlier 'homosexual' movements that had sought assimilation with heterosexual society. Gay liberation was instead concerned with never having to assimilate again. Gay villages developed as the physical embodiment of this new ideology. They also allowed for the formation of voter blocks necessary to gain political representation. Queer men who were located in, or passed through, these spaces were able to openly proclaim their difference from heteronormative society. A 'coming out' of 'the closet' was therefore spatially possible (chapter 1). As Harry Britt, a gay activist in San Francisco argued: 'When gays are spatially scattered, they are not gay, because they are invisible' (quoted in Castells 2004: 272). Spaces such as gay villages were necessary for queer men, both to socialise and for political representation. These places offered a form of queer visibility and transgression of heteronormative space by spatial agglomeration.

As discussed in chapter 2, popular images of groups of white queer men in Cape Town would seem to indicate that they too have developed a particular rendering of this spatialised form of gay liberation (although to varying degrees of success), by creating their own space – the De Waterkant gay village. Every year in Cape Town a Gay Pride Festival takes place through the historically segregated white city – and is attended mostly by white queer men (chapter 6). These men are both visible and represented as distinct from other spaces and bodies in the city centre. While, as we will also see in chapter 5, this spatialisation is not due simply to Western influences – although such influence must surely be seen as very relevant – but also to more local historical and race-based nationalistic issues, it is important to understand here that such a spatialisation takes with it a particular – and by no means universal – conception of the gender binary. These men are therefore commonly represented by a particular spatial model that conditions queer sexuality around sexual object-choice rather than overt and sustained cross-dressing and femininity.[33] While, as with men in the West, it would be incorrect to assume all white queer men in Cape Town are overtly masculine (or as discussed in chapter 2, that by any means all wish to associate with the space of the gay village), they nonetheless are not understood by many to view their sexuality as one that requires sexual relationships with heterosexually-identified men. As the interviewees above extolled, sustained cross-dressing, as found in outlying suburbs of the Cape Flats, is absent from the gay village. And indeed, one need only look at the front covers of *Detail* newspaper (Figure 3.7), the free publication for queer men in Cape Town distributed in the gay village, to see similar overtly masculine images to those found in queer publications distributed in many other urban gay spaces. A popular image for others in the city of this group of men is that of a community free to socialise; possessing a unique visibility separate from heterosexual society (and hence not openly attempting to have sex with heterosexual men to complete an effeminate gender identity); not cross-dressing on a regular basis; and all publicly (on some level at least) expressing a queer identity, place them in sharp contrast with effeminate cross-dressing coloured men and the 'straight' men they wish to have sex with. As some coloured queer men discussed, cross-dressing men are sometimes understood as being pressured into cross-dressing and mistreated by heterosexually-identified men. By contrast, white queer men who frequent a space such as the gay village are understood by some interviewees not to be represented in this way.

Indeed, as Amanda Swarr's (2004) nuanced discussion in relation to white queer South Africa deftly highlights, a different historical legacy to coloured cross-dressers means that cross-dressing in anything other than cabaret shows or on clearly delineated stages can become easily associated with 'outmoded' and indeed 'culturally regressive' sexual identities (see also chapter 5 for more on this comparison, its historical evolution and its distinctly race-based and exclusionary undertones): 'The sex-gender-sexuality system under which urban white gay men operate values masculine gender identities ... Despite acceptance of drag in commercial performances, transgender identities are often rejected and ridiculed' ... [continuous] drag queens are seen as inferior and inappropriate' (p. 82).

Yet in outlying suburbs of the Cape Flats, visibility and hence transgression of heteronormative space is achieved in an altogether different way to

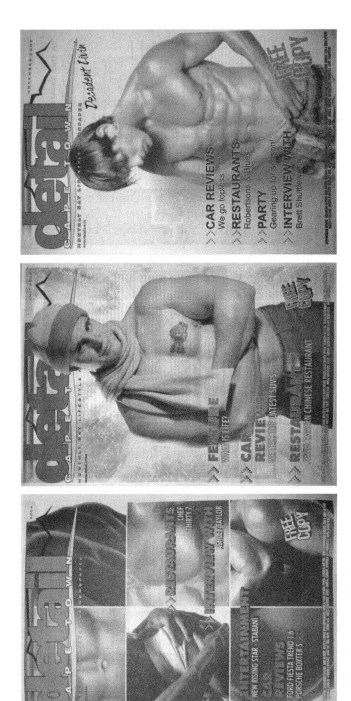

Figure 3.7 Front covers of *Detail* newspaper.

the groups described by Swarr. Groups here have a different history to many white queer men in the central suburbs of Cape Town: a history where widespread and overt cross-dressing was not only accepted, but also used to promote elements of coloured culture. While disliked by some, its detractors were never able to rid the community of it. Politically, cross-dressing is directly tied to the memory of struggles over District Six and the formation of coloured communities. Coloured cross-dressing has continued to maintain a prominent position within these coloured communities. The gender binary has therefore remained vital for both queer men and heterosexual society to articulate sexuality. This, in turn, has led to a different conceptualisation of queer spatiality for coloured cross-dressers. Rather than creating a demarcated space, coloured cross-dressing men have achieved visibility and wider community safety through an outward performance of effeminacy from within heteronormative space. As the above sections have shown, many of these men are able to lead open and free lives, where they are easily accepted by the wider community. For these men, the agglomeration of individuals in a physical space is not – and never has been – required. Instead, a 'coming out' within space is achieved by bodily performance. Indeed, cross-dressing men's sexual desire for heterosexually-identified men would make attempts at spatial agglomeration pointless. Sexual activity with heterosexually-identified men would be severely limited if they chose to remove themselves spatially and ideologically from heterosexual society. The articulation of queer visibility in the gay village and on outlying parts of the Cape Flats is therefore different in each space. Spatially, heteronormative regulation is broken down differently in these two locations, by attempting two different strategies at becoming visible. Yet both groups are able to achieve openness and safety.

It must also then be realised that the different visibilities in each location illustrate and inform how queer men in the two communities perceive the heterosexual/homosexual binary and hence sexual identity categories in different ways (see also chapter 1). While some coloured queer men point to the alleged freedom of what they refer to as white queer culture over that available in some coloured queer communities, both in reality remained structured by the options available to them. For example, as the quotation by 'WILLIAM/27' in the previous section explains, some coloured men assume that heterosexually-identified men who have sex with cross-dressing moffies are 'still in the closet'. These men, it is argued, are having sex with other men, yet not admitting their 'true' sexual identity. From a Western gay liberationist perspective, these men could fall into the 'bisexual' sexual grouping. Within Western sexual politics, this group are often viewed negatively by both heterosexual and homosexual society. From a heterosexual perspective there is often a call to assume that a bisexual is 'just experimenting, he's really straight'. From a Western gay liberationist perspective, bisexuals are 'just not all the way out of the closet yet' (Hemmings 1995 and 2000; James 1996). Heterosexually-identified coloured men who engage in sexual activity with coloured cross-dressing queer men could easily be categorised in a similar way. As described in chapter 1, there is, in other words, incongruence between their sexual activity and their sexual identity. This group fail to fit within 'the closet' schema.

In turn, such a view can also dictate that those cross-dressing men who have sex with heterosexually-identified men are in fact only furthering a situation of 'false-consciousness' whereby congruence between sexual activity and sexual identity can never be reached for the heterosexually-identified man.[34] Rather than confront heteropatriarchy, coloured cross-dressing men are only furthering it. Yet again, it becomes possible to argue that such a view remains firmly entrenched within 'the closet' schema – a schema focused around understanding a subject and their identity that blindly looks towards identity congruence and a particular reading of liberation as the end product. Such a view only goes to marginalise communities that have been able to explore different variants of the heterosexual/homosexual binary and create different spaces of empowerment and acceptance.

Indeed, the heterosexual/homosexual binary and hence sexuality in communities associated with cross-dressing coloured men is based instead around a strong and particular reading of gender identity and sexual identity (which is itself affected by a particular history of transnational migration, cultural mixing, race-based segregation, exploitation and discrimination). For heterosexually-identified men, sexual identity is defined and regulated through an understanding of the importance of their masculine gender identity. For these men, there is no need to 'come out' since for them, they were never in 'the closet' to begin with. The wider coloured community is well aware that these men may have sex with cross-dressing queers. For the wider community as well, a proclamation of a queer identity is to drag and act in an overtly effeminate manner. Men who perform a masculine gender identity therefore do not see the need to view themselves as anything other than heterosexual. By comparison, and as the work of Amanda Swarr (2004) has pointed out, significant segments of white queer culture in South Africa can in fact be seen to remain equally 'constrained' due to the fact they would most likely 'rank' cross-dressing men unfavourably. A different historical legacy to that of coloured queer cross-dressers means that bodily performances of sustained overt effeminacy as a means of queer visibility can often become heavily sidelined in white queer communities (Spruill 2004; see also chapter 5). It would further vilify white heterosexually-identified men undertaking sexual relationships with queer men. To assume a stance that 'ranks' coloured cross-dressing as either more or less 'liberated' than any other queer visibility must therefore be acknowledged as being undertaken from a particular position in relation to 'the closet' that itself can draw on particular elements of different racialised histories.

Nevertheless, this discussion should not discount the possibility of mistreatment of some coloured cross-dressers by some of the heterosexually-identified men they have sex with. Indeed, such violence itself points towards broader inequalities across the sex-gender spectrum well documented in South Africa (see for example, Dunkle et al. 2004; McEwan 2005; Vetten and Bhana 2001). But to argue that the possibility of mistreatment of queer cross-dressing men is a reason to discount cross-dressing would be to ignore the successes this group have achieved in relation to the wider community. Rather than argue that cross-dressing is a culturally regressive act in comparison to the types of visibility promoted in a space such as the gay village, attention should instead be drawn to finding ways of further empowering cross-dressing men. To view cross-dressing queer men in such a light would help illustrate that the types of visibilities represented in the gay village and on some outlying parts of the Cape Flats are both structured by gendered dynamics. It would also expose how some coloured queer men who reject cross-dressing as a culturally regressive form of queer visibility do so from a position that favours masculine queer performances without necessarily exploring how they too are structured (and at times limited) by the gender binary, 'the closet' and also history.

Conclusion

In some coloured communities, concepts of sexual identity and gender identity, tied to a specific spatial appropriation of heteronormative space, have led to different ways of becoming visible than in some historically white communities. What it means to become visible and the mechanisms deployed to achieve it in each community can be decidedly different. While some coloured men view cross-dressing in a negative light, especially when compared to what they understand to comprise a white queer culture in the city, it is equally possible to argue both have been successful at leading open lives, relatively free from discrimination. Both are also constrained by the options available to them.

The history of coloured cross-dressing in Cape Town is one that stretches back to at least the middle of the twentieth century. It is also a history closely associated with the development of coloured culture and coloured collective memory. This history, however, is one that has always been socially ranked in relation to white society. During apartheid, coloured moffies were constructed by the coloured middle-class as an example of all that was 'degenerate' about working-class coloured lifestyles. Today, some coloured queer men view cross-dressers within their own community as less free than their white queer neighbours in the city. Race and class have continued to delineate cross-dressers within Cape Town as a separate and socially less desirable group.

For many foreign tourists who visit Cape Town, it is then perhaps right of them to consider it a small city. A particular spatialised model of masculinity tied to discrete queer spaces is but one way of expressing queer sexuality in the city. Yet this expression is one that many wish to associate with. During apartheid, some coloured groups saw benefit in associating with white society. Post-apartheid, some coloured groups continue to see white queer culture as something to aspire to. During both periods, beliefs as to the 'superiority' of certain aspects of white society helped engineer these views. Yet in both time periods these views failed to explore the successes coloured queer men have had at leading open and visible lives within their own communities.

Chapter Four

How to be a Queer Xhosa Man in the Cape Town Townships

Introduction

Travelling to what, during apartheid, were designated black African townships takes the visitor along a different path from that to the outlying apartheid-designated coloured areas of the Cape Flats. Rather than branch south along the peninsula, the journey follows the N2 highway or Klipfontein Road, east, out towards the airport. Taking the N2, as many do, is the fastest way out of the city. Away from rush hour, travelling inland as far as the famous university town of Stellenbosch can take as little as an hour. The airport or Nyanga township could be reached in about twenty minutes. Yet, for the visitor, choosing such a route would result in missing out on an experience that, perhaps more than any other, encompasses the legacy of urban spatial zoning in Cape Town. Beginning at the Leisbeek Parkway close to Main Road (chapter 3), Klipfontein Road travels through the apartheid-designated coloured area of Athlone. The main roads here are wide and uncluttered, with well-kept palm trees helping to divide the four lane highway. Regular traffic lights and unhurried drivers foster an almost leisurely feeling as drivers gently flow inland. Yet when crossing the M10 road close to Manenberg Police Station the composition of people and houses suddenly and dramatically changes. Formalised housing and wide open streets are abruptly replaced with a narrow two lane road and the beginnings of the Guguletu township, a historically apartheid-designated black African area. The disparity between the two areas could not be more complete: As the road runs further east, shacks and sand covered roads are now common occurrences.

To continue on, journeying further into the townships along Lansdowne Road helps give first time visitors an appreciation of the sheer enormity of the ever growing Cape Town townships. Travelling through the midst of an at times chaotic mass of dwellings can easily become an overwhelming experience. It is in these types of dwellings, many without running water or electricity, that nearly half of all Cape Townians live. And it is the contrast between these types of dwellings and those just a few kilometres away that helps the outsider understand the unfairness and injustice that for so long defined the city and the country. It is also in these still disadvantaged locations that the home of the last group of queer men important to this study is to be found.

This final chapter in Part One of this book therefore devotes itself to uncovering both the way black African queer men in Cape Town have been able to prosper and the unique barriers they face in leading open and visible lives. Like the previous two chapters, it will also offer explanations as to why groups have chosen specific paths to become visible in urban heteronormative space. Specifically, it will explore how within Cape Town townships, the diversity of black African queer visibilities were in large part created and subsequently strongly affected by both the legacy of apartheid regulation and the way apartheid itself suddenly ended. Yet more so than with either the study of white or coloured queers in the city, this chapter will also highlight how colonial and apartheid regulation may have helped, at the beginning of the twenty-first century, to galvanise homophobic discourses among certain elements of black African society. It will therefore be argued that apartheid spatial regulation not only limited the options available to queer black African men in the city for the majority of the twentieth century, it also laid the foundations for strong and sustained contemporary homophobic beliefs. It will also consequently be shown that the forcefulness with which homophobia is felt among black African queer groups in the Cape Town townships is one of the main reasons why they have chosen specific strategies to become spatially visible to their communities.

The Black 'Threat' and the European 'Contamination'

The oppression of black African groups by the white minority government in South Africa represents the single most defining element of South African history. As previous chapters have explored, apartheid (or 'separateness' in Afrikaans) was based on an ideology of spatial separation between 'Bantu' (a common apartheid term for black African groups) and European groups. Apartheid ideology was rationalised by the white state on the idea that South Africans could only live harmoniously in the country if kept apart from each other. For the white minority government, this separateness would help keep all that was European and more 'civilised' protected from what they perceived as the 'uncivilised black masses'.[1] Yet this policy of separation led to decades of civil unrest and the transformation and almost destruction of black African communities and culture (Clarke and Worger 2004; Worden 2000). While white leaders tried to assure the populace that spatial separation was all that would occur through the logic of apartheid, the reality was that it resulted in the continued oppression and subjugation of black African (and coloured) groups by a tiny fraction of the country's population. At the same time however, such policies have also helped foster a belief among some that queer sexuality itself is directly tied to control of black African groups by the Dutch and British. It is therefore the aim of this first section to contextualise the processes of apartheid and preceding racial policies for black African groups in South Africa, and especially Cape Town, and the logic that is still used by some today to argue that 'homosexuality is unAfrican'.

Since colonial times, black African groups have been displaced from their lands as first Dutch settlers and later British conquerors moved out east across the country from their initial landing at the Cape. Systematic discrimination followed early contact, especially after the discovery of diamonds in the 1860s and gold in the 1880s in the Transvaal region and the need for labour (Etherington 1979; Thompson 2001). The British, to limit the degree to which black African workers could negotiate wages to work in the intensive mining industries, simply conquered the still independent African states in southern Africa, confiscated the bulk of their lands and imposed cash taxation on them (Cope 1986 and 1989). This had the effect of forcing those black African individuals who had previously chosen to work on the mines to now work there on their employers' terms. Those that moved to urban areas for work were forced to abide by discriminatory laws that forced the price of their labour to the lowest possible levels. Migration by black African labourers to mines and to urban areas therefore became a central tenet on which the British and Dutch were able to sustain the economy. After the formation of the South African Union in 1910, the government instigated the 1911 Mines and Work Act, further excluding black African workers and limiting them to the lowest paid jobs in the mining industry (Davies 1976).

In the Cape however, a slightly different story was developing. Unlike areas further east and further north, what later became the Western Cape, where Cape Town is situated, had proved unreachable for the majority of black African groups in pre-colonial times. The arid and semi-arid conditions that insulated the area had limited the degree with which it could be settled by groups elsewhere (Ross 1999). Indeed, in pre-colonial times, only the Khoisan (chapter 3) in the Mediterranean and Pluvial climate zones, behind this buffer zone, inhabited the Western Cape. As Western (2001) has shown, the influx of black African individuals to Cape Town, even after the arrival of Europeans, is a relatively recent phenomenon.[2] Until the ending of apartheid, Cape Town was overwhelmingly a coloured city. Today, however, the number of black African individuals – and specifically Xhosa – is increasing, as they search out employment and other opportunities in the prosperous city of Cape Town.[3]

The first large scale arrival of black African migrants into Cape Town therefore occurred through the British colonial administration, which brought black African men by train to work in the city's docks during the latter part of the nineteenth century.[4] Early on, black African workers were spatially segregated from the rest of the city, with a 'Native Location' on the then-outskirts of the city, at Ndabeni.[5] Due to Acts such as the 1923 Natives (Urban Areas) Act, black African individuals were only allowed to remain in the cities as long as they had employment. Black African workers coming to urban areas to seek employment could only stay for a limited period before being forced to return to rural areas. If they failed to leave the cities, they could be imprisoned.

The first planned 'location' (later, 'township') for black African groups in the city was established in 1927. Langa (meaning 'Sun') was built to replace Ndabeni, which was seen as unhygienic and decrepit – especially in contrast to the growing neighbouring white suburbs. A highly regulated settlement, the labourers who inhabited Langa were subjected to harsh controls which made trading illegal and forced all visitors to report to a superintendent. Overwhelmingly Xhosa in make-up, places such as Ndabeni and Langa helped create the first instances of 'home-boyism' – a bond created by common geographical location. A divide was therefore created among Xhosa groups, between those who were urbanised and those who were seen to be from rural locations, or to have arrived in the city more recently. As Bickford-Smith et al. (1999) point out, there soon developed perceptions among those who lived in Langa that 'country girls' were considered 'backward, uncivilised and coarse', whereas urban black African women were considered 'brighter and more polished'. The urbanisation of the Xhosa in Cape Town, however limiting and repressive, nonetheless helped to create a class divide between urban and rural that has persisted to the present day (see below).

As chapters 2 and 3 have argued, apartheid was conditioned largely on the need to separate black African groups from white groups, and on the protection and isolation of the white nation. The earlier controls limiting black African migration to the cities were therefore further enhanced with the deployment of government Acts after 1948. Far more forcibly than with coloured communities, the South African state attempted to limit political representation, economic opportunities and movement around the country for black African individuals. While coloured groups were limited in the type of employment they could undertake, black African groups were even more forcibly reduced to the lowest levels within the economy.

As the apartheid state developed, increased concern was placed on the possible influx of black African workers into the urban (and predominantly white) centres. In the 1950s the state therefore began a process to displace as many as possible to 'Bantustans' or 'homelands', away from the urban centres such as Johannesburg, Durban and Cape Town.[6] These homeland areas had originally been defined by the colonial British government and established as 'reserves' under the Natives' Land Act of 1913. Now they were to be resurrected and acknowledged by the apartheid state as the traditional black African (and hopefully, later, independent) lands separate to the rest of the country.[7] Homelands were consequently set up for different language groups, with the Transkei and Ciskei in the eastern part of what was the Cape Province (today part of the Eastern Cape) designated for the Xhosa (see Figure 4.1) (Platzky and Walker 1985).[8]

Black African workers in Cape Town and other cities who were unable to find jobs were deported back to their 'independent' homelands. Yet the homelands proved to be even harsher to live in than the townships in the cities (Christopher 1997). As an example: white populated areas of the

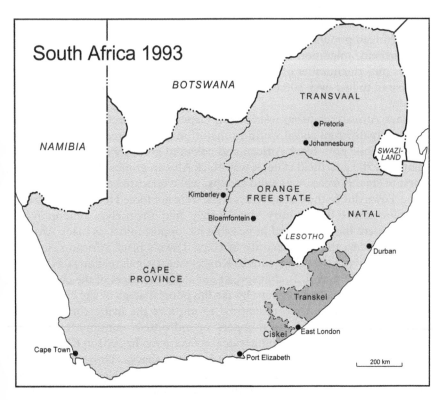

Figure 4.1   The location of the Transkei and Ciskei in relation to Cape Town.

Cape had a population density of 2 per square kilometre. In Transkei there was a density of 55 per square kilometre and in Ciskei a density of 82. Therefore, despite the implementation of the pass laws, black African workers from the eastern part of the Cape Province continued to arrive in Cape Town, desperate to find some form of employment and to escape the poverty and hardship in the homelands. The huge demographic growth of the city therefore could only be maintained by the creation of several new and illegal townships on the edges of the city, such as Crossroads and Modderdam. Initially the state responded by rounding up those without permission to be in the city and bussing them back to the Eastern Cape. They also attempted to remove these illegal settlements, in some cases (such as with Modderdam) successfully (Bickford-Smith et al. 1999).

By the 1980s however, growing international awareness of the plight of black African groups in South Africa forced the state to create a new planned township, Khayelitsha, seventeen miles from the city centre on the distant edge of Cape Town. In 1986 the pass laws were repealed under mounting international pressure and ever-growing black African civil unrest. Today, Xhosa individuals from the Eastern Cape have continued to migrate from rural areas to Cape Town. Between 1982 and 1992, the black African population of Cape Town more than doubled. With the end of apartheid, migration has continued to increase. The most recent full census puts the number of black African individuals in the city at 900,000, compared to just over 100,000 in 1975, an increase of over seven hundred percent.[9]

Black African township residents in Cape Town therefore often inhabit an entirely different social world to that of many coloured and white individuals. While both black African and coloured groups were discriminated against by the apartheid state, it was black African groups that suffered the worst of state policies. Coloured groups, while relocated to the outskirts of Cape Town due to the Group Areas Acts, were not forced to move hundreds of miles across the country should they find themselves unemployed. Neither were they as limited in possible job opportunities as black African groups. Today, the vast majority of Cape Town's black African residents continue to live in townships such as Khayelitsha, Guguletu, Langa, Nyanga, and Philippe (Figure 4.2), that spread out along the edges of the city, along the N2 (Figure 4.3). These are by far the poorest areas of the city. While the ANC government has attempted to improve the living conditions of township inhabitants, large numbers of individuals continue to live in informal shacks without running water or electricity. In 2001 in Khayelitsha 64 per cent (55,301 dwellings) were informal shacks. Only 20 per cent (17,286 dwellings) had piped water inside their homes. Nearly 24 per cent (20,205 dwellings) relied on paraffin, candles and other fuels, rather than electricity, for lighting.)[10]

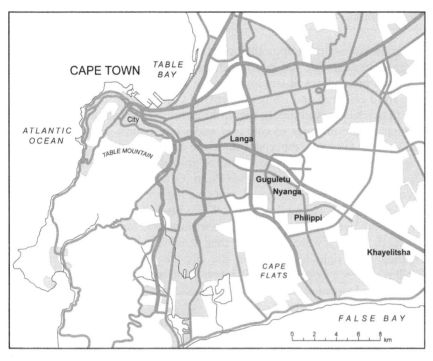

Figure 4.2 The location of some of the major townships in Cape Town today.

Figure 4.3 Informal shacks in Cape Town.

Yet the townships, despite their poor living conditions, continue to grow. Large-scale migration has continued from rural areas where living conditions and possibilities of employment are even bleaker. However, in comparison to coloured and white residents in Cape Town, these new arrivals, and those that arrived before them, do not posses the same local cultural heritage as the majority of coloured and white groups in the city. Places like District Six have, especially since the end of apartheid, helped in the creation of a shared history for coloured groups in the city.[11] The centre of Cape Town and places such as Sea Point, Green Point and the City Bowl have a long history of segregated white habitation. Today they continue to be dominated by white inhabitants. While black African groups also have a historical legacy in Cape Town, their numbers, for the majority of the twentieth century, were far smaller than those of coloured or white groups. Further, their right to remain in the city was by no means guaranteed (unlike coloured and white individuals); for many there was always the possibility of forced relocation to the Transkei and Ciskei, and a life of even greater poverty.

As might be expected, in comparison to other racially defined communities in South Africa, little direct research was conducted during the colonial and apartheid eras about queer identities or more generalised same-sex sexual practices among black African groups across the country and those in Cape Town in particular. Yet what little does exist points clearly to the fact that same-sex sexual activity was not only known about among many groups but was also accepted, with qualifications, among some. Some of the earliest direct evidence of this comes from the South African mines during the late nineteenth century.[12] As the above discussion has briefly mentioned, colonialists in South Africa attempted, through confiscation of lands, to force black African individuals to work on gold and diamond mines. These mining compounds were conditioned on the regulation of migratory labour (Campbell 2003 and Elder 2003). Men spent several months at a time working on the mines away from their homes and families, living in cramped and overcrowded mining hostels. By the beginning of the twentieth century reports by the British such as the 1907 Taberer Report had began to document the apparently widespread occurrences of same-sex, age-stratified sexual activity on the South African mines (Epprecht 2001 and 2004).

Youth in these same-sex relationships were commonly referred to in the mines as 'wives' (Sibuyi 1993). And in some cases these young men would be proposed to upon entering the mining compounds by more senior mine workers or 'boss boys'. Upon acceptance (often facilitated by bestowing gifts such as clothes, blankets and even bicycles), the 'wife' would be expected to wash dishes and look after the more senior mine worker, the 'husband'. Sex would also occur between the two partners, both penetrative and by the rubbing of the more senior partner's penis between the thighs of the younger 'wife'. These relationships or 'mine marriages' were taken very seriously by those who took part in them, with some documented cases of senior mine workers going so far as to pay lobola (bridal wealth) to the wife once they returned to their homes (Moodie 1988).[13]

Age therefore was augmented by gender-defined roles during the construction of mine marriages. Similarities can therefore be drawn between these black African sexual relationships and that of coloured cross-dressing queer men in Cape Town, discussed in chapter 3.[14] However, unlike coloured cross-dressing queer culture, cross-dressing and overt effeminate gender performances do not appear to have been as common. Neither were these relationships as strongly regulated by a form of queer identity in contrast to heteronormativity. In other words, it is unknown how far a variant of the heterosexual/homosexual binary – described in chapter 1 – delineated these men. As Murray and Roscoe (1998) point out, stronger similarities can be drawn to the construction of same-sex desire in ancient Greece where leg and facial hair indicated it was no longer appropriate for a relationship to continue.[15] These activities were also by no means merely a minority practice among mine-workers. Marc Epprecht (2004) suggests that in some cases 70 to 80 per cent of men at the mines took male sexual partners. Reasons suggested include a wish to mitigate loneliness, economic benefit, and the re-enactment of traditional gender roles that were becoming less common among actual females as the century progressed (Moodie 1988). Added to that list must be same-sex desire (McLean and Ngcobo 1995).

Yet whatever reason these men had for engaging in same-sex sexual activity, it remains nonetheless possible to conceptualise the formalised social construction of these relationships as, if not the direct result of, then at least augmented by colonial and apartheid rule. While some evidence from the period points towards relatively common same-sex sexual relationships between black African men in groups such as the Tsonga (who today inhabit the Transvaal in South Africa, Mozambique, Swaziland and Zimbabwe) prior to mining work, a popular view remains that white colonialists have been 'responsible' for the widespread proliferation of this activity among black African men due to the mining and migrant system. As Marc Epprecht (2004) has explored in great detail, this view stems from a common and misguided colonial trope which positioned black African groups as 'childlike' and hence in need of protection from more 'developed' and 'civilised' white rulers.

Yet this view also emerges from more concrete rationalisations. For example, Elder (1995) has discussed how apartheid architects saw distinct benefits in allowing same-sex relationships to continue in mining hostels, despite action they were taking to curb the 'queer conspiracy' within white society at the time (chapter 2). Indeed, such activity among black African men would actually only go to help the Nationalists' ideological cause, by containing black African sexuality and limiting the possibility of sexual activity with white women. Mining hostels were therefore regarded by the apartheid state as spatial containers that successfully regulated the sexual activity of black African mineworkers:

> The closed system of mining life in South Africa saw the emergence of sprawling white family residential estates alongside hostels accommodating thousands of black African male workers. The presence of white miners' wives, daughters and mothers alongside thousands of black men who had no sexual outlet not only poignantly demonstrates some of the internal contradictions that racked racial capitalism, but also the root of homosexual tolerance. (Elder 1995: 60)

It is also evident that the forms of sexual expression associated with migrant hostels were, in general, not condoned by wider black African society. While it was clearly known by some that mine relationships would occur when men were distanced from their families, these relationships in general were not promoted away from these environments. As Mathabane (1986) (discussed in Donham 1998) has noted, when growing up in Soweto on the outskirts of Johannesburg in the 1960s, hostels for migrant workers in the city had become well known for same-sex sexual activity. Parents would warn their children not to go too near these hostels, lest they be 'swept aside and smeared with Vaseline and raped'.

Such findings could in some circles be seen to erroneously assist a contemporary sector of South African society in linking colonial rule and European influence with the propagation of same-sex sexual activity (Reddy 2002). Further, today same-sex sexual activity is also directly named and identified as separate from heteronormative society. Here, 'homosexuality' as an 'affliction' emerges in a similar way to the development of sexualised differences among other societies, described in chapter 1. It therefore becomes dangerously easy for some contemporary political leaders to assume that same-sex sexual activity, anachronistic and medicalised 'homosexualities' and contemporary queer identities are only promoted in South Africa because of outside European encroachment. As an example, a particular spin on this argument came from the Congress of Traditional Leaders of South Africa (CONTRALESA), an influential political group within the country, in their submission in opposition to the proposed same-sex Civil Union Bill in 2006 (see also chapter 6):

We maintain that throughout Africa the indigenous people have had their traditions, cultures and languages invaded by foreign elements that have used force to disorientate them and prevent them for utilising their own traditional norms and values to maintain peoples and order in their communities. Africa has paid a heavy price. Unfortunately, as African majority governments have been voted into power using euro-centric 'democratic' constitutions, they have generally refused to give recognition to their own traditional norms and values . . . As traditional leaders we have had occasion to raise the matter of homosexuality in several of our forums. Even at the level of the South African Development Community Council of Traditional Leaders the matter has been raised as part of our human rights seminars. While admitting of the existence of the problem, all those present were agreed that homosexuality is neither condoned nor promoted by any of their cultures . . . We object to the certification of the Constitution on the basis that it is Eurocentric and will lead to undesirable consequences such as the Constitutional court judgement in question. (CONTRALESA 2006: 7, 10 and 13)

In another, and perhaps more (in)famous example, Winnie Mandela used a similar leap in logic during her trial for kidnapping in 1991. At the time the wife of future South African president Nelson Mandela, she was found guilty of four charges of kidnapping and a further four charges of being an accessory after the fact of assault. During this trial it was alleged that in the 1980s Winnie Mandela and her team of personal bodyguards had been terrorising township residents, kidnapping, torturing and murdering those who had not supported her increasingly radical and violent political views. What is striking about this case, however, is not simply that it marked the first official recognition of illegality and corruption on the part of Mrs Mandela. Rather, that Mandela's legal defence argued that she had simply been 'protecting' the individuals she was alleged to have kidnapped and assaulted by removing them from the presence of Reverend Paul Verryn, a Methodist minister. It was alleged that Verryn was sexually abusing boys and young men in his care (an allegation that later was found to be false). As Holmes (1995 and 1997) points out, the Mandela defence lawyers invoked an astonishing cognitive leap by associating same-sex sexual activity and the identity label of 'homosexuality' with maltreatment of defenceless and underprivileged people. In such a way, homosexuality itself (through its now assumed association with sexual abuse) could be linked with wider forms of oppression of the poor. Same-sex sexual activity and, by association, those who employed the identity label of 'homosexual', were constructed as different forms of colonial abuse. Therefore, Winnie Mandela's actions would hopefully be seen to fall within the wider (and morally far less reprehensible) anti-apartheid struggle. Indeed, so successful were the defence in re-imagining the trial as one about the colonial imposition of same-sex sexual activity and identities on black African peoples, rather than about assault and murder, that placards outside the court supporting Winnie Mandela proclaimed 'Homosex [sic] is not in Black Culture'.

In summary then, segregation and exploitation of black African groups by white rulers due to colonial and later apartheid ideology unmistakably had an indelible effect on the country as a whole and on 'non-white' communities in particular. As is clearly known, abuse on the part of white colonialists and apartheid architects helped to disrupt and in some cases almost destroy entire cultures. The importance of the mining industry to the country and the necessity for migrant labour resulted in large numbers of black African workers becoming dislocated from their homes and placed into close quarter living arrangements. Yet evidence in this section also suggests that black African male workers were in some instances able to form sexual relationships with other mine workers during such racial discrimination. T. Dunbar Moodie (1988 and 2001) and others have offered several explanations as to why these relationships developed. They may have been due to sexual desire, economic need, or perhaps to counter loneliness and fear. The proportions that made up these reasons may never be known. What is known however, is that these relationships were acknowledged by white authorities and developed under conditions imposed by them. It is also the case that for some today within South Africa it has been perilously and simplistically easy to frame the discrete existence of 'homosexuality' (both in reference to more generalised same-sex sexual activity and as an – admittedly anachronistic – identity label) as an 'unAfrican' phenomenon, by arguing it had no place in African communities prior to European encroachment. As the above examples have highlighted, it can therefore be seen as due more to colonial rule and black African exploitation and maltreatment than due to actual 'home-grown' reasons. In part it is therefore admittedly profoundly ironic that one of the founding tropes for this argument stems from a white racist belief that black Africans needed 'protecting' due to their 'childlike' inclination. Yet it is with less irony that this argument takes from one of the most draconian periods of South African history the belief that black African queer groups today are in some way exhibiting a false consciousness derived from white violence and mistreatment. Such an argument not only attempts to foreclose any discussion of how same-sex sexual relations have been a part of black African communities in southern Africa, it also robs contemporary queer-identified groups of any 'authentic' voice with which to speak.

In reality, such negative beliefs fail to acknowledge the truly remarkable ways in which same-sex desire was understood – and in some cases, named as separate to a dominant heteronormativity and accepted – by different black African groups during apartheid. It therefore becomes vital to briefly examine what is known about such diversity before focusing on the very unique situation found in Cape Town.

The Possibility of Qualified Acceptance

To successfully counter other commentators who argue against an African tradition of same-sex desire requires an exploration of groups that were less directly affected by white action. It further becomes important to locate groups that named their sexual difference as precisely that – as existing in distinction from wider heteronormative society. While the search for 'authentic African homosexualities', as Neville Hoad (1999 and 2000) informs us, should not be relied on too heavily to counter 'traditionalists' (see below), it must also be remembered that such searches can help give real legitimacy to contemporary communities – especially when they search not for 'authenticity' but for examples of acceptance by the wider community. This is of added importance when it is remembered these queer men lived not in the pre-colonial period but a mere two or three decades ago.

For the late activist Simon Nkoli (1993 and 1995) same-sex desire in Soweto, Johannesburg was understood to exist as a discrete sexual identity, but was also viewed largely as a predicament associated with bewitchment. As he explains in the following quotation, shortly after telling his mother he was attracted sexually to men, she decided to take him to see a sangoma or traditional healer, in the hope that he might be 'cured':

> Once my mother had cooled off, she decided that I needed to be cured. And so began my year-long tour of sangomas . . . [the sangoma] put her bones down and said 'Hmmm, dangerous.' I laughed. I remember how I laughed. She said, 'Your child has been bewitched.' (Nkoli 1995: 250–251)

For some other men, especially in the townships around Johannesburg, another belief to explain their difference to the rest of society was that these men were in some way hermaphrodites. A common word by the 1980s in these townships was to describe a male individual with a public declaration of same-sex desire as an isitabane or its slang derivative stabane. As De Waal (1995) explains, this word came to mean something akin to 'queer' but the literal translation actually means hermaphrodite. A physical 'deformity' such as hermaphroditism offers some form of rationalisation (similar to being bewitched) to explain difference within a community. It therefore not only names these men as different and places them into some variant of a heterosexual/homosexual binary, it also safely locates them into a category of pre-existing explanation. And as Linda Ngcobo,[16] himself an individual who is referred to as a stabane, explained:

> In the townships they used to think I was a hermaphrodite. They think I was cursed in life to have two organs . . . For them [the wider community] there

must be some physical reason for being homosexual, you see. Then it is part of nature. It is not a man against God. (McLean and Ngcobo 1995: 168–169)

Directly linked to this idea of hermaphroditism was the role played by gender in understanding sexual identities. As Donham (1998) has argued, if an urban black African boy during the 1960s and 1970s in Soweto showed signs of effeminacy, then the only explanation was that he was in all possibility actually a woman, or at least if not 'entirely' a woman, then following Herdt (1994), some form of 'third gender'. As with coloured communities discussed in the previous chapter, it appears that wider society was constructing effeminacy in men as something that marked out these individuals as different. Even if boys or young men who were outwardly effeminate and possibly attracted to other males had male genitalia they would still be raised by their parents as 'girls'. Some of these men also engaged in cross-dressing to the extent that they would wear female clothes at home. Further, as Louw (2001) has documented in Natal (now KwaZulu-Natal) on the east coast of South Africa in the 1950s, this gender construct was further institutionalised through actual weddings between Zulu partners. Here the 'passive' partner was termed an isikhesana, and the more 'dominant' and masculine partner an iqenge, terms that are still used by some communities today (Reddy and Louw 2002).[17] Similarly, in Johannesburg, the term skesana was used to denote effeminate queer men and the term injonga used to describe masculine (and often perceived to be heterosexual) men the skesana had sex with (McLean and Ngcobo 1995). These arrangements of gender and sexuality, as with some coloured communities, made it easier for the wider community to understand and even accept these men both as different from heteronormative society yet also still a part of the community.

The common thread of community rationalisation therefore connects concepts such as witchcraft, hermaphroditism and effeminate gender identities. Each of these concepts helped the community come to terms with a group of men who were seen and identified to be different, yet in ways that could fit into pre-existing explanations about the world. These rationalisations therefore can actually go to serve two directly oppositional purposes. In one interpretation they reinforce the belief that some queer identities – as they are understood today in contemporary South Africa – that function as distinct entities separated off from, and in direct and sustained opposition, to heterosexuality (with rights enshrined in the Constitution – see chapter 6) are an alien import. All these historical rationalisations, in other words, were able to draw on other elements of black African community tradition, norms and wider experiences to explain a group of men who were different to the majority yet crucially *accepted within it*. By way of comparison, the overt visibility of queer sexuality today in some townships (see below) most certainly is not accepted and hence is perhaps easier to dismiss as 'alien'.

Yet another and perhaps more compelling interpretation would argue that witchcraft, hermaphroditism and effeminate gender identities allow contemporary men with queer identities a history that does not compartmentalise their sexuality to a specific period in history or reduce their experience to some form of foreign contamination. When a history of same-sex sexual activity among black African groups in South Africa – and the creation of delineated identities – is revealed not to have simply come about because of outside intervention, it would therefore seem to be far harder to claim, as Winnie Mandela's supporters did, that 'homosex is not in black culture'. Further, it must be borne in mind that the search for these sexualities in South Africa's past is not simply a search for 'indigenous' culture wholly removed from European 'contamination'. Rather, it is a search for examples of communities coming to terms with the idea of sexualised difference and therefore a search for examples of acceptance.

Nevertheless, it would appear that the qualified acceptance found in the above examples did not always extend to communities in places such as Cape Town. While many Xhosa men ended up working in mines elsewhere in the country, the actual black African population of Cape Town was much smaller than those in other areas during apartheid. Further, as the following sections will explore, the rationalisations used by black African communities in and around cities such as Johannesburg and Durban with terms such as stabane, skesana and injonga do not seem to have been as common for predominantly Xhosa communities further south.

Hence, when it comes to the specific case of Cape Town an additional element is necessary to understand why some continue to hold strongly negative views of contemporary queer sexuality: the ways in which groups have become known about post-apartheid. The following sections therefore examine strategies deployed to understand sexualised difference historically within the Cape Town townships and the continued struggles associated with recent queer visibilities.

Ivys and Pantsulas on the Cape

There exists very little historical information about how communities understood or related to either same-sex sexual activity or queer identities in the Cape Town townships. Unlike Johannesburg or Durban, where a limited amount of research has described the historical lives of township residents termed stabane, skesana and injonga, in Cape Town no such studies have been conducted. However, it is clear that predominantly Xhosa groups in Cape Town have developed their own queer identities and visibilities since the 1980s, that show both continuities and discontinuities with what has been found among groups elsewhere.

Xhosa groups in Cape Town have historically tended not to employ overtly gendered labels such as skesana and injonga or to use terms such as stabane to name themselves. In Cape Town, during the years leading up to the end of apartheid, they used the word 'Ivy'. This term developed in unison with the more heteronormative 'Pantsula' and both were considered by the wider community to denote music, dance and fashion styles rather than particular sexualities. While gender played a key part in the understanding of these two identities, it was not used to nearly the same degree as with communities elsewhere. Ivys were seen to 'take care in their appearance' and Pantsulas were men who dressed and behaved in more overtly masculine ways.[18] Yet unlike Pantsulas, Ivys also frequently engaged in sex with other men.[19] (The term Pantsula has since re-emerged in a more commodified and commercial form and is associated with famous South African rap musicians such as Hip Hop Pantsula).

During the 1980s, Ivys were aware that within their group men were having sex with other men. Conversely, while Pantsulas have remained a group not especially related to any form of queer sexuality, their emergence during the same period as Ivys and their mirroring of gender roles often led respondents to mention them when discussing Ivys. Crucially however, the sexual activities of Ivys were not known especially well by the wider community. Because of this, Ivys were not in a position whereby they had to 'justify' a sexualised identity to the wider community, or find a social space within it from which they could complement heterosexual society. In other words, there was no need to seek a form of qualified acceptance because the wider community did not view them as a group representing sexualised difference. Further, while the word Ivy is clearly a female name, these men did not consider themselves (and also were not considered by the community) to be 'women'. Effeminate gender identity was not understood as part of an Ivy identity. An Ivy identity was not perceived by the wider community to be a 'sexual' identity. Instead, they appeared alongside Pantsulas simply as another (admittedly less overtly masculine) group interested in modern dance styles and fashions. As these individuals, themselves Ivys during the 1980s in Cape Town, explained:

> So I will go around with them . . . although then it was not something which I would say we are gay. We called ourselves as 'Ivys'. You know? Where we will wear white pants, yellow shirts, pink – You know? We always used the white colours, very bright colours . . . An Ivy, it was someone who dresses with white jeans, tight white jeans, tight tops . . . Ivy is a lady name. The way you dress, your hairdo, your shoes, your perm, your S-Curl [hairstyle], yes. It's also part of what you do with your hair, to

be identified . . . Ja, it was a black thing. There were [also] Pantsulas, guys who'll wear jeans and tackies [training shoes] and tracksuit tops. You know? Sweaters – guys who are very straight and who dress the dress code, with tackies and jeans and lumber jacket. And the Ivys will be identified by wearing tight white jeans, you know, pink shirt or yellow shirt, or red. And your hair, you have to do your hair, you know, like, 'Afrodisia', or you'll do what is called perm your hair, you know, and shave your beard, your moustache. You must be kind of plain on your face, and so. So that's how I was introduced to those people.   WESLEY/39

So because most of those guys that were Ivys, they were gay people, but it never comes to the wider community that they are gay people, because there's no gay people, any to their minds, that exist in our townships in those days.   UNATHI/39

And as another individual explained about Ivys and Pantsulas and the way Ivys were defined rather by their association with a particular US pop star, than by a sexualised identity:

The Pantsulas were more – were an opposite of the Ivys in terms of style, because the Ivys were more feminine and the Pantsulas were more, like, township boys with Brentwoods [designer label] pants and All Star [designer label], you know . . . I think Michael Jackson was also, like, another influence which made, like, people – The way Michael Jackson dressed, or dresses, it was like a trend that was easy to follow then, you know, because it was like long perms and curly, shiny, greasy hair, which Michael Jackson looked like, so it was OK. It was acceptable in that way, because, 'Ooh, the Michael Jacksons! The Ivys! The Michael Jacksons.' So it was easy to categorise that group then.   MELISIZWE/34

By the early 1990s however, the term Ivy had started to lose its prominence within the Cape Town townships. Two important considerations are important here. First, the wider community was beginning to understand that Ivys were in fact having sex with other men:

I think, to me, the way I see it, I think the people started to be very, compare the – they said put gender on it, because it's tight, it's like something that was not supposed to be weared by man, it's supposed to be – I think, and then it lose that touch, and then people, they tried to analyse it too much . . . And also now people started to identify themselves clearly as gay people, rather than something else. And then, ja, it's really different, a lot of things. And then that was the end of it.   UNATHI/39

Second, and as the end of the above quotation suggests, there was a change in political regime. The end of apartheid and the freeing of Nelson Mandela from prison ushered in a new era of sexual identity politics in South Africa. While this has been acknowledged to have affected white queer men in the city and their subsequent political freedoms, it has been less well understood how this helped to fundamentally realign the social construction of sexuality among black African men in Cape Town.[20] In effect, the end of apartheid created a situation whereby Ivys ideologically relocated themselves far more strongly onto a variant of the heterosexual/homosexual binary and hence were able to name themselves as distinct from heteronormative society.

I think that changed mostly right after the elections in 1994, where you'll find most black people are expressing themself, who they are. I think also the speech which our president made when he got out of jail – of prison, Nelson Mandela, where he addressed the issue of sexual orientation. I think that's when most people came out. That's when most people accepted themself as who they are. WESLEY/39

The address this interviewee is referring to was Nelson Mandela's Inauguration as President of South Africa in Cape Town on 9 May 1994. This, along with the creation and ratification of the New South African Constitution in 1996, must be viewed as a defining moment in the way men in the Cape Town townships were able to characterise themselves and employ identity labels around queer sexuality. President Mandela stated on that day:

In the 1980s the African National Congress was still setting the pace, being the first major political formation in South Africa to commit itself firmly to a Bill of Rights, which we published in November 1990. These milestones give concrete expression to what South Africa can become. They speak of a constitutional, democratic, political order in which, regardless of colour, gender, religion, political opinion or sexual orientation, the law will provide for the equal protection of all citizens. They project a democracy in which the government, whomever that government may be, will be bound by a higher set of rules, embodied in a constitution, and will not be able govern the country as it pleases. Democracy is based on the majority principle. This is especially true in a country such as ours where the vast majority have been systematically denied their rights. At the same time, democracy also requires that the rights of political and other minorities be safeguarded.

After this moment, Ivys felt far more able to visibly express to the wider community that they were sexually attracted to other men – and hence they took on some form of public queer identity. Through the enshrining of the protection of individuals based on their sexual orientation into the constitution, black African men in the Cape Town townships could, for what seems to have been the first time, move into a far more visible position within society. Unlike similar men in the Johannesburg or Durban townships, Xhosa men in Cape Town had never been in a position that allowed them, or required of them, to visibly express a sexualised difference. This is in part reflected by the apparent fact that words to describe such difference were not frequently used in the Cape Town townships prior to the ending of apartheid. As several interviewees discussed, there simply were no words to describe queer sexual identities, since as far as township communities in Cape Town were concerned, there were no queers. While it would be a mistake to say that black African men in Cape Town never came across words such as 'moffie', 'homosexual', 'gay', 'stabane', 'skesana', 'injonga' or 'queer' during their lives leading up to the un-banning of the ANC and the ending of apartheid, it is important to appreciate that they never applied them to themselves in a way of which the rest of the community would have become aware. Instead, they used words such as Ivy to describe themselves, words that were linked more to a style of dress, the type of music and the type of dancing these men engaged in, rather than the sexual activities they were involved in.

It is, nevertheless, possible to hypothesise that this lack of understanding from the wider community was also driven by homophobia and stigmatisation towards those who were viewed as different. As a young Xhosa individual explained about the community's historic understanding of male hostel mining communities:

Because even in the previous days, our fathers were working in the mines. Possibly they were gays, but you had to be in the closet until you die. Nobody's supposed to know.   BILLY/24

While it remains unknown quite how Cape Town township inhabitants viewed same-sex desire during the whole apartheid period – and how it may have varied between township locations – it does appear that during the final decades of National Party rule distinct queer identities among Xhosa groups were not discussed and quite possibly assumed not to exist by the majority. All this changed in the early 1990s when men felt more able to assert a queer identity in ways previously impossible.

Creating Competing Visibilities

The ending of apartheid and the opening up of cities in South Africa to free black African migration has changed the composition of Cape Town considerably. Since the early 1990s Cape Town has seen far greater numbers of Xhosa and other language groups (as well as individuals from neighbouring countries) moving to it. At the same time, there has been a relatively large expansion in the number of men visibly expressing distinct queer identities within the townships. These forms of visibility can be separated into two main groups: Those who cross-dress, termed colloquially as those who engage in 'drag' and are identified as 'drag queens', and those who do not.

There is some evidence that the current practices of men who engage in drag date back to the dying days of apartheid when some Ivys were already starting to cross-dress, in ways similar to coloured cross-dressing queer men. While the exact date that these men started cross-dressing was not possible to ascertain, it is possible to see some influence coming directly from the city of Johannesburg and coloured communities in Cape Town.[21] As one interviewee discussed, he was dragging in the townships during the 1980s. He largely became aware of this form of sexual identity expression when he spent time in Johannesburg, trying to find out more about queer lives there:

> *Ja, then you don't know gay life, you don't have a 'degree'. So, I wanted a 'degree'. Uhm, so [X] said to me, and [Y], [Y] is a professional nurse . . . come let's go fetch your clothes, they went and the evening [in Johannesburg] I washed and washed and started putting nail polish and makeup and all that [it was the] 80s . . . [I] came back to Cape Town, wearing a dress, wearing a wig and I knocked on my grandma's door . . . and my mother screamed, she cried.*   JAMES/52

Indeed, this point, that Johannesburg was a place in which cross-dressing was fostered among black African queers, was also echoed by other interviewees, who saw the longer history and greater size of Johannesburg in relation to Cape Town as being important factors conditioning an understanding and visibility of queer desire.

> *Yea, I think because Jo'burg [Johannesburg] has been there for a long time, they have big townships and there's everybody there, so Cape Town's just grown now, Khayelitsha is just new, this place is just new. Only Langa and Nyanga and they were very small towns here, just to come and work in the kitchens, helping, so but Johannesburg has been there for a long time and people are working in mines and people are staying in, what you call those places? Hostels, so that's where it started, hostels, mines, whatever, long time ago.*   KEVIN/32

And as another interviewee explained, there is also a perception that coloured cross-dressing queer men and coloured queer men generally are more sexually liberated than queer men in the black African townships.

> *And the coloured community, they are gays at once. Nobody – They don't give a damn. You see, like, us, we have all these cultural norms that we have to abide to, even though you can say, 'Yeah, I'm living my life', but sometimes you have to abide to certain circumstances, you know? Otherwise you're going to be in shit, you know? But the gay – The coloured community, they are free. You find that from the age of five, six, there a person understands, their parents, even their lifestyle. Actually, I think to them, it's more appreciated. I think so.*   BILLY/24

This view of coloured queers as being more able to publicly and visibly express a form of queer identity has also been used to explain why black African queer men started cross-dressing in greater numbers in Cape Town. The end of apartheid saw fewer restrictions being placed on race group mixing. When this occurred, coloured conceptions of queer visibility started to find their way into the townships.

> *It became big in the townships, because it's like uhm, people used to go to clubs you know, and then they saw uhm, coloured people wearing wig and whatever, and then they come back and also wear wig like coloured people.* KEVIN/32

Influences both from Johannesburg and local coloured culture have helped condition an understanding of cross-dressing as an acceptable form of queer visibility. As would therefore be expected, similar views to those put forward by coloured cross-dressing men (see chapter 3) were expressed to explain why they now wish to engage in it:

> *Dragging is kind of fun . . . It's kind of like, finally, it's me. I love the way I am. It's my drag, it's my make-up.* MALCOM/19

And as this young man, who himself does not cross-dress, but knows of many who do explained:

> *I think it's because it's been a long time in the township that it's been, like, you can't – It's been restricted, so people – I think people are tired of hiding themselves. So whichever way they'll express themselves, is in. Yes, they can walk around with women or kiss or do whatever, but anybody can do that in the streets. But then if they dress up, if they're seen walking on their own . . . you can tell if a person is gay, especially men.* LEE/25

Yet, from the late 1980s, running parallel to a public display of cross-dressing as a form of queer visibility has been a view held by some men that sexual identity need not be tied to effeminate gender performances. While the exact reasons as to why this trope would have developed so strongly alongside (and oppositionally, see below) to cross-dressing were not possible to ascertain, it is important to note several key influences. First, as with cross-dressing within some coloured communities, it need not always be the case that such activity be condoned by all queer men there. A desire not to cross-dress can be due to a wish not to associate with femininity or to risk wider community censure. As Rankhotha (2005) has argued in relation to Zulu queer men elsewhere in the country, queer sexualities in township locations can allow for a fluidity around gender roles not possible in heteronormative society. It therefore becomes possible to see that a certain degree of self-reflexivity about their own positionality in relation to hetero-sexual society and in relation to gender roles allows Xhosa queer men the option to cross-dress or not. Indeed, as Graeme Reid's (2006) work on black African men in Mpumalanga shows, a desire to both subvert and emulate heteropatriarchy can exist in communities with rigid masculine heteronormative performances.

Second, throughout the 1980s black African queers were not only made increasingly aware of coloured queers in Cape Town, but also of the now overtly visible and openly masculine-identified white queer male commu-nity (chapter 2). While some gay bars in the city did allow the entry of coloured and black African queers during this period, not all were willing to do so, even when licensing laws permitted (Leap 2003; see also chapter 5). Of perhaps more importance for cross-community interaction were the nascent attempts from within predominantly white queer organisations during the final years of apartheid to establish links with black African queer men in the Cape Town townships.[22] Groups such as 6010 (now Triangle Project, see chapter 6) and now defunct groups such as the Organisation of Lesbian and Gay Activists (OLGA) and the Association for Bisexuals, Gays and Lesbians (ABIGALE) made important strides in accessing and supporting queer black Africans. Also, for a brief time in the 1980s a small group of black African queer men were able to form the African Gay Association (AGA) in the Cape Town townships that itself was able to form links especially with OLGA (Holmes 1995; McLean and Ngcobo 1995; Nicol 2005). These groups were also assisted by the more established Johannesburg organisation, Gay and Lesbian Organisation of the Witswatersrand (GLOW). Queer visibilities centred on variants of masculinity were therefore further strengthened within townships due to influence from particular notions of sexual identity tied to the gender binary that themselves emerged from a desire to segment off and relegate sustained effeminate behaviour (chapter 3 and chapter 5). As this individual explains, workshops by groups such as ABIGALE on self-esteem and self-efficacy appeared to be vital in assisting many black African queer men during the period:

> Well, these workshops started with ABIGALE, which it was a gay organisation, and we were assisted by a gay organisation from Johannesburg. It was GLOW. . . . And I think by networking we could really get a sense of who we are . . . issues which are really crucial for us: for instance, build up our esteem, motivate us and also do kind of development, you know, develop ourself so that we can be . . . we can face the world positively, and also, I think, motivated us also to be educated, you know, go to school and be what you want to be in the professional field. WESLEY/39

By the early 1990s there were two contrasting queer visibilities in the Cape Town townships, neither of which had been as possible during apartheid.

Influences from outside black African Xhosa communities initially helped in part to condition the development and propagation of these two groups. Yet as with coloured communities on the outlying parts of the Cape Flats, cross-dressers today are often held in low esteem by those who do not cross-dress. And as with coloured communities, this view is closely associated with issues of class. Yet unlike coloured communities, this view is also strongly related to other factors including age and the fear of homophobic violence.

The Delineation of Visibilities

When it comes to queer visibilities in the Cape Town townships, one of the most striking facts is the relative youth of those who engage in drag. Those who are older, men in their 30s, tend not to drag, viewing it instead as something akin to a 'developmental stage of queerness'. This is clearly different to coloured cross-dressing culture, where age does not seem to be a significant factor in the choice of queer expression. By contrast, for black African queer men, drag becomes far harder to justify as they get older:

> Yes, it's like, uhm, I don't know how to put it, but uhm, they are immatured. The time you realise that you know I'm a guy, I'm a guy, and then you tend to do things other ways, uhm, so it's just that there's that youthness in them, that hot blood that pushes them wherever they want, to go to do. LINDIWE/33

These youth are also perceived by some older men to give little respect to their elders. Within Xhosa culture this issue of respect is understood to be of particular importance. Xhosa groups, unlike for example Zulu groups, have a rite of initiation that occurs when men reach maturity. This process, referred to as 'going to the bush', involves surviving for a month in rural areas – 'the bush' – and also being circumcised. When an individual returns, he can be referred to within the community as an 'Indoda', a term that literally translates as 'man' (as opposed to 'boy'). Indodas within Xhosa culture are therefore men to whom respect should be granted.

> Ja, some young drag queens, they just call you with your name, and they become very loose, loose, sort of, you know. And you can judge, when you sit and have a drink with them, that there's a little respect which they lost, you know, because they took themself as, 'Ag, we are the same', and all that. Which is true, we are the same, but there's that level of who's older than who, and, you know, did you go to the bush or you did not go to the bush? WESLEY/39

Yet this issue also goes beyond mere respect. Young men who tend to drag are viewed by others as acting recklessly within the townships. This behaviour is often accentuated by dropping out of school due to homophobia present there. Instead of going to school, many of these youths spend their time drinking alcohol in shebeens (informal taverns):

> *The younger ones, they are all drag queens . . . For me uhm, it's very painful [to see them] once they drop out of school, they become 'models' of the shebeens.* JAMES/52

When a degree of youthful disrespect is combined with alcohol-fuelled expeditions to local bars, it becomes clearer to see why some men who do not cross-dress look unfavourably on those who do. Yet decisively, cross-dressing itself places these young men in a position of risk of verbal and physical attack. Cross-dressing, as discussed above, is still a very recent widespread development within the Cape Town townships. Unlike within Johannesburg townships, where a degree of qualified acceptance of effeminate gendered behaviour has been in place a lot longer, heteronormative society in Cape Town is only now having to come to terms with this new visibility. When a lack of understanding and acceptance is added to somewhat antagonistic behaviour by cross-dressers to begin with, confrontations can easily occur with heterosexual men. Sometimes men who cross-dress are attacked and killed because of these confrontations.[23] By comparison, coloured communities, because of the long legacy of moffie culture, tolerate and even accept cross-dressing men. This is not the case in the Cape Town townships:

> *I'll say, ja, it's like forcing yourself into something which that person doesn't like . . . So that's how these queens [cross-dressers] start to be dangerous for them [heterosexual men], actually, because straight people start to throw glasses in their face, throw them with a beer, that, 'Hey, you, fuck, why you looking at me?' You know? 'I'm not a moffie', or, 'I'm not gay.' You know? . . . I will see they go flat out with their drinking and start touching people's private parts, kissing unexpected, hugging, you know, touching. I think that's what makes straight people not to like queens.* WESLEY/39

> *Sometimes, you see, if the drag queen, and then he get a boyfriend, and then, if he go there, to the shebeen, then the other people who's going to come, people, like, think it's a lady, but it's not a lady, you see? That's why other people killed a drag queens. Yes. They think it's a lady.* BULELANI/32

This is then seen as reflecting badly on other men who openly proclaim a queer identity yet do not cross-dress.

Hey, those people that . . . dress like queens, I really don't understand about them. I don't like them at all, because why, I don't think they are – They cause the trouble, because why, some of the guys or the women outside, say, 'Look at that stupid, that moffies! They dress like – they dress like us.' And, OK fine, they talk to them. So when someone meet me, say, around, or maybe in the taxi rank or around outside, maybe they just give me only one dirty look, because of other people that they dress like queens. So which means that they spoil this line of affairs.   SIZWE/32

This is of added importance in the Cape Town townships, since unlike in coloured communities, black African queer men who do not cross-dress also sometimes seek out sexual relationships with heterosexually-identified men. As chapter 3 noted, it is overwhelmingly the case that cross-dressing coloured moffies are the group which wish to have sexual relationships with heterosexually-identified men, in part to supplement their effeminate gender identity. By contrast other coloured queer men and those who frequent a space such as the city's gay village do not have to associate having sex with a heterosexually-identified male as such an important part of their own identity. In the Cape Town townships, both black African men who cross-dress and some of those who do not were noted as having sexual relationships with heterosexually-identified 'straight' men. While, as the third quote below illustrates, this is not uniform across all groups, it should be realised that if cross-dressing black African men are viewed negatively by heterosexually-identified men, there can also be a fear among queer men who do not cross-dress that such views will carry across to them. (By contrast, it was very rare to find queer men who do not cross-dress wanting to have sexual relationships with cross-dressers.) Indeed, as this particular interviewee explained, it is not always the case that non-cross-dressing queer men 'date' or have sexual relationships with other non-cross-dressing homosexually-identified men.

[In answer to 'who do men who aren't drag queens but are homosexually-identified "date"'] Like, what can I say? In the townships, where I am, like, gay men date straight men. I haven't seen a gay man dating another gay man, you see?   BILLY/24

And as this queer man who does not cross-dress explained:

I had an affair with a straight guy, but who had a girlfriend. So it was that on and off. You know? You have to understand that that person is straight, as he say, he's got a girlfriend, but, ja, he does give you his time, his chance, you know, when you want to be with him.   WESLEY/39

Yet, in other examples, queer men who do not cross-dress also said they would not have sex with straight men because they feared it would mean being 'used' as cross-dressers are perceived to be (here, similarities can again be seen with some more affluent coloured rationalisations in chapter 3). As this interviewee explained, when discussing why some queer men have sex with 'straight' men, and why he would not want to:

> *Because it means that we [queer men generally] are tools to be used for someone's sexual satisfaction, and then to be left just like that. That's the message that it gives them ['straight' men], and that's why it keeps on happening . . . That's the impression it gives them, and that's why it keeps on happening, and they kind of – Ja, it basically means that we are incapable of relationships. That's what it boils down to, and that's what it encourages, and it's so fucking degrading. I don't have a – There is another term for it, but it's – it is degrading, totally degrading, for them [queer men] to sleep with those ['straight' men].* PHILANI/25

The combination of age and the fear of homophobic violence against cross-dressers helps to keep groups of queer men distanced from each other. For many queer men who do not cross-dress, cross-dressing is not only perceived as a form of youthful indulgence, it is also something that brings with it the real fear of physical violence. Yet this divide between those who drag and those who do not is also mediated by one important factor, also prevalent among coloured communities: that of class. Indeed, a commonly noted feature that helps demarcate different groups of queer men in the townships is that of employment. The legacy of apartheid continues to affect the employment opportunities of black African groups, despite programmes of affirmative action initiated by the ANC. In Cape Town, nearly fifty percent of black African individuals of working age are unemployed, compared to five percent of whites.[24]

While class can be viewed as important social construct in any group's construction of itself, it tends to be very clearly marked among township inhabitants. For queer men in the townships, the divide is not between varying levels of wealth and/or prestige, but between having absolutely no money or resources and having some. For queer men, this class divide is also strongly influenced by age. As mentioned above, a group of younger queer men who have dropped out of school and who cross-dress is now emerging. This group, who also tend to be unemployed, are becoming increasingly distanced from more established and relatively more wealthy men.

> *The reason why . . . when someone would say 'I'm working at this position, I'm earning so much money, so [X is] not working, so I can't go out with [X], then I had to go out with [Y], because [Y] is working and he's got a profession, a profession just like mine', and whatever. That's what is happening, that's why there's so many groups in the township, that's why you'll find so many groups uhm, what can I say uhm, isolated. I don't know whether it's right, you know, isolated groups in*

townships, just because of like the young people, they go along together, you know, they go out together, and then, people like us you know, who are not working, they go along together . . . There's that classiness of uhm, who you are, and what you're doing, and that's it. KEVIN/32

Sometimes, even though, like, some of those who work are a bit older, nè, and those who don't work, some are at school like, the age group difference, I think it's more than the class. I think there's – that's the age group difference. BILLY/24

These class distinctions are also mediated by perceived differences associated with how long individuals have spent in Cape Town. As mentioned above, there has long been a distinction between those who view themselves as more urbanised and those who are perceived to have recently arrived from more rural areas (often assumed to mean from the Eastern Cape – and possibly apartheid-designated former 'homelands'). Today, among queer groups, this distinction continues, affecting how groups are able to socialise with each other.

But lot of gay people, they like, we can't go to [X's] place because [X] is a tribal, a tribal is someone who comes from the Eastern Cape, someone who's got . . . that Xhosa thing, who has all the cultures from them, ja. LINDIWE/33

Men who have spent longer in Cape Town view men from the rural Eastern Cape as now being freer to express their sexual identity. For queer men from the Eastern Cape, arriving in Cape Town signals an independence to visibly display their sexual identity in ways they would not be able to in more rural locations. Importantly, men from the more rural Eastern Cape are understood by men who have lived longer in the city as more likely to engage in drag. In turn, some men who have spent longer in Cape Town continue to see cross-dressing as something they themselves have already experienced and, hence, no longer need to engage in. Similarities can therefore be made with the belief among some that younger cross-dressing men are progressing through a 'stage' of identity formation. As these individuals, both of whom have lived in Cape Town for over a decade, explained:

Because, like, a lot of gay people now, there's a lot of, a huge influx of gay people from the Eastern Cape, and the 'Capetonians' will sort of outclass those ones, because, like, the Eastern Cape is mainly known to be backwards . . . In terms of – not more, less cosmopolitan than Cape Town, and – Yes, they do drag more, because, like, all of them, they're very comfortable dragging . . . It's because they just feel – It's the bigger city. Maybe they feel they are out there, they're free. You know, it's like . . . it's, like, the big city: 'I feel free, I can be gay, I'm away from the family, and nobody's going to talk about me.' And yet in the smaller towns, people do – Dragging, it could be, like, a huge drama . . . Ja. You know. And – But that's not how I think [now], because, I mean, I think men and men is fine. You know, it's – it doesn't have to be – I don't have to be like a woman . . . I think it's just growing up. MELISIZWE/34

It's a 'scapegoat' to come to the city, because the city, not necessarily for gay issues only, just like people following traditions and all that stuff. It's not too much [in] the city. At least you can get away with anything. So it's difficult, I mean, [in] the rural areas. So it was nice for people to come in here, thinking that, 'OK, I'm out of home, I'm here . . .' UNATHI/39

There are several explanations as to why cross-dressers and men who do not cross-dress remain socially separate from each other. The creation and subsequent delineation of these two queer visibilities remain, however, largely the result both of the way apartheid was able to regulate Xhosa groups and the way apartheid itself ended. For example, the development of queer men openly and visibly expressing any form of queer identity occurred suddenly, and only once Nelson Mandela had been freed and the new constitution was in development. Prior to this time, Xhosa men in Cape Town were in general unable or unwilling to openly proclaim an identity in opposition to the rest of the community. The rapid development of queer visibilities within the Cape Town townships have further been the result of interactions with groups who were previously kept largely spatially separate from each other due to the naming and regulation of 'race-based' difference during apartheid. Influences from queer coloured and white communities post-apartheid have had clear effects on black African men in Cape Town. (And as chapters 5 and 6 will explain, black African visibilities and invisibilities also influence other groups.) Further, the expansion of queer visibility within Cape Town townships coincides with the influx of Xhosa individuals from the Eastern Cape, where apartheid planners had tried to forcibly locate them. Post-apartheid, the distinctions between cross-dressers and non-cross-dressers have been augmented by several factors. Age and class, in different yet intertwined ways, have helped keep a group of older, more established men who have tended to live for a longer period in the city separate from younger men who may have immigrated to the city more recently and are also more likely to drag. Yet this distinction is also strongly mediated by the perceived fear of homophobic violence. To understand this particular dynamic more fully, it is essential to explore in more detail some of the reasons why homophobia has remained so forceful within the Cape Town townships.

Homophobia and the Creation of Social Nodes

While there is evidence that points towards homophobic violence in all three of the racially-defined communities under study, it is among black

African township men that this violence is most forceful. Cases of gang rape against black African queer men, along with premeditated beatings and frequent verbal attacks were often documented during the research period.[25] Sporadic and seemingly unprovoked incidents were also noted, including spitting and throwing of objects such as house bricks at queer men walking along streets:[26]

> *I mean, it's very high, in a way that if you go out there, in some areas, where people don't have an understanding of gay people, it's either if you talk about the issue, you can get kicked out or you can be beaten up . . . It's very risky to go out and being unknown and go to the totally environment that you don't know at all.* MARTIN/32
>
> *They just beat them and some – kill them by – by guns.* BEN/32

As mentioned above, in some black African communities there existed, prior to the end of apartheid, the possibility of qualified acceptance developing. Such acceptance allowed men who were represented as different the opportunity to find a niche within the wider community without fear of societal retribution. Within Cape Town, this opportunity does not appear to have been as readily apparent. Rather than express the existence of queer identities to the wider community, large numbers of men in Cape Town instead used terms such as Ivy that kept the reality of queer desire relatively hidden from outsiders. The end of apartheid and subsequent state acknowledgement both of the existence of and need to protect queer groups changed this dynamic. For the first time queer men in Cape Town have been able to openly proclaim a sexualised difference to the rest of the community. Yet this sudden shift has not given Xhosa communities themselves much time to come to terms with the now very visible idea of queer desire. As already discussed, this has led some non cross-dressers to choose not to associate with those who drag – a group whose very perceived flamboyance leaves them open to hostile heteronormative regulation.

Homophobic violence therefore occurs when visible queer men come into conflict with Xhosa and wider black African value systems. Here, rather than have time to adapt to new forms of queer visibility, community norms have been confronted and challenged from within over a relatively short period. As previously discussed, the very visibility of cross-dressers within townships therefore serves to increase the chance of negative reaction from some within the heterosexual community. Rather than make queer men 'safe', as noted within coloured communities in the city, cross-dressing only goes to highlight the very newness of this group. The homophobia associated with cross-dressing is also furthered by elements of what respondents refer to as local Xhosa tradition (and wider black African culture in South Africa) which place great emphasis on overt masculinity as a defining characteristic of manhood and boyhood – with effeminacy remaining solely associated with women. In such a climate, the onus is placed firmly on cross-dressing or effeminate gendered queer men to remain invisible – a situation that it appears is lessened within some other communities where qualified acceptance has been in place for longer. If Xhosa men do not remain invisible, then they face the full brunt of homophobia from the community. As this individual who used to cross-dress but no longer does explained:

Ja, homophobia was very quite bad. Even if they would see there's a child who's gay, you know, they will be – the boy will be beaten up, you know, because he has to hide it. And people will talk and say, 'Hey, you moffie!' You know? 'It's not a good thing, and we don't appreciate gays.' And so. So it was hard. It was not easy for me to explore my sexuality, especially under the Xhosa culture . . . Xhosa culture, you have to behave like a man. Whatever you do, you've got to be very manhood and you've got to fulfil your Xhosa tradition, where, when boys and men are together, you have to do customary things, where boys must go fetch wood, must be able to work in the garden, must be able to assist other boys. Or even your sport has to be a boyish sport. You cannot play a girls' sport. So that was a kind of hiding for me. So I couldn't express myself at all. But going around, going around with other friends which are – were gay, then it was a very good thing for me. WESLEY/39

And as these two individuals, neither of whom cross-dress, explain, there remain strong motivations for remaining within 'acceptable' community norms:

The thing is that as Africans, or as Xhosas or whoever, is that a man was to marry another girl, have children, and their children reproduce and multiply. And then if that's not happening, then they've got a problem with it. If it's men sleeping with men, they've got bigger – resistance. And then – So that is why – It's like, if the family is not growing because of this one guy that does not want to sleep with a girl, then it is a big problem. Then, if you're not changing from that, then you're going to get cut off. So that is why a lot of gay guys live on their own. LEE/25

When you go through that door and go out, there's someone is going to look at you, and he or she is going to say something funny, but you are not going to hear that thing. Once they knew that you are gay. THABO/23

While violence and emotional stress are serious concerns for queer men, these problems are also compounded by a belief held by some that these men are soft targets for crime. In large part this belief stems from an assumption that queer men are less likely to fight back if robbed. There is a belief that queer men will be more likely to behave 'like women' when attacked than like a heterosexually-identified man. In other words, the high visibility of cross-dressers to the wider community acts as a gender-defined social marker that becomes transplanted to all queer men. As this individual, who does not cross-dress, explained:

> *But then, if people are watching you and know that you're not going to do anything, because they tend to think, like, 'These guys are women, so they won't be able to fight back, so we'll just mess up their stuff.' And then – So if they break into your house, you're not going to do anything but go to the police station, and there they're going to find out – or they're going to see that you're gay, and they'll not take any steps further than when you went to the police station. So it feels like they're targeting . . . because the straight guys in these areas are very much powerful and dangerous, so if you mess with them, then it means . . . you're going to get killed.* LEE/25

Violence against queer men is also more likely to occur because perpetrators are aware that local police are unlikely to take the claims of queer men seriously. As with elements of the wider community, it appears that police within townships are not immune to homophobic judgements about queer men. As this interviewee explained, specifically about violence against cross-dressing men:

> *Mm. For example, let's say, maybe – You see, gays are assaulted everywhere they go, almost everywhere, ninety percent chances wherever they go out. If you go to a police station to report a case, they laugh at you. Even the police can say, 'I'm not supposed to represent you.' You see? And people judge you. Just let's say – Mm – You're just being misjudged wherever you are. And unfortunate are those who don't have family support, because at least it's better when somebody at home understands you, but most of the time, even our families don't understand. You find that you are just on your own, depressed, everything.* BILLY/24

When queer men no longer feel part of the broader community, when they are easily attacked due to their sexuality or because they are seen as soft targets for crime and when police refuse to intervene, it becomes easy to see how great importance is placed on wider social groupings of queer men – groupings that provide not only solidarity but also safety. Within townships, social nodes of queer men are hugely important for different groups. Social nodal groupings act both as a form of protection against general crime and violence directed specifically at queer men, and as important cohesive structures to help affirm the identities of these men after they have been rejected by the rest of the community.

Several groupings were noted within different townships, and each was found to be conditioned by a different type of queer visibility. Each grouping was headed by a social nodal leader who was well respected within the local area and had their own shack or house for other queer men to meet in. As this interviewee who socialised with the social nodal leader in Nyanga, but is also aware of key individuals in Khayelitsha and Lower Crossroads, describes:

> *[Z] is a, how can I explain him? Everybody feels, I mean that, I like him so much . . . He's very sweet, he doesn't look at you straight and say look at yourself, I mean he welcomes you the way you are, that's what I like about him . . . He's always keeping his shack nicely, you know, whoever comes is welcome, I like him. . . . So like in Crossroads it would be [X] and in Khayelitsha it would be [Y], and in Nyanga it might be [Z].* LINDIWE/33

And as this interviewee explained:

> *It has something to do with the resources, because if you have a house, definitely you are going to be the leader of this whole thing. Because the people, they don't have space anywhere, so you have, that they use your space, and so you – It's only one person who coordinates these things.* UNATHI/39

A degree of wider community acceptance and respect was clearly important for these groupings to exist. Because each social nodal leader was respected in the wider community, men who visited the homes of these individuals were far less likely to be mistreated by neighbours. Hence, these locations provide a vital degree of social safety, in otherwise dangerous environments:

> *I think in essence it's due to the fact that, you know, there's – for instance in this community, there's this one gay guy who is, like, out there. Everybody knows that he's gay and he's open and, you know, he does everything that he wants to do, basically. And people know about it and nobody bothers him. And so that, in its own, serves as an inspiration to others who are closeted or, you know, like, who are young and, you know, that, who are already gay, and that they have somebody that they look up to.* NKOSANA/27

One of the social nodal groupings in Khayelitsha, which was also the largest, was understood mainly to be comprised of younger queer men who crossdressed. A second node in a different area of Khayelitsha was noted as being associated more with employed professional men. A grouping in Lower Crossroads was centred around men who had recently immigrated from the Eastern Cape and no longer cross-dressed, or had never crossdressed. The last node, located in Nyanga, was encompassed more mature queer men some of whom had once cross-dressed but now chose not to.[27] This last node had been in existence for considerably longer than the others. As such, it had existed under different leaders since at least the late 1980s when it was more associated with cross-dressing. As these friends of the original leader explained:

Then after that in Cape Town I met this guy, ah, his name was [X]. He was like, uhm, they used to, he was a, they used to call him 'Boss', a queen, a queen of the gays, a gay queen you know . . . because he was the first gay guy in the township in Nyanga, yeah, I mean he was the first guy to come out being gay in Nyanga. KEVIN/32

He used to wear dresses, even – We went to another gay friend of ours who passed away, I think, a year before [X] passed away. But [X] was wearing an African dress and tying a big hood, like the traditional Xhosa woman would wear, and that's who [X] was. XOLO/40

Men who belong to a grouping also tend to live close to the social nodal leader, or travel to visit the leader's dwelling on a regular basis. As noted by the following interviewees, these leaders are viewed very highly by the men who socialise with them. For many queer men, these leaders provide both a degree of moral support and refuge. As these two interviewees explain, both discussing the leader in Lower Crossroads:

So now, when I stay here next to him, so I just know, I mean, he just tell me every-thing, how to handle a relationship, how to go to the nightclubs, how to meet some other gay people, how to handle an affair. Something like that. SIZWE/32

Like, they are my friends, just friends, like gay friends, you see? What I do, like – A friend is a friend, no matter it's bad – in bad times and good times, not only when it's nice and maybe you've got money and – Someone who's going to help you, like next to you, someone who can share something, like if you've got a problem with your family, who can help you, advise you and something like that. That's what me and [X] that's what we are doing. You see? That's why I said he's my only friend. BULELANI/32

There are undoubtedly some similarities between the configuration of social nodal groupings in former black African townships and the way some cross-dressing queer men socialise in some of the outlying Cape Flats coloured communities. Groupings help to protect individuals and affirm their identities. However, unlike coloured communities, queer men in the former townships require nodal structures first and foremost because of their newfound visibility. In comparison to some coloured communities, social nodes in townships are needed for physical protection and to offset social ostracisation caused by a wider community still trying to come to terms with open displays of queer sexuality. Further, as noted in chapter 3, those coloured men who do not cross-dress are generally from more economically advantaged areas and do not see the need to group together in their daily lives. In black African townships, economic circumstances and community opinion would appear not to vary to the same degree. It is subsequently far harder for queer men to live without the support and solidarity offered by these groupings. In a community with high levels of homophobia, it is fair to argue that men who openly proclaim a queer identity need all the social support they can get.

And so it is this general need for protection from violence, tied to a powerful need for social support from other queer men, that mark out the Xhosa queer visibilities studied here as distinct to either white or coloured variations studied elsewhere this book. The very visibility of Xhosa queer men is mediated by homophobic violence that helps keep queer groups located around specific points – social nodal homes – in different townships. Queer identities are therefore spatially regulated not only by a variation in the way space is appropriated more generally – either at the broader urban level (as with some white queer men) or at the bodily level (as with some coloured cross-dressing men) – but by the way both these variations among black African queer men are affected by violence and rejection. Social nodes allow men with similar histories to socialise safely with each other. Queer visibility in townships remains focused in specific locations, spaces where queer sexuality is relatively protected. Different townships are therefore marked by different types of visibility. While issues such as class and age (tied to additional factors such as rural to urban migration and desired sexual partners) continue to delimit different groupings of queer men, it is homophobia that ultimately reinforces these divides and spatially separates groups from each other.

Conclusion

This chapter began by exploring how the history of colonial regulation and apartheid spatial control in South Africa has gone to perpetuate a belief that 'homosexuality is unAfrican'. Within this discourse, same-sex sexual activity more broadly and same-sex identities are both represented as colonial impositions – both as an exploitation of black African groups and as an imposition on 'traditional' black African values. Some scholarly work has also pointed out that the mechanisms put in place by colonial control and apartheid regulation may themselves have created environments that allowed the development of certain codes and rituals associated and male same-sex desire. The power of the 'unAfrican' argument remains its ability to align itself with broader grievances surrounding European colonisation in the country.

Such an argument, however, fails to acknowledge the way in which queer men were able to exist among different communities during apartheid – in communities that were less directly regulated than mining compounds or same-sex hostels. Recorded examples from cities such as Johannesburg and Durban point to the ability of men to function successfully within their own communities. It may therefore be more equitable to argue that homophobia, rather than homosexuality, is what is truly 'unAfrican'.

But equally, as Neville Hoad (1999) has argued, there remains a problem in trying to 'search' for 'authentic' queer identities away from those which have been influenced by Western forms of queer culture and politics. The search for the 'authentic' can end up playing directly into the hands of homophobes who are able to argue that any contemporary queer identities in South Africa must in some way be influenced by, for example, Western impacts. The search for the authentic and the 'indigenous' can help put into relief their difference to identities that exist in Cape Town today – to the detriment of all those who have become visible post-apartheid. A far more interesting approach is therefore not simply to argue that there were queer identities prior to colonial rule but rather to explore what methods were actually used by the wider community to accept those who positioned themselves as different. Rather than simply attempt to argue against the unAfrican argument, this chapter has consequently also tried to show that visible queer men were able to exist within some communities because those communities were able to conceptualise those men in ways that were not threatening. Anecdotal evidence exists that shows that in communities away from the mines a form of qualified acceptance was possible. If the 'unAfrican' argument is to be confronted, it will not be done by looking for 'authentic identities' in opposition to 'Western/European' identities. Neither will it be achieved by simply ignoring the specificity of local communities through an (at times) unfounded concern over 'romanticising' difference. Instead it will be done by showing that communities in the past have understood same-sex desire and queer identities and that there is nothing to stop them doing so again so as to link current queer visibilities with a rich history.

Within Cape Town, however, the development and acknowledgement of visible queer identities post-apartheid has resulted in strong and sustained homophobia from certain sectors of the wider community. The creation of a delineated sexual identity around a variant of the heterosexual/homosexual binary has forced the wider community to examine this group of men in a way it previously did not have to. Unlike the anecdotal evidence presented for cities such as Johannesburg, it appears this group was not discussed or rationalised in Cape Town to the degree found elsewhere. This therefore also suggests that a certain rigid and oppositional rendering of the heterosexual/homosexual binary located around the naming of particular forms of sexualised difference quite probably was not in place or not as strongly enforced among Cape Town Xhosa groups during the colonial or early apartheid period (see also chapter 1).

Post-apartheid the simultaneous development of competing visibilities – as some men have chosen to cross-dress on a regular basis while others have not – has therefore been spatially regulated by the real threat of severe homophobic violence. In other words, a particular formation of heteronormative regulation post-apartheid, backed up by sustained homophobia, has not only been augmented by the suddenness of queer visibility – it has also strongly affected how such queer visibilities can develop. The sudden overt visibilities of queer men post-apartheid are therefore marked by specific groupings of men within demarcated locations in different townships. The problem of applying 'the closet' emerges when it is realised that for a long time the configuration of sexuality in some of the Cape Town townships did not require a 'coming out' of 'the closet' since a binary and subsequent anxiety either on the part of the men in question or the wider community does not appear to have been firmly in place. It is further called into question when the diversity of queer experiences post-apartheid and the divergent visibilities of social nodes are examined. A search for 'authenticity' and 'congruence' between a sexual identity and sexual activity become muted concerns when viewed in the historical light of Cape Town township experiences. As Part II of this book will show, some of the contemporary needs of queer men in the former townships are also in many ways distinctly different from those which have emerged from more Westerncentric liberationist (and commodified) concerns which spring more directly from issues located around a teleological progression from 'the closet'. For some these needs have been partially sidelined and made invisible, while for others, the recent emergence of black African queer visibilities is starting to affect the way others wish to view identities, social justice and meaning of sexual politics.

Part II

Interactions

Chapter Five

Social Invisibilities

Introduction

Part I of this book devoted itself to exploring the lives of queer men in three communities during and after apartheid. Each chapter explored the historical and contemporary details of these men's lives to understand the sometimes remarkably different paths they have taken to become visible in heteronormative space. The visibility associated with the space of the gay village, perhaps the most overt to the wider world, was shown to be due to several reasons, including a form of political apathy that today helps keep different groups of white queer men separate from each other. Yet a sector of this community, more than any other, represents for many in South Africa and elsewhere an archetype of newfound freedom synthesised with what some see as a 'globalised' version of queer life. For queer activists and commentators around the world, Cape Town is the poster child of successful liberation from oppression. Subsequent chapters therefore attempted to counterbalance the emphasis that has been placed on these identities and sexualised spaces by delving into the sometimes contrasting lives of queer coloured and black African men. A particular group of coloured cross-dressing queer men in Cape Town were shown to have taken a different path towards openness and visibility. And as such, these men have been successful in ways that do not delimit their visibility in the urban environment to specific spaces. For coloured moffies, the community itself has been appropriated. Many black African queer men, by comparison, have created for themselves visibilities strongly marked by the fear of homophobic violence – itself in no small part a result of apartheid regulation. Yet further, both coloured and black African men have two competing queer visibilities (cross-dressing or not cross-dressing), which are powerfully configured around issues such as class, age and migration. These factors are also strongly regulated by the way apartheid was able to categorise and spatially contain different groups.

Yet as chapter 1 discussed, visibility is not simply dictated by a queer group's relationship to heteronormativity. The different queer groups represented here also interact with each other and so, inevitably, create new configurations of visibility and invisibility, anxiety or complacency. As argued earlier, it is these interactions that can help mark out another dimension of what can be termed queer visibilities.

The end of apartheid has made such interactions far easier. As such, Cape Town could almost be seen to represent a ludicrously skewed social experiment. What would happen, someone might ask, if you had three competing forms of queer visibility living and evolving alongside each other, but separately, and then one day you took away the barriers?

This simile, while terse, does nonetheless get across the point that for the majority of its history, one city has had three different communities living in varying degrees of isolation from each other. To take this point further, not only were they relatively isolated from each other, they also had foisted onto them half-truths to help justify the need to keep them separate in the first place. What would happen, one may ask, when an entire superstructure of misinformation, fear, exclusion, mistreatment and ignorance begins to crumble?

But this is not just a hypothetical query. The outcomes of these interactions have real and in some cases devastating effects on queer men. Post-apartheid, now that the walls have come down, some communities are able to prosper, while others remain at times sidelined. As this and the following chapter will show, the interactions between groups of queer men in Cape Town from different racially defined communities take with them a history of discrimination, suspicion and, in some cases, ignorance. As other geographers whose work has been characterised by concerns over social justice have described, appreciating how benefits and burdens are distributed unevenly across different marginalised communities remains a central issue when exploring disenfranchised communities (Harvey 1973 and 1992). As the remainder of this book will explore, Cape Town's history perfectly encapsulates this problem from the perspective of contemporary queer men.

Socially, this chapter will show that the most prominent form of queer visibility in the city today, that associated with a group of men in the De Waterkant gay village (chapter 2), can itself make some coloured and black African queers partially invisible. The following chapter will explore how, politically, distinct barriers remain for broader participation in organisations and political events. These invisibilities are due both to the interactions of these queer visibilities and also to the histories of these communities that led to different queer visibilities developing in the first instance. Yet also, in the following discussions (and particularly in chapter 6), the heightened visibility of different groups also means there exists the possibility of self-reflection, questioning and 'queering' about the dominance of the needs of any one community and any one visibility.

Breaking Down the Fortifications

It would be easy, and dangerously crude, to begin or to confine a chapter on social race group mixing in South Africa solely to a discussion of how white South Africans continue to employ old racist constructions about other groups. Such an approach would end up being nothing more than an easy and sloppy shorthand for a far more complex array of issues that continue to affect how groups view each other. As will be shown, these issues encompass economic and class considerations, assumptions about gender identities and a degree of unawareness about different communities.

It should also be recognised that rapid change continues to take place in and around the gay village in Cape Town. Over my four years of research in the city, opinions and misconceptions about different communities continued to change, develop and diminish (and then sometimes grow again) in quick fashion. The findings reported here therefore, as with all research, need to be seen to represent one specific instance in the development of social interactions between different communities in the city. They are not meant to suggest that communities will never be able to come together. Neither, clearly, are they meant to suggest that such findings relate to all groups from any one artificially created 'race group'. They are however meant to highlight that a history of mistrust and inequity should not simply be assumed to have vanished. The history of these different communities in relation to each other due to apartheid cannot simply be discarded. And neither, for the communities themselves, are the instances described here likely to be quickly forgotten.

Further, it should be remembered that the power to discriminate or exclude different racially defined groups is not solely confined to any one queer community. Indeed, as chapter 3 has already explored, historically, some coloured communities have held strongly negative views about black African communities. As Western's (2001) highly praised work has noted, it remains possible for some individuals who represent themselves as coloured to remain tied to an apartheid-inspired race-based 'ranking' system, whereby black African communities remain perceived as socially 'inferior' to coloured communities. A form of what Cathy Cohen (1999) might term secondary marginalisation can exist, whereby coloured individuals can perpetuate the socially ranked spectrum that was put in place during apartheid.

Although infrequently voiced to community outsiders, race-based assumptions by some within the coloured racial grouping can help position the coloured community into what they see as a more favourable social position vis-à-vis their black African neighbours. While the following quotation should not be seen to indicate such feelings are uniformly accepted, they were nonetheless discussed by several respondents over the research period:

> *The coloureds seem to think that they are a class above them [black African groups].*
> *They think they are a little bit whiter then them, so to say . . . They might not have*
> *the bone structure, or the hair . . . It's the way we grow up in our home environments*
> *and it all impacts on your thinking later. They just all seem to have that thinking.*
> *Most of them. [You] don't see a lot of coloured drag queens or gays go out and mix*
> *with blacks. They don't openly speak about it, but they think they are stupid. And*
> *that they have no brains.*   BRADLEY/35

For some coloured queer men, there is also the belief that homophobia in the black African townships is so great it would be foolhardy to attempt to socialise there:

> *And you've got that in the [black] African culture is that when your parents find*
> *out that you're gay, they will immediately kill you. It's because of their religion*
> *thingy that they believe in when man mustn't be [with another man. If you do]*
> *they will kill you. It's the – ja. And it's actually very scary, because I mean this is*
> *a free country, and everybody should be free in this country, ja.*   STEVE/25

> *They [coloured queer men] are scared . . . They don't understand. They are ignorant*
> *[of black African townships] and they are scared.*   ROBIN/36

Reciprocally, it was noted that some black African queer men see coloured culture more generally as being based on an inherent insecurity about their position within the nation. This is then believed to give rise to feelings of isolation among some coloured groups. From a black African queer perspective, this helps maintain several assumptions as to why there continues to be relatively little mixing between the two communities:

> *Because they [coloureds] were confused before. They were taught Afrikaans so*
> *much . . . They told themselves that they belonged to the white side. But what hap-*
> *pened after the [free] elections, they realised that, 'We're not white, we're not black.*
> *The whites are pushing us away and the blacks are pushing us away.' You know?*
> *So – I mean, there is that sadness.*   LINDIWE/33

> *Because they also have lost their culture. You know? Coloured people always have*
> *put themself always as white. So they're also, kind of, scared of getting involved with*
> *us, and things like that. So it doesn't become easy. You know? It doesn't become easy*

because of the acceptance and the stigma. . . . I think the apartheid has played quite a very big role of dividing people in South Africa. That's why coloured people were second-class citizens, next to whites, and black people were third, right at the back. . . . Coloured people always talk, 'Ooh, I cannot go to Nyanga. I cannot go to Guguletu.' But we [all] can go everywhere . . . When it comes to a racial – racial conflict or discrimination, I feel that coloured people still feel that black people are black people and they must be separated from them. They still think they are second-time-around citizens in this country, which is not [correct]. WESLEY/39

Apartheid ideological beliefs continue to have an effect on the opinions that some within coloured and black African communities have of each other (Western 2001). The perception that coloured communities 'lack history' is a powerful trope and has already been discussed, from a coloured perspective, in chapter 3. Equally, the use of 'race' as a marker of alleged other social characteristics, while clearly misguided, has a very long history in the country (chapter 1). While these views may once have originated among white colonists, it now seems they have found their way successfully into other communities. It must however be remembered that these views should not be taken to represent those of all members of these communities (just as it should be remembered the queer visibilities discussed in this book do not represent all members of any group). Nevertheless, neither should they simply be discounted. They were, after all, felt strongly enough to be voiced by several interviewees. At the same time, however, it should also be noted that exclusion by white groups towards coloured and black African groups is also a reality. While by no means evident among all white queer South Africans, exclusion of coloureds and black African queer men does exist. A history based on systematic discrimination, that created ideologies and beliefs focused solely on vilifying difference and celebrating subservience, cannot be immediately undone or forgotten. The forcefulness with which discrimination occurs will naturally vary between different individuals and between different groups. So too are their stark variations in the rationalistions used to explain the mechanisms and results of exclusion by some white queer men.

The issue of exclusion on the part of some white queers towards coloured and black African queers is of added importance in this context because of the limited spaces in which different racially defined groups can interact. As the other work and quotations above help illustrate, there exists relatively little mixing between coloured and black African queers in their respective communities. Because of this, one of the few spaces in which all three groups come together is the De Waterkant gay village, a space located in a part of the city that is still demographically overwhelmingly white South African.[1] Indeed, it should also be borne in mind that many coloured and black African queer men feel that white queers rarely visit their communities. As these black African queer men explained specifically about the fears white queer men have of visiting black African townships:

> *[They do not come] Because it's – one, they don't feel safe, and understandably. And two, there's not much relations with black gays and white gays.*   LEE/25

> *It's fear, ja. It's a fear, ja. It is, ja. It's fear, because that's not how we were brought up. They were brought up to be told that black people are very dangerous, you see, and all that stuff, ja.*   XOLO/40

> *There's still that not trusting each other well, especially when it comes through the white side. It's so easy for whites to come to the township and sit and wine and dine. They will rather say to you, 'Come to town.'... Even to socialise with people in the township it's easy, but whites who are born and bred in South Africa, it's not easy for them... They fear death.*   WESLEY/39

> *[It's] remnants of the past, unfortunately, are still with us. OK? So the townships have been known to be this just awful place where crime is just at its, you know, at its highest and, you know, bad things happen to white people when you go there. You know, those are some of the, you know, the word that gets around, that, you know, like, so I'm thinking that that plays a big part in that, in white people being afraid to go into the townships.*   NKOSANA/27

Conversely, both from some coloured and black African respondents, there exists a favourable view of a lifestyle associated with a group of white queer men represented spatially in the gay village. As chapter 3 has already explored in the context of coloured men, there is a perception among a particular group that queer lifestyles associated with white men are freer and less inhibited than their own. A similar view was held by some black African queer men, although unlike coloured queers, this group tended not to view white queer culture as more alluring simply because men were not 'forced' to cross-dress. As chapter 4 laid out, cross-dressing is not as prevalent or as uniform across black African former townships as it is within particular coloured communities. Within the former townships, cross-dressing as a form of queer visibility exists side-by-side with large numbers of men who do not cross-dress. Both groups, through the development of social nodes, are made visible within townships. The reasons why black African queer men sometimes see white queer men as representing lifestyles more favourable than their own therefore centre on different considerations.

One of the most prominent perceptions of white queer men by black African queers was that this group were less likely to encounter extreme cases of homophobia as frequently as themselves. Heteronormative regulation is not believed to be as rigid as it is in the former townships. For some this therefore also means that the space of the gay village is viewed as a location where they are able to openly and visibly express an identity denied to them in their own community. Similarities can therefore clearly be seen with representations some white queer men in South Africa would seem to have of the De Waterkant gay village (chapter 2) – and representations black African queer men have of the city more generally. For some black African queers and for some white queers, the gay village remains the epitome of freedom and safety. As this township resident explains:

> *I was kind of in that situation so basically what I'm trying to say is be extra careful. So, gay people in the township, that's more risky. What if they turns into trouble – the gay village was there . . . I decided to go there, you know – just to know more, get to understand it and see – because it is difficult not only for because of safety I couldn't really be safe with township people.* PHILANI/25

And as this following conversation with two township residents makes evident, white society more generally in South Africa can sometimes be perceived as more liberated and accepting towards queer sexuality. While chapter 2 has documented the problems faced by white queer men during apartheid – and specifically, the discrimination they faced from a Christian, isolationist and nationalist doctrine – there was at least an implicit knowledge among white society about the existence of homosexuality as a discrete entity. During the same period this knowledge appeared not to exist as strongly among the Xhosa in Cape Town. Following from the discussion in chapter 4, this lack of knowledge helps drive antagonism towards men who visibly express their queer identities within the townships.

> LINDIWE/33: *It's much easier for whites to be gay. I mean, it's because – I won't – What can I say? Is that their parents already know about life, you know, what's going on in life, and they know this is 2004. Before it was 2003 and 1998 and 1977, so they know what's happening. They've got history and they know the changings.*
>
> ANDREW: *Why don't black people know the changes?*
>
> LINDIWE/33: *What can I say? I will say education.*
>
> KEVIN/32: *It's just because of, like, black people never got the chance to express themselves because of the apartheid.*

Both for some black African and coloured queer men, there remain in place several powerful motivating factors to explain why they would wish to associate with, visit and socialise in the gay village in Cape Town. Despite the widely divergent histories of each community, the space of the De Waterkant exists as a potent draw for not only some white groups but also some black African and coloured groups. While by no means felt by all coloured and black African respondents, there is still a perception that white queer men, most visibly located within the gay village, are less constrained by factors that condition life in their own communities. For black African queers in particular, the gay village is held in high regard as a space far less homophobic than their own local world. For some coloured queer men, as chapter 3 has argued, the gay village is viewed as a space where cross-dressing is never a prerequisite of acceptance. Instead the gay village is a space where some degree of masculinity, rather than overt femininity, is the accepted norm. Yet despite beliefs as to the benefits to be enjoyed in the gay village, and despite common perceptions as to the openness and accessibility of the space (chapter 2), coloured and black African queers who attempt to access it can find distinct limitations placed on them.

The Power of the Rand and the Weakness of Solidarity

The most basic and also one of the most limiting factors that can stop some coloured and black African queers accessing the gay village is simply that of distance. Coloured communities on distant parts of the Cape Flats such as Lavender Hill and Mitchell's Plane and black African communities in any of the townships are spatially located several kilometres from the centre of the city. For black African queers in the former townships in particular, there are severe problems in being able to travel to the city centre at night. Public transport in Cape Town after nightfall is sporadic and sometimes dangerous (Clarke and Crous 2002; George 2003). Economically, it therefore becomes problematic to be able to reach the gay village and travel back home later in the evening. At night there are very few, if any, minibus taxis (the most popular and cheapest form of transport in South Africa) from the City Bowl to the townships. A private taxi could easily cost R150 (£12.50) – a sum of money far in excess of what even employed individuals in townships would be willing or able to pay.[2]

Yet while physical distance remains an important limiting factor in accessing the gay village (and city centre, generally), there are also other equally forceful issues that affect the ability of some black African and coloured queers to socialise in that space. From their own perspective, these issues are directly linked to a history of racial discrimination in the country. By far the most striking factor that several black African and coloured interviewees described about the gay village was how they felt they had easily ended up being made to feel socially inferior because of their race. As a vivid illustration of this issue, respondents from the townships and Cape Flats gave numerous accounts of how they were denied entry to certain clubs and bars in the gay village. As these two black African queer men explain:

And even if you go to these white clubs, Andy, white people will still look at you, like, 'Ooh!' Like, you know? Then, 'Look who's coming in!' And, you know, they will even push themself one side. You know? Like, you can see, you can feel, you can feel it, you can see it. I remember once we went to [X]. I had my visitor from the Eastern Cape . . . We were turned back at the door, and say, 'No, you cannot come in.' And we questioned that. Why? And they said, 'No, it's only for club members.' And I said, 'But we are gay. What kind of club members? Where can we register as members? Where can we register?' Said, 'No, the manager's not here to do the registration and things like that.' You can see, it's a fumbling, it's fumbling what they are saying. There's no such – You can see, you can sense that, ag, they're just fumbling. We were turned back.   WESLEY/39

It's racism, basically. It is pure racism . . . Which is quite sad, because a lot of people would come, maybe, from Jo'burg [Johannesburg] or the Eastern Cape or all the way, and they want to go to the gay club, where they can be free. And now they go to the gay club and they're denied access to the place. You know. So it's still racism.   MELISIZWE/34

And from a coloured perspective:

Because, I mean, sometimes my friends – not my closest friends, but people that I know – they're, like, not allowed to go in. Why? Because they're not regulars. Now, how do you become a regular if you're not allowed in the first place? I mean, it's confusing.   DOUG/20

Basically they wouldn't let me in because of my race, and this was justified on the grounds that I was inappropriately dressed, which, of course, was bullshit.   WILLIAM/27

Such statements appear to make plain a perception of exclusion based on skin colour at certain establishments in the gay village. For some queer men, race becomes a marker that makes entry into certain establishments problematic. And indeed, when taken to court, one club that was singled out admitted to a door policy which allowed for 'exclusion based on [the individual's] race' (Kassiem 2004; Lane 2005). Yet some who frequent the gay village have also disputed these claims. As one writer argued, the issue is not so much about race as it is about economics:

Listen, I don't believe that there's much racism going on . . . I know that there was an incident . . . In fact, Behind the Mask [a gay news website in South Africa]. There was an article written, or a posting to one of the newsgroups at Behind the Mask, and it specifically related to, I think, [an] incident in Cape Town with a club story. 'Why did they charge entry? Why don't they allow everybody in? Why can't poor people go in? Why don't they make special provision for poor people?' etcetera. And I think the major problem here is that what people are tending to overlook is that a five-star hotel does not make provision for poor people. You can either afford it or you can't. It's based on class in terms of living standards or whatever. GEORGE/39

However, such an argument fails to grapple with the more pressing issue of skin colour being used as a marker of exclusion. The argument put forward by respondents who had been denied entry was that they were being excluded first and foremost because of their skin colour, which only by association led to the belief that these individuals were economically disadvantaged. Indeed, as the following quotation from another bar owner, DYLAN, highlights, skin colour in some instances is simply being used as a shorthand for economic disempowerment:

I've had people coming to complain to me, black African customers, saying that they are not let into certain clubs. And [an individual with a PhD, no longer living in the townships] said to me, 'Well, it can't be because of my clothes, because I'm probably earning a salary ten times what the doorman is earning.' DYLAN

The argument that exclusion from clubs is due mostly to economic considerations also comes under attack when it is appears that some bars and clubs in the gay village have purposely put their alcohol prices up to limit the number of black African and coloured queers visiting. Indeed, the following quotation from another bar owner, SANDY, clearly suggests that economics in an abstract sense is not the only reason why some black African and coloured queers are denied entry to these spaces:

I mean, it's not even a year ago that [X], my manager, was kicked out of [one of the clubs]. They wouldn't let him inside. I mean, how dare they? . . . And you know what else they're doing? They put their prices up to prices that are just not acceptable. R14 for a beer is not acceptable. It's as simple as that. Why should they be R14 a beer? You know why? Because the poorer communities can't afford R14 a beer. Why should they pay R14 if they can pay R5 or R10 wherever else they want to go to? SANDY

The comments of these two bar owners, when taken together with the view of some black African and coloured respondents, seems to reveal the belief that far more is at work than simply economic imperative in keeping certain individuals out of some bars and clubs. It thus also becomes important to re-examine some of the main issues raised in chapter 2, as to the dominance within the gay village of a lifestyle associated with a particular class of urban male. It appears that the class-based nature of exclusion discussed among white queer men in chapter 2 and perceptions of race collide when some black African and coloured queers attempt to access particular spaces. As the following interviewee, who personally knows one coloured individual who was denied entry to a club, explains:

MICHAEL/21:   *They, well, recently discriminated against a friend of mine who's of colour – who's coloured, specifically – And, you know, they just said that they wouldn't allow him in – And the reason was that he was dressed – they say he was dressed too down-market, which was a complete fallacy. He was dressed better than all of us. I was wearing gym trainers, blue jeans and a sport jacket, a Nike – a Levi sport jacket zip-up, and I got in. Hardly glamorous, but I'm as white as snow, which is the problem. Basically the subtext of that refusal of my friend was that it was synonymous with being a down-market coloured problem. Yes, he's coloured, and perhaps they were just trying to be sensitive towards him. Little did they know that he probably earns more than most people in the club. He's an actuary for a top institution, highly qualified, highly intellectual, a fantastic all-rounding human being, you know. One shouldn't even need to justify that. The fact is he was denied to come in and the subtext was, 'He's coloured.'*

ANDREW: *So this club is predominantly white?*

MICHAEL/21:   *Well, they were trying to keep it with that up-market – You know, there's this other [issue] as well. 'Up-market', in the context of gay culture, is a white professional who goes to gym, who drives a good car . . . But this is this market, and this sort of white contingency of up-market, good-looking gay clones, or gay cultural clones. And they're also linked to a very much larger amount of people from London, from all over, from Germany. They all sort of are on the same sort of cultural wavelength. They're almost a subculture on their own, you know.*

Put another way, being understood as part of the coloured community in this instance did not mesh with a lifestyle and culture, described in chapter 2, which has come to dominate representations of the gay village. It would appear that both coloured and black African queers, no matter how 'well dressed', risk being excluded from clubs simply because of their skin colour. Their skin colour in this instance does not act simply as a racial marker of their alleged economic disempowerment, it also acts as a marker of their inability to conform to a cultural identity strongly associated with a particular class-based archetype of urban queer male. A particular group of white queer men in Cape Town (the 'clones' in the above quotation) are striving to emulate a no doubt essentialistic class of queer identity that itself is derived from images in part derived from overseas. Coloured and black African queer men are sometimes viewed as not 'up-market' enough to take part in this attempt.

The need to appear 'up-market' need not only be seen as problematic for black African and coloured queer men. As JONATHAN, the owner of another club explained, efforts by a doorman keen to keep the bar 'up-market' easily resulted in the exclusion of certain individuals because they were perceived to be inappropriately dressed. As he explained with this one example:

> *And you never know who's going to arrive at the door next – Jean-Paul Gaultier was refused because he had sandals on. You know. The doorman still had that mentality of, if you wear a suit, then you can come in, but if you wear sandals, no.* JONATHAN

The problem, however, is that unlike internationally famous French fashion designers, a number of black African and coloured queers felt they were not being denied entry at certain establishments because of footwear. Instead, as highlighted above, the perception of some was that they were being denied entry to certain places because their skin colour labelled them out for exclusion.

Economics clearly does play an important part in the reasons why both some black African and coloured queers are restricted in accessing some venues. Indeed, statistics in the country show that when taken as a whole, coloured and black African workers have lower average incomes than white South Africans (Figure 5.1). Further, if they live a long way from the City Bowl, then they obviously will have to pay a premium in transportation costs to the gay village. But these concerns are only secondary. In some instances it seems that if a black African queer man who lives in a former township is able to afford to visit the gay village, he may still be denied access both because his skin colour indicates perceived economic disempowerment and because of a perception that his skin colour implies an inability to subscribe to a particularly powerful queer visibility in the city. Nevertheless, as this white interviewee explained, the economic power of individual coloured or black African queer men who attempt to access the gay village may at times not be nearly as important as the assessment by some within that space that only white queers are able to emulate or strive towards a strongly class based and 'exclusive' queer identity:

> *But I suppose it's a comment on the ingrainedness, the level of routedness, of racism in South Africa that, you know, it still exists in the space [the gay village] that you would think would be enlightened and egalitarian and welcoming. But um, ja, to some degree the gay village in somewhere like Cape Town is one that looks towards cities in the world and does especially look towards London and then, you know, its brand consciousness, its what car you drive, what sort of corporate position you hold. And many black people don't fit into, um traditionally fit into, those sort of moulds.* CHRISTIAN/31

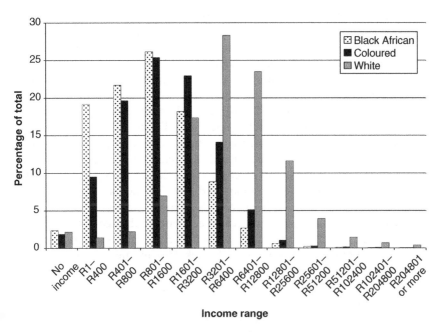

Figure 5.1 Monthly income amongst the employed aged 15–65 by population groups in South Africa (data taken from 2001 South African Census, http://www.statssa.gov.za).

The exclusion from queer venues due to skin colour is not of course solely restricted to Cape Town, it has been well documented in many other cities. As Knopp (1997) has explored, spaces associated with a particular commodified form of queer identity have often been seen as exclusionary and directly racist towards 'non-white' groups. For example, a process of 'carding' has been documented in the US, whereby African Americans were specifically targeted for excessive amounts of identification before being allowed entry to clubs (Nero 2005). In these instances, it appears that a large number of 'non-white' queers may cause an establishment to 'lower its tone' – whereby it will find it harder to be associated with a form of queer identity linked to economic power and privilege.

The power of the Rand within the Cape Town gay village therefore represents a constellation of issues that can help keep some black African and coloured queer men out of that space. It cannot be denied that some coloured and black African queers may well not have the same level of disposable income as some white queers. The legacy of apartheid cannot simply be forgotten. Real material economic inequalities between groups cannot be equalised overnight. As discussed above, these factors by themselves do not constitute 'racism'. Nevertheless, a narrow take on the economic argument remains unable to explain the perceived exclusion some have described here – and the court case brought against one particular club. It fails to excuse the possibility that some coloured and black African individuals are being excluded because of a perception that these groups are unable to 'buy into' a particular commodified take on what is seen by some as an 'exclusive' queer culture.

In such instances apartheid-enforced class differentials can be reinscribed onto skin colour. While apartheid did initially force a ranking between different racially-defined communities, it now appears that those differentials can at times be maintained through a rendering of skin colour forcibly tied to class. At an extreme, such a rendering can lead to the exclusion of individuals from certain bars and clubs in the gay village who are deemed unable to take part in such an 'upmarket' project. This therefore is a form of exclusion that draws clear precedents (although not necessarily direct lineage) from actual state-imposed racial segregation as occurred with apartheid policies. Coloured and black African queers can sometimes therefore be excluded both because of real economic disempowerment and because of the reading of economic and cultural disempowerment as tied to skin colour.

For some coloured and black African queers, their exclusion from venues in the gay village is simply a racist manifestation. And it is without doubt a racist manifestation when race remains forcibly associated with preconceptions about wealth and class. Yet the exclusion of coloured and black African queers within the gay village also goes further. While economics remains the most powerful limiting factor for these groups, other, specifically South African factors, also play important roles in keeping certain groups of white queers the most visible in the De Waterkant.

Gender Identity as Exclusion

As already discussed in chapter 3, representations of masculinity, as opposed to overt and sustained effeminacy, remain an important element within sectors of contemporary Western queer culture, located around, for example, particular urban gay spaces. Bodily gender performance is regulated within certain queer spaces to the extent that cross-dressing and effeminacy are no longer as prominent as they once were. The history of 'nancy boys' and 'fairies', well known during the early-to-mid-twentieth century in Europe and North America, was soon set aside as queer culture continued to change, becoming increasingly focused on achieving sexual political rights (Chauncey 1994 and Houlbrook 2005). As Wilchins (2004) has explored, the legacy of overt effeminate behaviour within the new gay rights movement was often viewed more as a hindrance than a source of inspiration.

At the same time, however, this is also not simply to say that there is *no* effeminacy within these queer spaces. 'Camp', for example, when tied to extravagance and démodé and effeminate behaviour, can itself act both as a political tool and a marker of social visibility within some queer cultures (Sontag 1967). As the documentary work of Jennie Livingston (1990) has shown, drag and cross-dressing can still exist within this realm. But such representations have become increasingly and safely separated from the more 'mainstream'. Indeed, for many, these representations remain enmeshed within specific sites and events such as Pride marches, drag balls and cabaret shows – a situation that has also already been documented in South Africa (chapter 3). More broadly as well, issues of gender remain separated from more 'mainstream' sexual political issues, so much so that transgender rights have evolved as a separate category of political advocacy. (Indeed, this fracture is further sustained and complicated by the separation of 'cross-dressing' from either transgender rights or more common 'gay' rights.)

As Heidi Nast (2002) has argued, the construction of such delineated identities can also be seen in part to be the result of different nationalist projects. In South Africa this can perhaps best be illustrated in the way apartheid and earlier colonial isolationist tropes surrounding white masculinity have been framed in relation to the alleged effeminacy of coloured queer men. While chapter 3 went to significant lengths to highlight a more egalitarian view to understanding queers who side more with either side of the gender binary, this section will show how there still remains feeling among some that a raced masculinity tied to queer identity is still for some more 'favourable' than a raced femininity tied to a queer identity.

For some queer men in Cape Town, there therefore exists an awareness of difference between those who exhibit overt and sustained effeminacy and those who do not. This awareness, when taken to an extreme, can manifest itself as an aversion to all that falls outside the remit of a particular rendering of 'masculinity'. For some within Cape Town, this aversion is strongly associated with elements of coloured culture. Again, race and queer visibility combine to exclude a particular group of men. As the following interviewees explain, stereotypical and indeed essentialistic renderings as to the effeminate coloured queer male help both to delineate the differences between these two racially defined groups and position a particular white visibility as the more favourable of the two:

You know, there's gay coloured culture, which is a whole sort of contingency on its own. I don't know enough about it . . . The general feeling I get is that they are associated with being trashy queens by the white guys, in a way. Very subtly, but not – On a very subtle – Well, it is obviously racist level, it's almost associated, you know, these coloured or Clora [Gayle[3] for 'coloured'] queens are associated with being slightly – They're from the other side of the tracks. Let's put it that way – It's sort of very camp. The coloured queens are – if they're queens, are associated with being a lot more camp, a lot more out there. MICHAEL/21

Um. I think there are a few stereotypes and that's about it. The coloured stereotype of the overly camp coloured moffie – in contrast there's a strong sort of macho identity or stereotype or archetype on the white gay scene in Cape Town. Um and so yes to some extent you can say that coloured guys are typified as being very camp. CHRISTIAN/31

But then just a lot of coloured gay men that are just sort of camp and effeminate, and that is perhaps looked down upon from [other queer men] who doesn't – who's no different from his straight counterpart, but just happens to do different things in the bedroom. CRAIG/25

While many coloured gay men do find value in claiming a social space and express-ing themselves in a blatantly homosexual cross-dressing way that challenges social norms, I think many white guys are intimidated by the perceived risk of presenting themselves as being – as being less stereotypically masculine. MORRIS/42

While clearly a stereotype, the trope of the effeminate coloured queer man can retain great purchase among some white queer groups. It would there-fore appear that a particular rendering of essentialist white masculinity can at times come into conflict with the representation of the coloured effemi-nate male body. Indeed, Amanda Swarr's (2004) work on the politics of cross-dressing among white communities in South Africa clearly highlights how the policing of 'whiteness' remains strongly reinforced by a policing of the gender binary. If a white queer individual were to cross-dress it would be assumed to occur only as a theatrical art form. 'Drag artists' among white communities are therefore contrasted with what Swarr notes are understood as 'common drag queens' among other racially delineated com-munities. From this perspective, powerful parallels can also be drawn with Anne McClintock's (1990) work on the importance of apartheid national-istic rhetoric to promote and maintain white masculine control, domination and survival. In this instance the logic of racial control was also used to justify manipulation over the roles of men and women in the protection of the 'white nation' against all possible threats (see also chapter 2). As Nast (2002) points, out such readings of heteropatrichial control can easily become transplanted in some form onto queer groups, in the process re-inscribing pre-existing forms of exclusion onto new groups. Masculinity therefore, from one possible white queer perspective, it seems today must either be repeated and reinforced or consciously parodied in specific spaces such as drag cabaret shows. While clearly not applicable to all individuals, it can nonetheless be seen that to some, to fall outside this logic, to fall outside the spaces where such performances can occur – to take on some form of cross-dressing identity – is to signal weakness and femininity –

which at an extreme can lead yet again to the 're-ranking' of queers on archaic apartheid racial scales.

It is also however true that very few (if any) cross-dressing coloured queer men wish to visit the gay village. In part this again is an issue of distance. Many coloured cross-dressers live in areas many kilometres from the City Bowl. Yet it is also tied to a belief among some coloured cross-dressers that the normalised masculine gender performances displayed within that space boarder on the 'inauthentic'. For coloured cross-dressing men, masculinity can remain tied to the role of the penetrative partner ('top') during sex. Queer men who do not associate with this idea remain a difficult group for some cross-dressers to identify with – existing within an at times different heterosexual/homosexual binary relationship more closely tied to 'the closet' (chapter 1). As this interviewee who cross-dresses, vividly and succinctly explained about the problems he sees in the masculine displays within the gay village:

> *It's exclusively butch. There's very few gay boys that is actually in drag. Only for tops. Ha! And all of them are fucking bottoms! . . . That is the assumption. Because most of them are fucking receivers of revenue.*   ROBIN/36

Here, a reversal of the rationale used by some white queer men helps exemplify the way gender performance keeps queer groups separate in Cape Town. It also highlights again how the histories of some coloured and white queer visibilities emerge from different ideological roots as regards how to appropriate heteronormative space. These different beliefs, strongly tied to race-based classifications, can help reinforce the dominance of a group of white queer men as the most visible group within the De Waterkant.

Ignorance as Exclusion

While gender performance acts as one of the primary factors affecting the visibility of some coloured queers in the space of the gay village, another entirely different factor plays a primary role in limiting the visibility of some black African queer men in the same space. Indeed, in contrast to generalised and essentialistic effeminate representations of coloured queers by some white queer men, black African queer men appear to be characterized by a more generalised lack of understanding. While by no means the case for all, for some white queer men who inhabit or pass through the gay village, black Africans are known about by their very unknownness. This representation is first and foremost fostered by a historical legacy that influences a general lack of contact between white and black African groups in

South African urban space (Durrheim and Dixon 2001; Moodley and Adam 2000; Saff 2001; Turok 2001). It is therefore perhaps hardly surprising that some white queer men would be limited in their abilities to relate their queer experiences to those of black African queers. As the following two quotations illustrate, beyond some limited appreciation that queer visibilities are not easily accepted, there appears to be very little knowledge of township life:

> *My knowledge of the gay community in the coloured areas or the gay community in the black areas is much more limited than my interface with gay people who come, whether it be from a poor or an affluent white background. Because one – I mean, particularly, even today there are – I would be very reluctant to try and go into a poor black area without somebody taking me around, because I really would – I would just have an anxiety about it . . . So I'm afraid my comments are perhaps a little bit race – They are race-based although not racist-based. I think that's probably the best way of putting it.   MONTY/53*

> CRAIG/25:   *[The gay village is] very, very white, or not – OK, it's not – There are no South African township black people. I don't – I've very rarely met anybody from townships. If you meet black people, they are urbanised and – You know, when I would say urbanised I mean now living in central Cape Town or the suburbs of – or they're from other places in Africa or from Europe or America.*
> ANDREW: *Why do you think that is?*
> CRAIG/25:   *Because there's such a strong division between – Well, first of all, there's – Cape Town is always described as a gay city, which is always very funny, because, I mean, if any gay – If you're white or coloured, but, ja, it's definitely not a great – You don't look out over the townships and think, 'Oh, look at those big, gay, happy places!' It's not an inviting environment from – for gay people. And I'm always aware of how small our little world is, with our little clubs and our small little strip of Atlantic Seaboard and City Bowl, and how small that is in the grand scheme of things, ja.*

Yet this lack of knowledge is also reinforced by an acceptance that the legacy of apartheid regulation makes it very difficult for white individuals to get to know black African queer men either now or in the near future. Comments such as those described in the quotation below therefore operate both as a justification for lack of contact between groups and as an explanation as to why the prospect of getting to know many black Africans queers will remain limited:

> *I think apartheid totally fucked us all up. Because people are too fragmented and live behind walls and that they don't easily reach out to others – and you find that they are divided culturally, lets say, skin colour, black gay and white gays don't really mix, coloured and blacks, and then you get different whites. You've been in*

Cape Town, you know what I mean, you can see it for yourself . . . I would have liked to have more friends in the townships, but I hardly venture out into the townships. Which is probably my own fault, but I mix with a wide variety of English, Afrikaans speaking, young and old. People from various professions and various skin colours, although predominately white I must say, and that is something I can't just change that overnight, can I?   GARATH/38

And as this bar owner freely volunteered about some of his own patrons, ignorance and preconceptions only go to limit interaction between communities. When describing how his regular patrons view black African queers who do attempt to socialise at his bar:

They think they're rent boys [sex-workers], basically. The minute they see a nice-looking black or foreign, like, a West African or anybody who's – who's, like, smart and cool, they automatically think he's a rent boy.   SANDY

There is also, for some, little awareness of any direct discrimination against black African or coloured queers. Despite acknowledgement by some black African and coloured queers that the gay village can racially discriminate against them, some white queer men at times appear oblivious to these grievances. In part this lack of awareness is able to continue because spaces within the City Bowl and adjacent areas have always been demographically predominantly white.[4] As Part I of the book explored, as state legislation such as the Group Areas Act came into force in Cape Town, black African and coloured groups were forcibly removed from areas close to white habitation. The end of apartheid has not resulted in the sudden integration of different racially defined groups. For white queer men who frequent the gay village, there is therefore an understanding that the space has historically always been white. The lack of black African and coloured individuals in that space and a lack of awareness of any marginalisation they might feel is therefore easier to rationalise. This in turn provides a rationalisation not to have to confront the apparent social invisibility of coloured and black African individuals in that space – despite increased awareness of queer diversity. As this white interviewee deftly explains:

They [other white queer men] don't view it as racist partly because white people have always lived and grown up in an all white environment. The paradigm within which they think is well, you know, this is just normal. The fact that black people are not there and that black people hang out in the township is somehow made [easier to understand] . . . other spaces in Cape Town are similarly white so people don't find it that much of a logical inconsistency when they go to the gay village, they don't have the sense that the gay village should embrace all people across socio-economic strata on the basis of this one unifying factor. So it's simply that they see the gay village as no different to the rest of Cape Town socially and therefore it's not a problem I don't think as much as it might otherwise be for them. Um, but also I think it's also that way because a lot of white people in Cape Town are racist and they would prefer simply not to mix with too many people of colour. I think it's as blatant as that. Ja.   CHRISTIAN/31

When an acceptance that contact between racially defined groups will remain limited is combined with a further perception that the space of the gay village has remained normalised as predominantly white in composition, it becomes plain that some black African queers can easily remain socially invisible within that space. Indeed, it appears that a general lack of understanding – or ignorance – both towards the problems faced by black African queers within their own community and towards the problems faced by black African queers when they attempt to access the gay village defines a significant element of the perception of this group.

Conclusion

As the last part of the above quotation by 'CHRISTIAN/31' illustrates, it becomes hard to dispute that there is, from some members within the white queer male community in Cape Town, a degree of outright discrimination towards other groups. The continued linking together of economics with skin colour, and the linking of class-based perceptions as to the exclusivity of a particular rendering of Western-influenced queer culture with skin colour, were strongly articulated by many respondents. Yet as the previous two sections have attempted to explore, direct and overt racism is not the only factor that limits the access black African and coloured queers have to the space of the gay village. It has therefore not been the aim of this chapter to simply regurgitate intellectually tired arguments concerning racism among a certain segment of white South Africans to explain what is occurring in the gay village. Neither, conversely, has it been to deny the very materiality that goes to construct the sometimes exclusionary racialisation of space. Either stance would tend to obscure a whole myriad of cross-cutting issues that are both just as powerful at making invisible coloured and black African groups and also relate directly to the way these groups have been able to become visible (and the problems that they have faced) in the first instance.

As explored in this chapter, the perceptions of some coloured queers as overtly effeminate are associated with the way that group was able to appropriate heteronormative space and hence become visible within its own community in ways different to some groups of white queer men. On the other hand, the perception of black African queers as unknowable is augmented by the way apartheid was able to categorise and spatially contain groups. The line as to where these beliefs cross over into being termed 'racist' is not a clear-cut one. At one extreme, if black African and coloured queers believe they are not allowed into clubs because of their skin colour, racism becomes easier to identify. At another extreme however, when some white individuals almost sheepishly attempt to explain the historical justifications as to why they do not have many black African queer friends and do not see how they will have any in the future, the call of overt racism becomes far harder to justify.

What does remain clear however, is that some black African and coloured individuals can easily become excluded from the space of the gay village – and that at the same time the gay village will remain, for the foreseeable future, the most likely space where all three groups will be able to socialise with each other. Nevertheless, an exploration of the rationalisations used by various white groups as to why others can remain excluded from that space also points towards a certain level of reflection and indeed even anxiety as to their own position in relation to the gay village and other communities. If nothing else, the attempts by all these men to understand their own position in relation to others in the city since the end of apartheid points to a growing awareness of difference itself – even if that difference remains hard to understand or even at times to identify.

Visibility and invisibility therefore work together in different ways when groups with different histories attempt to socially interact. The ending of apartheid – the breaking down of artificial barriers – has not straightforwardly helped to socially unite different groups. However, the effects of invisibility also reach far beyond social interactions. As the next chapter will show, queer invisibility does not only work in the social arena, it has also presented distinct problems (and also possibilities) to groups and organisations with more overt political agendas as they come to terms with an ever greater awareness of difference.

Chapter Six

Political Invisibilities (and Visibilities)

The previous chapter set out to explore how different queer visibilities in Cape Town have been able (or not) to socially interface with each other. Issues of race, gender, class and appropriations of urban space interlinked to help keep some black African and coloured queers socially invisible within the space of the gay village. It was shown that both different communities' visibilities and the factors that lead to those different visibilities can continue to keep communities separate from each other. Such findings also help us to see how different queer groups struggle to rationalise what is occurring in the gay village, highlighting instances of anxiety and complacency. Such findings, however, would seem not necessarily to gel well with the popular representation of Cape Town, and indeed South Africa, as a liberated and accepting space for queer sexualities.

In large part it has been historical factors most strongly linked to apartheid ideological and spatial control which have shaped the fortunes of each male queer community studied here. The development of an 'exclusive' visibility most strongly associated with some men in the gay village in Cape Town, as chapter 2 has shown, has come about in part because of the inability of the South African white queer community – that which was most strongly regulated by the apartheid state – to develop its own cohesive local queer community during apartheid. Post-apartheid, historical factors have continued to affect why sections within this community have been ready and willing to associate with and draw inspiration from particular elements of a queer culture that had its roots in certain urban sites in the West. A particular take on gender identity and spatial appropriation are the two examples given here of how this community can contrast with and overshadow those produced and reproduced elsewhere in the city.

Yet in other ways as well it becomes possible to see how this visibility might have difficulty interfacing with other visibilities in the city in ways that move beyond simply the social. Indeed, as Bell and Binnie's (2006) work on the geographies of sexual citizenship points out, questions of responsibility and problems of assimilation remain central in understanding the political imperative of citizenship rights. Issues of rights and duties can not simply be framed in relation to the state. They also have to be framed in relation to other groups of citizens. Such debates, located within concerns over social justice, can remain focused within an urban environment, as groups attempt to gain rights through, for example, protest within heteronormative city spaces. Or debate can occur more readily at the level of national discourse. Here issues of nationalism and its relationship to sexuality-based rights become more pressing. Yet at both scales, issues of who is being represented and why must remain key.

This chapter will therefore offer three investigations of both the problems acknowledged by queer organisations and activists in being able to represent difference, and the innovative solutions they have tried to deploy to overcome them. These examples, when seen together, will help illustrate how different communities interact and play out in relation to each other in divergent ways, offering instances where a 'queering' of many of the beliefs around particular visibilities and rights-based claims becomes possible. To begin, this chapter will look at the oldest and most well established social support organisation in all of Africa for queer individuals to see what issues it has come across in its attempts to service different queer communities in Cape Town. It will then move on and explore one of the most well known forms of urban sexual rights political action, Pride, and discuss how the event has developed in Cape Town. It will then examine how the same-sex marriage campaign and passing of the Civil Union Bill in 2006 helped to galvanise queer individuals across different communities in the city and the country on a scale previously unheard of – in the processes allowing communities to show solidarity in the face of heteronormativity and homophobia in a way previously impossible. Yet at the same time the very visibility of queer groups during the same-sex marriage campaign will also be shown to have led to a dramatic stimulation of homophobic rhetoric. The methods by which queers were made visible due to the marriage campaign also granted space for others to critique the deployment of sexuality-based rights in the country in ways they had previously been unable. This chapter will therefore conclude by returning to some of the issues raised in the first part of this book: the problems faced by queers in South Africa today remain not only related to group interaction, but also continue to be defined by deeply felt homophobia.

Offering the Services of Triangle Project

Triangle Project (originally called 6010 and then GASA 6010[1]) began when a group of queer men during the early 1980s in Cape Town came

Figure 6.1   Triangle Project offices located in Mowbray in Cape Town.

together for issues of social support. Counselling and medical services soon formed the core work of the organisation. Such work was then furthered by the advent of the AIDS pandemic which was noted initially among white queer men in the 1980s in the city (Pegge 1995) (see also chapter 7). The organisation, now located in the Mowbray suburb of the city, was the first in South Africa to respond to the AIDS crisis and is today the largest social support organisation of its kind in southern Africa (see Figure 6.1) (Triangle Project 2007).

But by the late 1990s Triangle Project also had to come to terms with a perception among some in the former townships that it was an organisation heavily skewed towards white groups. With its roots in the lives of white men during apartheid, the organisation found itself faced with particular problems in branching out, especially to help black African men who were starting to become increasingly visible in the city. Perhaps the single biggest issue the organisation faced during this period was in finding new and innovative ways of integrating its social support programmes with the needs of black African queers.[2]

In part this problem has been inherently spatial. The Triangle Project offices are located between the Mowbray and Observatory suburbs of the city, close to the CBD/City Bowl. This location makes it very easy for those who live in the central suburbs of the city to reach the organisation. For those who live in the outlying Cape Flats or the former black African townships, the offices are harder to reach. As one black African man explained about the organisation:

> *What can I say? I think the location is the major problem, because, it's in the town, you see? Let me say so, because it's Observatory, and we are far in the township. Some of us, some people, I think, don't know about Triangle. I think so. They don't know. Some – What can I say? Maybe some would love to come, but don't know how.* BILLY/24

To try and combat this problem, the organisation set up a satellite office in the Guguletu township in December 1996. This office, while initially successful, soon started to develop problems. The space of the Guguletu office had been set up to offer a safe and secure environment for black African men to engage in counselling sessions. However, it soon emerged that the space was being used mainly for socialising, rather than for services. As the director of the organisation explained, when discussing the problems of getting more involved in the black African townships:

> *[The Guguletu Office didn't have] a structure of appointments. People would pop in there when they needed something. The programmes that the organisation tried to run there weren't successful there . . . Even though a counselling service was put in place in Guguletu and staff were specifically hired to give a counselling service in Xhosa from that space, the other issues around the issue of counselling within a black community played such a role that people in fact would rather still come [to town] and speak to someone who spoke in their second or third language, for the anonymity of going to another space.* DAWN BETTERIDGE

Despite attempts to service black African township individuals by starting a special office designed for their needs, the endeavour proved unsuccessful. As chapter 4 has highlighted, groups of black African township men often socialise in social nodes. These nodes are inherently close-knit. Because of that fact, those who are involved in these nodes are known about by other members of those same (and quite possibly, other) nodes. Should a member of a node wish to visit the Guguletu Triangle Office for a private counselling session, there would be the strong risk of that individual's friends finding out, and possibly questioning that individual on a personal matter.[3] This would also have been an issue for those individuals that had not publicly proclaimed some form of queer identity and/or feared homophobic responses from the community if they were seen going to the Guguletu office. These issues proved very problematic for an organisation such as Triangle Project, whose work was primarily dependent on the need for confidentiality. This point was also made by one of the black African workers at the Guguletu office:

> *I know a lot of people in Cape Town that would rather leave the services in the township and go and use the one in town. And now, with gay communities, it was, like, really difficult, because it was smaller, and people don't want to be identified. If somebody want to come out, some people will go there and, like not say anything, you know, and then run away, you know.* MELISIZWE/34

Clearly problems existed for black African queer men in being able to reach the centrally located Triangle Project office in Mowbray. Yet equally problems emerged in locating an office directly in the middle of a community where social ties among certain queer men proved so strong.

A second and far more successful strategy was therefore implemented, whereby a social nodal leader (chapter 4) was himself trained first as an outreach worker for the organisation and then employed as a full-time member of staff. Rather than directly confront the differences between more individualistic counselling methods and the group social interactions of queer township men, Triangle Project decided instead to integrate one of those groups within its own structures. This approach has worked largely because social nodal leaders are granted (or rather, have earned) a very high degree of respect among their social circle. As discussed earlier, these nodes work both to offer a degree of safety and also a degree of validation for men who are a part of them. Leaders within these groups are therefore both trusted and seen as able to help queer men when they need assistance. They are, in other words, a close approximation to social support councillors – but working within a framework far more closely associated with mutual support.

Over time this model has developed into the 'Safe Spaces' programme, whereby the outreach worker acts as a facilitator to weekly meetings within the townships to discuss social issues that might be affecting queer men. These meetings take place either in the home of a known queer individual or in a neutral and safe space such as a community library. These spaces are therefore already known about within the community for purposes other than Triangle Project meetings. They therefore do not necessarily have the same type of stigma attached to them as the formalised office space of the unsuccessful Guguletu office. In effect, these meetings have helped to create a new more formalised model of social node – but one that still retains a degree of informality combined with camaraderie. As these two attendees explain, the importance of the space is very similar to the importance placed on social nodes:

We were talking about different issues, things that I was learning that I didn't even know. And it's kind of a feeling that you are in within your family, people that understand you, people that you can share with . . . Most of the people could come to Safe Spaces, and you're meeting new people each and every time you go there. PETER/32

Because if you have got a problem, they are trying to – the people [are] trying to solve your problem. They like – they – What can I say? Maybe it's a [relationship], you've got a problem . . . when you go there to the Safe Space, then you talk about it. You get some people give you some advice. FRANK/29

These meetings can then act as a bridge between the informality of a social node group and a more structured and appointments-based service offered by the main Triangle Project offices. By so doing they are able to incorporate the immediacy and spontaneity of help that would be found in a friendship group with the more sustained and long term support found in clinical counselling or service provision. As outreach worker Mabhuti Makangeli explains when discussing the differences between the type of help often sought by black African queer men and the type of support that can be offered by various wider Triangle Project services:

Because people, like, they think that, like, especially in black community, people, if they've got a problem, they want the problem to be resolved now. But [in] the Safe Space, we discussed that . . . you have to follow this procedure and this, so that it can be solved . . . [Sometimes] you can't resolve the problem right now, because you have to go in this and this and this way . . . We have to take time. MABHUTI MAKANGELI

This strategy has not only helped in the servicing of black African queer men, it has also helped improve the perception of the organisation as one that does not only cater towards individuals in and around the central suburbs. By reengineering its approach towards service provision, Triangle Project has been able to reach a far greater number of black African queer men who, historically, have been limited in their ability to access (or been wary of) the organisation.

Access to social and medical support in a city defined for centuries by racial exclusion has, for a long time, proved incredibly vexing for Triangle Project. Indeed, it should be remembered that the organisation itself has its roots among white communities in the 1980s who needed support both to live with the policies of an authoritarian state and to face the emergent threat of HIV/AIDS (chapter 7). In twenty years the organisation has been witness to dramatic shifts in the country, and as such has been more than willing to try to adapt to new and growing concerns. The ending of apartheid has made it easier for it to gain access to black African and indeed also coloured communities. Yet especially for black African communities, the social worlds and also needs of that group seemed for a long time at odds with the type of (and implementation of) services Triangle Project has traditionally offered. The eventual success of the Safe Spaces programme is therefore an acknowledgement that the relationships between queer men and between queer men and wider heteronormative society in former townships can at times be distinctly different to those found among men elsewhere. These relationships are directly related in the way each queer group presents itself to the community. Such different visibilities help both to frame the previous problems faced by Triangle Project and now the successes they have had in working *within* the social worlds of these queer men.

Yet the growing relationships between township queer men and Triangle Project have also gone a lot further. While social, psychological and medical services have been and will remain important for men in township environments; it is also the case that many of the problems that arise for them stem directly from explicit and persistent homophobia. A pressing need for township queer men is therefore to be able to live in environments freely without fear of community violence. It therefore also becomes important to see how an organisation that has remained overwhelmingly focused on social support during the past twenty years has started to develop a more political stance towards homophobia in townships. And further, it is crucial to see how it has been able to make visible to the wider community the existence and needs of black African township queer men. But before that discussion, it is worth first looking at the development of an event that, in contrast to Triangle Project, has tended to shift its focus from directed politics to celebration.

Being Proud of Cape Town Pride

Pride marches and Pride parades have their roots in 1970s North America, with the emergence of a new type of open gay culture and gay politics. The development of openly gay communities in cities such as New York and San Francisco were centred on a new form of political consciousness that sought to directly confront and overcome decades of homophobia, prejudice and semi-secrecy. The very first Pride march occurred in New York in 1970 as a commemoration of the Stonewall Inn riots the previous year which had effectively ushered in the era of overt gay identity political struggle (Kates and Belk 2001). Over the next few decades Pride events would spread out across North America and then across the globe. Events would also grow to encompass not only a march or parade but also often a week of celebrations and events designed to promote and give validation to forms of queer sexuality in otherwise heteronormative and/or hostile communities. By 2007 there were nearly two hundred events scheduled to take place throughout the year in places as diverse as Traverse City, Michigan, Reykjavik, Iceland and Colombo, Sri Lanka.[4]

The importance and relevance of Pride has remained its ability to make public that which is often viewed as confined to some degree to the private sphere (Brickell 2000). Pride events therefore attempt to destabilise heteronormative assumptions about sex and sexuality in a very public way. Pride festivals and marches are also therefore concerted attempts to establish safe spaces through visibility, often moving outside traditional Western constructions of gay villages (Davis 1995). Because of this, Pride festivals and marches can be viewed as inherently political activities that attempt to bring visibility to queer sexuality across space. By challenging heteronormativity in public space, their aim is also to create awareness and develop political power for queer groups.

Yet, as others have explored, it is also possible to see Pride as an increasingly commodified spectacle. Just as chapter 2 discussed in relation to some white queer visibilities in Cape Town, a focus on consumption and leisure as markers of a particular lifestyle space have become increasingly important for events such as Pride. For Alan Sinfield (1998) and Mark Simpson (1996) Pride can now seem marked more by its corporatisation, regimentation and self-congratulation than by any form of coherent political consciousness. There is therefore an awareness that Pride today in many parts of the world is notable more for its ability (within limited parameters) to entertain and give validation for rights already won than for its skill at politically challenging heteronormativity. And as Lynda Johnston's (2005) thoughtful work on the politics of Pride discusses, there is also a constant danger, even in the most sexually liberated of spaces, for bodies and performances at Pride events to simply be read through Julia Kristeva's (1982) notion of abjection, whereby heteronormativity is at once drawn to and repulsed by the allegedly disruptive displays of Pride marches and parades. When Pride marches focus on repeating the same representations in ways that are at once different to heteronormativity yet also increasingly familiar, the power of Pride as a politically destabilising tool becomes subdued. It is not hard to imagine how this problem is only accentuated in queer spaces located first around leisure and consumption.

Nevertheless, it is also evident that in some environments where public displays of queer sexuality are more recent, Pride events have been able to maintain their public power to confront and visibly destabilise societal assumptions and beliefs about sexuality. One need look only at recent events in Russia (Harding 2007; Human Rights Watch 2007) and Israel (Urquhart 2006) to realise that.[5] While these displays in communities away from North America and Western Europe can sometimes rightly raise neo-colonial concerns due to their assumption of modernist teleological progression and Western styles of citizenship (Hayes 2000; Binnie 2004), they do nonetheless also signify newly visible and often combative and overtly political displays of sexuality and desire. At two extremes, it seems today that Pride has therefore come to embody two divergent (yet not necessarily always distinct) themes. In one direction, Pride increasingly symbolises the successes of communities as they share in their newly won rights while at the same time being in danger of being read as less directly relevant to people's immediate lived experiences. In the other direction Pride is far more caught up in the immediate occurrences of queer lives, as it comes to signify a chance to express sexualities that at other times remain semi-hidden, severely threatened or totally invisible. It is in these communities that the struggle for sexuality rights and social acceptance is often far newer – and perhaps more dangerous. In the context of a city such as Cape Town, an interesting dilemma therefore starts to become apparent. As earlier chapters have shown, a diversity of queer visibilities tied to different radicalised histories, economic (dis)empowerments and legal recourse means that different communities perceive of themselves and their place in the wider community in very different ways. How might an event such as Pride, which would seem to vary both across time and across space, be able to work with and be energised by these different communities? Yet to understand how Pride in Cape Town has tried to grapple with this issue, it is first necessary to see how its neighbour further north was able, during the final days of apartheid, to organise a march when the rest of the country remained on the brink of civil war.

The first Pride in South Africa was held in Johannesburg in 1990, coming just eight months after the un-banning of the ANC. For many involved in the event there were genuine feelings of concern as to their own and their fellow marchers' safety. South Africa was still a country heavily fashioned on institutionalised mutual distrust. Consequently, despite the National Party's unexpected concessions, South Africa was still a place where an openly visible gay march might well have ended in violence. Yet at the same time and in many ways paradoxically, there was for many involved in that first march a growing realisation that the new political climate might well offer greater concrete protection of queers. The un-banning of the ANC by the National Party was viewed by many not only as a last-ditch attempt to regain control of the country, it was also seen as a central concession on the part of the old guard (Clark and Worger 2004; Thompson 2001). And the ANC itself had already made clear its views that queers, just like black African, coloured and Indian groups, should not be discriminated against (Tatchell 2005).

In comparison to events elsewhere in the world, the Johannesburg Pride of 1990 was a very small event. Approximately 800 people showed up to march, many of them wearing brown paper bags on their heads in fear of being recognised (Rundle 2006). Yet the event proved a success, not only in raising the awareness of queer issues within the changing South African political system, but also bringing together queer individuals from across racial communities around a common cause. Indeed this first event proved pivotal because it was an avowedly political gathering. It was an early attempt to politically and visibly fuse issues of racial discrimination with issues of sexuality-based discrimination in South Africa. As Simon Nkoli, the prominent queer and ANC activist, stated at the opening of the first Pride parade on 13 October 1990:

> This is what I say to my comrades in the struggle when they ask me why I waste time fighting for moffies. This is what I say to gay men and lesbians who ask me why I spend so much time struggling against apartheid when I should be fighting for gay rights. I am black and I am gay. I cannot separate to two parts of me into secondary or primary struggles. In South Africa I am oppressed because I am a black man, and I am oppressed because I am gay. So when I fight for freedom I must fight against both oppressions. (Nkoli 2006)

The optimism and excitement of this first Pride march were carried over to the next few years as more and more men and women took part. In 1993 the first Cape Town Pride march was held, when early queer activists there became heavily influenced by the successes occurring in the north. Organised by the now defunct ABIGALE group (see also chapter 4) it achieved a mix of individuals from across different racially defined communities. And just as with their cousins further north, the real and symbolic nature of this event should not be underestimated. In the year before the first democratic elections in the country, queer men and women from across the city of Cape Town marched past Parliament calling, as anti-apartheid activists had been doing for years, for the end of institutionalised discrimination (Achmat and Raizenberg 2006). A new queer voice was being heard in the country and it was a voice that seemed, in those early years, to be an inclusive voice. During the early part of the 1990s it appeared that South Africa was going to be a place where issues of race and issues of sexuality would be seen as equally important and directly related to each other.

Yet only a few years after this optimism seemed to peak, South African gay politics and political activism in Cape Town had started to fracture. Cape Town Pride was unable to energise the community and events occurred only sporadically throughout the rest of the 1990s. Meanwhile in Johannesburg the event that had kicked off the public drive to end all discrimination against queers was coming under increasing attack as it began to be perceived as a white middle-class affair. By the beginning of the new

Figure 6.2   A view into the gated party at the end of the 2004 Johannesburg Pride.

millennium, the event, in the eyes of many, had also ceased to be a political experience, becoming instead a carnival located around the historically white suburbs of the city. While, for a privileged few, levels of homophobic fear had also declined, it also seemed that the event no longer wanted to be associated or located within inner-city areas connected with black African inward migration. In 2004, the march occurred through the afflu-ent Rosebank suburb and ended at Zoo Lake, five kilometres away from the original location of the event in downtown Johannesburg. The 2004 event was capped off with a private party costing R20 to gain entry. Spa-tially and ideologically, Pride in Johannesburg had travelled a long way. Economically disadvantaged queers were forced to sit outside the security patrolled fence as more affluent partygoers 'celebrated' their 'equality' inside (Figure 6.2).

For many, including the Dutch author and key organiser of the 1990 Johannesburg event, Bark Luirink, Pride has been taken away from the black African queer community (Luirink 2006). Rather than exist as an inclusive event run as much by individuals such as the ANC member Simon Nkoli and the activist Bev Ditsie, it has instead become an event run by only an elite few. And as commentator and activist Shaun De Waal explored, this outcome transpired in part due to the very way in which Johannesburg Pride ended up trying to associate with what many saw as a politically muted, commodified and international version of queer identity. There was therefore a real danger that after legal rights began to be won, Pride in Johannesburg would begin to lose relevance to the majority of queer men and women in the region, instead simply devolving into a carbon copy of events that were already taking place elsewhere in the world. Writing in the *Mail and Guardian* in 1999, De Waal stated:

> We need to be aware of the gap between [southern African] specific conditions in an often authoritarian, paternalistic African polity and the way our Pride Parade structures itself according to First World models. [Johannesburg] Pride now has an official identity, a logo, a whole ad campaign behind it – and very attractive it is too . . . The intention, presumably, is to start building some kind of rival to Sydney's gay mardi gras, which has become a global tourist attraction and rakes in millions for that city . . . Glossy gay magazine *Outright* this month advises its readers to ignore the 'killjoy queer politicos' telling them not to have fun. Which is a trifle idiotic, since no one has ever told the marchers not to have fun – though, in the early days, we weren't doing it for fun. (De Waal 1999)

The following year Steven Cohen, the renowned South African performance artist (who once famously created controversy (and, indeed, visibility) when he marched in an early Johannesburg Pride with the slogan 'Give us your children. Those we can't fuck we eat'), provided a damning assessment of the state of Johannesburg Pride at the turn of the new millennium. The language he used to describe the event clearly echoes the concerns raised by others as to what Pride elsewhere had started to symbolise: 'Pride has died, my dear. It no longer has any political significance. It's just *decoration*' (Steve Cohen quoted in Trengove Jones 2000, emphasis added).

For some Johannesburg Pride had come to represent a copy of what Pride had started to evolve into elsewhere. Its very visibility as the first gay and lesbian Pride in southern Africa also means that it has helped give legitimacy to this model. But it is now a model that seems intent not to grapple with issues faced by many queer men and women in the city or in the country. Its location through gated white suburbs and, as exemplified by the statements of activists and artists in the country, its focus on celebration and tourism highlight how the local needs of queers have become increasingly invisible. Nationally figured as a celebration of gay and lesbian rights, it has instead become synonymous with a particular type of queer visibility to the detriment of others.

Nevertheless (and somewhat paradoxically), this refusal to confront the political has meant it has not had to worry about how its own politics plays out within traditionally black African or coloured communities. Indeed, its very lack of political engagement saves it from this concern. This has not been the case further south, where Cape Town Pride has at once been very successful at learning from the lessons of its neighbour while simultaneously coming to grips with other issues concerning the politics and the power of representation.

When Cape Town Pride started up again in 2001, there were a number of lessons it knew it could learn from the Johannesburg situation. To begin with, there was the feeling among some that Johannesburg Pride had become an overwhelmingly white and indeed elitist party, betraying its roots in the political struggle in South Africa. As Ian McMahon, the chairperson of the Cape Town Pride committee, explained about the perception some had in Cape Town of the Johannesburg events:

> *We feel that – obviously taking experience from Johannesburg in terms of they had their route in Hillbrow [first] and [then] Rosebank and all those sort of issues that they had, and we felt that they are so far away from the – Soweto that maybe they – Why does it have to be one parade in an area that is so extreme?* IAN MCMAHON

From almost the very beginning there was therefore a concerted effort to bring onboard members of the black African and coloured communities in an attempt to make sure the event was as inclusive and relevant to as many groups as possible. In 2004 a significant proportion of the event's budget was spent on transport to and from the black African townships and Cape Flats. Advertising also occurred on local radio in English, Xhosa and Afrikaans. Yet despite these efforts, it seemed that Cape Town Pride was initially unsuccessful at garnering the interest or the involvement of many black African and coloured queers. Despite spending approximately R11,000 on free and regular transport to and from the former townships and outlying areas of the Cape Flats on the day of the main events, very little of it was actually used.

It seemed that the renewed impetus behind the Cape Town Prides of the twenty-first century could not immediately offset a decade of sporadic marches and little community interest. While a few key individuals donated large proportions of their time and worked exceedingly hard to prepare for the annual proceedings, it appeared that the events in 2003 and 2004 found it difficult to overcome a general malaise and lack of awareness that Cape Town actually had a Pride event every year. Yet also, even some of those who knew of the event were still unwilling to take part. As the previous chapter has shown, there has developed a perception among some residents of the black African townships and predominantly coloured areas of the outlying Cape Flats that they are not necessarily always welcome within the space of the gay village. With the Pride parade itself taking place through this space, there seemed to exist a feeling that the event held little relevance to the lives of those who lived elsewhere in the city. As this township resident expressed, immediately after the 2004 event:

They should remove – move those things, now and again, into the township, conscientise black people in the township around gays. You know? [Must] everything happen in town? Only the rich would go there. What about the poor? WESLEY/39

In other words it was the geography of the city and the representation of its spaces as exclusively raced and classed that helped limit the participation of many queers. In 2006 and 2007 the Pride committee therefore tried a different tactic to gain participation, holding a parallel Pride event in the Guguletu township during the same week as the parade in the historically white city. As Brian Kruger, the director of the 2007 Pride explained, the Guguletu event therefore fits well within a broader remit of the new rein- vigorated Cape Town Pride to 'Unite Cultures' in an attempt not to leave any community isolated. Consequently, it has been specifically engineered to help gain participation from those queer individuals who, for numerous reasons, have been less visible at the city parade. The aim of the Guguletu event is therefore also to start raising greater awareness among the wider community of the very existence and legitimacy of queer men and women in the townships. By directly acknowledging the problems of homophobia faced by black African queer men in township locations, Pride has tried to make itself directly relevant to their lives. It therefore hopes in turn to gain wider participation:

I think that basically it's a larger community perception problem in the townships, which is that it is culturally incorrect to be gay in the black community. However, I personally believe that the black community is 20 years behind the white gay community at this stage, as far as acceptance and other issues around being gay are concerned. Pride is a celebration of 'Uniting Cultures in the city', and the same goes for the parade in Guguletu as well. However here we feel that focusing on awareness can go a long way to contributing to acceptance of gay issues in the townships. So it's also an issue of getting the word to the community at large that being gay is not as un-African as what people actually think . . . With the growth of Cape Town Pride we made a conscious decision to do a number of events in the townships. We felt it's the right thing to do and also felt that this was going to help make it a lot more inclusive than it was in the past, and this we did and will continue doing for Prides to come. BRIAN KRUGER

And yet this move by the Pride committee has also not been without its own problems. Indeed, in a country such as South Africa, the very idea of creating two separate events, located in different historically racially-defined spaces, might be seen as only institutionalising a historical divide within the city. This is especially pertinent when it is again acknowledged, this time by the Pride chairperson, that solidarity between queer men, as high- lighted in the previous chapter, is not as strong as it might be:

I mean, just chatting to people within my own social circle, people asking me – friends that are asking me, 'Well, why do we need Pride, because we've got all our rights?' And who have no – absolutely no idea of what it's like being a black gay person living in Guguletu . . . or Mitchells Plain . . . People also, I think, take – they seem to have a very cushioned view on life and work, and it's a very middle- to upper-middle-class white view, that they think, 'Hey, man, I'm out [sexually] at work, my family knows, my friends know . . . How great is life!' You know. And they don't realise that again, that life is different, that life throws out challenges for different people. IAN MCMAHON

As explained in the previous chapter, this is particularly problematic in a city such as Cape Town where large numbers of individuals who live in the historically segregated white city remain strongly adverse to travelling into the former townships. A situation is therefore in danger of emerging where black African queers remain concerned with the political struggle to confront widely held homophobic discourses within the country (see especially chapter 4) while those with the resources and the inclination to take part in the city celebration remain separate. In this way, it becomes possible to see Cape Town Pride as being representative of Pride in two eras. In some urban sites such as New York and San Francisco, the early struggle for acceptance and understanding by the wider heteronormative community gave to Pride events an air of urgency and political dynamism. Later Prides have tended to focus more on the celebratory and reaffirming qualities of the event. In Cape Town, this dynamic is played out among two communities with two different histories simultaneously in the same city. Further, the struggle that continues to exist within black African townships remains less visible at well publicised events in the historically segregated white city that both spatially and ideologically remain distanced from township life.

Both Johannesburg and Cape Town Prides have therefore come up against the problem of participation of different groups. For different reasons the visibility of black African and coloured queers has remained a constant point of tension within Pride parades and marches in these two cities. In Johannesburg, the event has evolved away from early political needs towards a commercialised tourist agenda. Economics and a changing parade route helped shift the focus away from the actual lives of the majority of queers in the city. In Cape Town, an appreciation of difference has led to a sustained attempt to overcome the problems associated with Johannesburg Pride and has met with some degree of success. That success however is also mediated by the historically defined spatial, political and cultural layout of the city. Just as chapter 5 showed, perception of different groups and the different needs of different communities have helped to keep them ideologically and spatially separate from each other.

As chapter 2 examined, a popular perception of Cape Town is of a city fully embracing its queer community. Yet as several respondents in that and subsequent chapters have described, such an image only relates to a small proportion of queer lives in city. In a similar vein, there is a legitimate need to examine who exactly is being represented at Pride events in Cape Town, and by way of comparison, in Johannesburg. In particular care must be taken to acknowledge the diversity of queer experiences found throughout the two cities. Just as chapter 2 discussed the problems of assuming that a particular popular representation of queer life could speak to all queer men, so too must it be remembered that a Pride event will speak to different groups of queer men in very different ways. Cape Town Pride has tried to acknowledge these distinctions and critically reflect on the needs of divergent queer groups with their associated different visibilities. And it is the fact that the organisers of Cape Town Pride have tried to work with these distinctions that has allowed for the development of a Pride event in a former township at all. In time events in locations such as Guguletu may well help foster acceptance for queers in otherwise unreceptive and antagonistic places. Yet as numerous examples in this book have illustrated, distinctions within Cape Town are so stark – and the needs of queers so divergent – that the creation of two Pride events may signal the continued separation of these two groups.

But there are also other ways in which the framing of sexuality-based rights in a country such as South Africa can lead to divisions not only, as discussed here, between queer communities, but also between queer communities and wider society. As the next section explores, issues of equality, nationalism, tradition and most importantly visibility collided with each other during 2006, sparking a level of debate about queer issues previously unimagined.

Same-sex Marriage: being Married to a Constitution

The story of the same-sex marriage campaign in South Africa is a story that encompasses many actors working in many sectors over a period of fifteen years. It is also a story that details the incredible successes the country has been able to achieve in the field of sexual legal equality – a struggle to make the needs of all queer groups known to wider society. Yet it is also a story of how deep-seated grievances from a large sector of the country concerning the very idea of sexual equality are only now coming to light. While it has always been known that the sexual equality clause in the 1996 Constitution would prove controversial, the degree of anger and betrayal felt by some during the passing of the Civil Union Bill in the country was for many unexpected. This section therefore has two aims.

First, it will show how success can be achieved in creating an awareness of the existence and needs of different queer groups around one particular issue. It will show how an organisation in Cape Town, Triangle Project, was suddenly in 2006 placed in a position to help energise queer men in former townships, predominantly coloured areas of the Cape Flats and historically white segregated areas of the city. In this way the marriage campaign was similar to the early Pride marches in Johannesburg, where a coherent political consciousness and concern was able to form within and between many different communities in the city. This concern was for one final push to achieve legal equality. Yet second, this section will also show how both the mechanisms to achieve the legal right of same-sex marriage and, intrinsically, the desire to make visible the needs of queer groups to wider society ended up galvanising sustained homophobic rhetoric against queers on a scale never before witnessed in the country.

To understand the importance of the same-sex marriage campaign to activist in South Africa – and later, to understand the passion with which it was opposed – it becomes necessary to look again at the transition to democracy in the country in the early 1990s. As the discussion above has already highlighted, the placing of sexual equality on the national agenda through an event such as Pride was fraught with the possibility of a very public homophobic backlash. However, other methods of gaining political and legal awareness of the needs of queer groups proved far less dangerous – and in many ways, far more successful. In 1994 the National Coalition for Lesbian and Gay Equality (NCLGE – later Equality Project) was formed to help coordinate lobbying for the inclusion of a sexual equality clause in the new constitution. Strategically, this group was able to develop some key discourses that had emerged after the unbanning of the ANC. As Hoad (1999) has explored, ideas of equality, rather than minority rights, were central to the eventual success of the campaign. The history of South Africa meant that minority rights would prove problematic, considering the country's long legacy of minority white rule. The history of the country also meant that so long as sexuality concerns were framed around equality in opposition to discrimination, they stood a good chance of being accepted. The new South Africa that was being created in those years was after all a country founded on a deep and long standing revulsion towards any form of discrimination (Botha and Cameron 1997).

The enshrining of the sexual equality clause in the constitution did not, however, occur without any opposition. Christian groups including the African Christian Democratic Party (ACDP) and the then Western Cape Premier, Peter Marais, both argued against its inclusion (Cock 2005). These negative views also seemed to be echoed by a significant sector of the wider public. An unpublished 1995 report discussed by Jacklyn Cock (2005) suggested that in the years immediately after the fall of apartheid, nearly 50 per cent of the population of South Africa would rate themselves as 'anti-gay'. A further 44 per cent were against giving queers equal rights in the new constitution (Charney 1995). The overall effect of such views was however limited. The inclusion of sexual equality in the constitution was not a process particularly open to extensive public participation (Lind 2005). Despite widespread societal misgivings, the sexual equality clause was successfully included paving the way for a succession of legal challenges to laws seen as unconstitutional by discriminating against queer men and women. In 1997, anti-sodomy laws were declared unconstitutional by the High Court of the Western Cape. In 1998, the Constitutional Court in Johannesburg upheld this ruling. In 1999, the Constitutional Court upheld previous provincial rulings that the Aliens Control Act (1991) was unconstitutional in its denial of immigration rights to bi-national same-sex couples. Despite a government appeal, the Constitutional Court upheld the ruling in 2000. In 2002, the Constitutional Court upheld the Pretoria High Court's ruling, which declared sections of the Child Care Act and Guardianship Act (1983) unconstitutional, allowing same-sex couples to adopt children.

By 2003, the last vestiges of the apartheid state's paranoia towards homosexuality, so heightened after the Forest Town raid a quarter of a century before (chapter 2), were finally being done away with. It therefore also appeared that the groundwork had been set for the last and perhaps most difficult change in South African law. In July of that year, Equality Project began holding workshops around the country aimed at stimulating grass-roots support among queer individuals for a change in the law to allow same-sex couples the right to marry. In July 2004, Equality Project along with 18 other co-applicants asked the High Court of Johannesburg to declare the common law definition of marriage and legally defined marriage formulas as unconstitutional. As Equality Project argued, the effect of those two provisions was to expressly prohibit same-sex couples from entering into the institution of civil marriage (Equality Project 2004). On 1 December 2005, the Constitutional Court ruled that both the country's common law definition of marriage and the formula of the marriage vow in the Marriage Act (1961) were inconsistent with the constitution and therefore invalid. The South African Parliament was given twelve months to alter the existing laws relating to marriage. The logic for this period of grace was a belief that the government itself would be capable of deciding how exactly to enact a change in law. As a note from the Court explained, it was held that:

given the great public significance of the matter, the deep sensitivities involved and the importance of establishing a firmly-anchored foundation for the achievement of equality in this area, it was appropriate that the legislature be given an opportunity to map out what it considers to be the best way forward. (Constitutional Court 2005: 4)

If however Parliament failed to alter these laws the Constitutional Court would use its power to automatically read the words 'or spouse' into the section of the Marriage Act which currently simply read 'wife'. In effect, this meant that by 1 December 2006 at the latest, same-sex marriage would be made entirely legal in South Africa. The question for the government was therefore not whether same-sex marriage should be made legal, but rather how same-sex marriage should be made legal. Yet as debate began again in 2006, this distinction seemed for many to become progressively more irrelevant.

Indeed, it did not take long for groups opposed to same-sex marriage to start publicly and fervently airing their views. Just one day after the Constitutional Court judgment the *Mail and Guardian Online* reported that the South African Council of Muslim Theologians had quickly moved to condemn the judgment. As this blunt (and in many ways, perversely contradictory) comment from the council's KwaZulu-Natal branch neatly summed up:

> It is ironic that the December 1 judgment of the Constitutional Court recognising same-sex marriages coincides with World AIDS Awareness Day – a day that bears testimony to the scourge of sexual promiscuity. (*Mail and Guardian Online* 2006)

Among several other organisations, including representatives from the South African Council of Churches, representatives at the Catholic Bishops Conference of Southern Africa, the ACDP and the Congress of Traditional Leaders of South Africa, the view that same-sex marriage was amoral and disrespectful would continue to fester for the next six months. Indeed the degree of displeasure about the oncoming law change became so severe that the government itself began to openly acknowledge that any new legislation was going to further polarize the country. Speaking to the *Cape Argus* in early August, the Deputy Justice Minister Johnny de Lange admitted, or rather foretold, a feared outcome of any new legislation: 'There are many issues in our society that actually can widen the social cohesion deficit in the country. This is one of them' (Quintal 2006). By early September the Civil Union Bill was finally tabled to Parliament. From this period until the end of November, South Africans would become embroiled in a national discussion not only about the possible merits or disadvantages of the bill, but also about the very foundations of what their constitution actually meant for them.

Queer groups and their supporters however, after reading the proposed Bill were plainly focused on one goal. While wide-ranging and clearly an attempt on the part of the government to fulfil the mandate of Constitutional Court judgment, there was strong feeling from many within the queer community and beyond that the Bill did not actually go far enough. Specifically, great concern was expressed about the creation of 'civil unions' for queer couples as opposed to 'same-sex marriage'. For example, the South African Human Rights Commission (HRC) stated in its submission to the Home Affairs Committee the following:

> The constitutional court decided to allow parliament to determine the legislative changes that would be necessary to cure the defects in the Marriage Act. In many ways the current Civil Union Bill does not give effect in the commission's view to what the court intended. Rather, the Bill appears to give effect to what was argued by the State in opposition to the recognition of same-sex marriages. *This is undermining of the court and offensive to gay people* . . . Firstly, a separate system of union is created for same-sex couples. This gives effect to the offensive doctrine of *separate but equal*. The separate register that will be created to record civil unions further enforces this. (Human Rights Commission 2006: 3, emphasis in original)

And as the Joint Working Group made up of fifteen organisations including Triangle Project stated:

> A civil partnership is effectively a *separate* institution from marriage. This is clearly evidenced by the face that lesbian and gay people are required to register a civil partnership on a separate register to heterosexuals . . . In our view the Civil Union Bill is objectionable both in what it does and what it fails to do: first, it entrenches inequality between lesbian/gay and straight people in our law which is indefensible; secondly, it fails to accord lesbian/gay people the full recognition demanded by the Constitution for their relationships. (Joint Working Group 2006: 3, emphasis in original)

The focus here was evidently on associating same-sex marriage with the broader principles of the constitution. As already noted, the sexuality clause in the constitution had itself come about because queer activists had been successful at linking sexuality-based discrimination with race-based discrimination. The idea of equality, in the face of an entrenched but waning apartheid system, was and has remained a marker of the new South Africa. For many queer activists in South Africa and their supporters there was a strongly held belief that anything less than marriage would not and could never be equal.

While an extraordinarily vigorous debate played out within the country's media, effort was also spent attempting to galvanise grass-roots groups. Within Cape Town this was mainly due to the efforts of Triangle Project in energising the city's queer communities. As mentioned earlier, this signalled a shift in the direction of the organisation, moving from social support into more overtly political projects. Outreach workers and senior staff appeared regularly on local and national radio programmes and were quoted in local, national and international publications. Triangle staff along with volunteers drawn from across different communities held pickets outside the Parliament building proclaiming the constitutional right for queers to be granted same-sex marriage (Da Costa 2006; Harrison 2006, Waxa 2006). While support on the part of an organisation such as Triangle Project during such a contentious period is not by itself surprising, the degree to which they became involved perhaps is. This was due to two factors. First, Equality Project, the organisation which had helped organise nearly all campaigns to change South African laws that discriminated against queer groups over the preceding fifteen years, had ceased to operate. This resulted in Triangle Project, as one of the supporters and co-signatories of the original application to the Constitutional Court, having to take over an advocacy role left vacant by the sudden demise of Equality Project. Second, Triangle Project now had an ever-growing number of volunteers and supporters from across different communities which could be called on to help raise awareness about the issues of the debate. As described earlier in this chapter, the developments over the previous two decades had led the organisation to try many different ways to access and socially and medically service queer groups. While, no doubt, many of these individuals may have become involved without the direct collaboration and endorsement of Triangle Project, their knowledge of the debate and their willingness to get involved was enhanced by their relationship with the organisation. Especially for queer black African and, to a lesser extent, coloured men in the city, this provided a new platform and a mechanism with which they could become visible to the wider community. As Glenn De Swardt, the Health and Research Manager of the organisation explained, specifically about the way the organisation was able engage with queer groups around this issue:

[after becoming more visible in profile after the decline of Equality Project we] forged a closer link between us and some of the populations we were servicing in the marginalised areas, previously marginalised areas, like the townships, where we were able to call on – no, activate groups in different township areas to actually come and protest with us and toyi-toyi[6] outside Parliament, which was, I think, quite empowering for them. They benefited from that . . . They were suddenly made very, very visible. They were suddenly put in the spotlight. They were taken to public hearings where they could speak to a portfolio committee on a government department, and their voice was given equal space to the leader of a political party in South Africa. I think that that's quite an empowering experience. And also we made great efforts to communicate with our constituents, if we can call them that, and to keep them informed. And obviously that was also driven by our need to have their – to keep them supporting us, but I think that we were seen to be fighting for a communal issue that affects everybody. GLENN DE SWARDT

The same-sex marriage campaign in Cape Town, through the efforts of Triangle Project, was successful in making visible groups of queer men that otherwise remain partially invisible in public and political discourses about queer sexuality. At the same time, it helped strengthen a feeling of solidarity between queer groups in the city. The marriage campaign was such a monumental issue in South Africa during 2006 that it was able to engage the interest not only of heterosexual society but also of many different groups of queer individuals. For Triangle Project, the same-sex marriage campaign therefore also helped raise, yet again, the profile of the organisation in the former townships:

> *I think that that sense of solidarity has been sustained. I certainly see more people popping in, more relaxed kind of interactions . . . coming in here and using the space, more with a sense of, 'OK, I belong here, this is also my space', which is quite nice.* GLENN DE SWARDT

By shifting its focus to deal also with more political issues, Triangle Project has become even more adept at accessing and working with black African queer communities in the former townships. The needs of queer men from former townships, as this book has already illustrated, are in many ways considerably different to those affecting more affluent groups in more formalised parts of the city. Rather than stay focused solely on issues of social and medical support, Triangle has instead broadened its scope to engage with the needs of black African queer men to confront negative societal perceptions. The debates around the same-sex marriage campaign allowed black African queer men and Triangle Project to raise the level of debate about queer sexuality both in Parliament and in the townships. By so doing it has been able to further earn the respect and trust of these men.

Yet on the other hand, the same-sex marriage campaign has also again highlighted widespread and deeply felt concern towards issues of queer sexuality and therefore, because of the unique way in which changes in the law to protect queers occurred, grievances among different communities about the constitution. While organisations such as Triangle Project were advocating that the Civil Union Bill should allow for same-sex marriage rather than merely same-sex civil unions, a significant proportion of the rest of the country was advocating that there should be no same-sex unions at all. Indeed, the South African Parliamentary Monitoring Group (PMG)[7] recorded widespread and sustained antagonism towards the Civil Union Bill at all provincial meetings set up to explore it. These meetings were initiated by the Department of Home Affairs (who were overseeing the Bill) and held throughout the country with the intention of engaging the public on issues of same-sex unions and to solicit opinion about the proposed bill.[8] Instead these meetings seemed to offer a very different opinion of the

South African population – of a people being given a rare public opportunity to question both the concept of same-sex unions and the new rights that had been granted to queer communities as a result of the constitution.

For example during the Gauteng meeting, those opposed to the bill on cultural or religious views proposed that the South African constitution actually be amended to 'protect' the sanctity of marriage as being between a man and a woman. In Limpopo, similar groups put forward the same proposal, together with the belief that a national referendum should be held and that the government fight 'moral decay'. In Mpumalanga groups argued that 'young boys and girls should be taught about African culture' and that more time was needed on the Civil Union Bill for thorough consultation. In KwaZulu-Natal it was again proposed that a constitutional amendment be instituted to protect the 'traditional institution of marriage' as that between a man and a woman. The same was suggested in the Eastern Cape along with the belief that a referendum should be held on the Bill and that 'Homosexuals should seek help from the church so they can change'. Similar groups in the Northern Cape and the Western Cape also proposed a national referendum and a change to the constitution to protect marriage as being between a man and a women.

By comparison, queer groups who also attended the meetings argued that the Civil Union Bill simply did not go far enough in promoting equality. At every single provincial meeting in the country queer groups argued that queer individuals required the same treatment as heterosexual individuals in their right to marry.

A very striking contrast therefore emerged from these meetings. From one perspective, it appeared (somewhat ironically) that there was widely held opinion that the government's proposed Civil Union Bill should be rejected. South Africa might therefore be the first country in the world to have united conservative religious groups and queer groups around a proposed rights-based Bill. But the provincial meetings also highlighted just how divided South African society remains around issues of sexuality-based equality. Arguments as to the 'sanctity' of marriage, the importance of 'tradition' and, at an extreme, the very 'unAfricanness of homosexuality' were juxtaposed with groups who argued that anything less than full same-sex marriage rights was a form of prejudice equal to apartheid discrimination. While South Africa had, over a decade earlier, enshrined the protection of queer groups in the constitution, a significant number in the country remained at best wary and at worst hostile towards any idea of queer equality.

As just one further example, the following excerpt from the *Sunday Times* reported what happened at the Department of Home Affairs' New Hanover meeting in KwaZulu-Natal:

From Muslim clerics to Catholic nuns to traditional Zulu leaders and Christian fundamentalists, they all spoke with one voice, a resounding 'no' to the Bill. Ironically, their rejection of the Bill is shared by the very people it is aimed to serve – the gay community. Outnumbered but not outsmarted, a small group of black lesbians, mostly representing the Pietermaritzburg Gay and Lesbian Network, defended themselves. For them the Bill is unacceptable not because it recognises their right to marriage but because it recognises it separately from heterosexuals . . . Nozizwe Shezi, a member of the nearby Mshwati community: 'Where will gay people get children from? I am a Zulu woman; for me to exist there were my parents, a man and a women. Now why do we need to change this order? A snake never gave birth to a human being. Why do we start this thing of a woman and a woman?' said Shezi to huge applause from the crowd. (Ntshingila 2006)

Such heightened feelings were also noted amongst queer groups in the Cape Town townships, where homophobia has remained pervasive. As these quotations highlight, there remains an acknowledgement that the ideals laid down in the constitution remain offset by communities still trying to comprehend the idea of sexuality equality. For some, there was a feeling that the same-sex marriage campaign had only increased feelings of ill-will towards queer individuals.

They [the community] still believe that it's not on [having same-sex marriage]. The same way they still believe that – the straight people, that it's not on to be gay in the first place, but because the constitution is there to back us up, then they see that they have no way out because we are not doing anything wrong. So I wouldn't say they accept it. They have to live with it because it's like that . . . especially in the Christian community. They would say, 'Ah, we don't know what this government is doing. How can they, the South African government –' That of – That what the people on the ground, that's what they are saying, that, 'We just don't understand this. First of all, these people –' us, that is, gay people, homosexual people – 'we accepted – I mean, they've got their rights in the constitution. Now they are legalising them to get married. What's going on? Where is Thabo Mbeki and Mandela taking us?' You see? XOLO/40

Just with the same-sex marriages, things have kind of hyped up and you can really see people where they are at, whereas in the past it was very quiet, but now it's almost like you're seeing new faces added to the kind of crowd that's, that's homophobic. LEE/25

By the end of November 2006, it was also clear that such feelings on the part of a particular sector of South African society were not going to be placated. A major oversight – and, as it turned out, a major problem – of the public provincial meetings held to discuss the proposed Civil Union Bill was that some variation of 'same-sex marriage' had to be written into law by 1 December that year. The Constitutional Court a year previously had already stated this. Yet the public meetings failed, it seemed, to acknowledge this point. In so doing, a sector of the public took it upon themselves to make their feelings heard about same-sex marriage in a way that called into question a key belief in the new constitution but that would make no difference to the final outcome of the deliberations. By comparison, queer groups were successful in pressuring the government to allow same-sex couples to marry. A last minute change was therefore implemented in the Civil Union Bill that would allow same-sex couples to call their union a marriage, rather than merely a civil union. It was voted on and passed by the National Assembly on 14 November and by the National Council of Provinces two weeks later. It was signed into law on 30 November, one day before the 1 December deadline.

Conclusion

As discussed in chapter 1, South Africa is only the fifth country in the world to have legalised same-sex marriage. It is also a country which, as discussed in chapter 2, is frequently represented as a liberated and accepting country for queer individuals. It is represented internationally as having one of the most liberal constitutions in the world. Cape Town in particular is now viewed as a city where queer sexuality is not only accepted, but also celebrated. Pride parades and the city's internationally famous gay village have helped propel the city into the upper ranks of international gay tourist destinations. For business and specifically tourism, there has been a conscious effort to brand the city in this way. For the ANC, the successful representation of Cape Town and wider South Africa have helped to legitimate its strategies post-apartheid and to favourably contrast the current government with the old regime. Nationally and internationally therefore, the marriage campaign has made it possible for the new government and the new nation of South Africa to position itself within a broader rights-based movement to end discrimination and hence to associate with other states committed to the same cause. As Nosiviwe Mapisa-Nqakula, the Minister of Home Affairs, was quoted as explaining:

> The Bill of Rights requires of us that we extend equality throughout our nation. It is not just same-sex couples who are excluded from fundamental rights; many under apartheid experienced similar discrimination because of the state's failure to recognise customary marriages. . . . It is this legacy that the constitution instructs us to redress . . . If we are to all accept the responsibility we have to our democracy, we must be willing to consider the needs, the rights and the dignity of others. (Mapisa-Nqakula 2006)

This is the new South Africa. It is a South Africa where tolerance prevails: acceptance of difference is acceptance of oneself in the new political system. It is a South Africa that prides itself on its new democratic and liberal institutions. It is a South Africa in which queer individuals are able to live freely. Indeed, the language used by the minister bears more than a passing resemblance to statements made throughout the same-sex marriage campaign by queer activists, as outlined above.

Queer activists and ANC officials alike are therefore rightly proud that the law now protects the rights of queer individuals to lead open and free lives and to marry. Yet these are also achievements that bear very little relation to the current lives of vast numbers of queer men and women in the country. For many, South Africa is still a country where being visibly queer is a very dangerous activity. The law may be on your side, but that seems of little consequence if, as shown in chapter 4, you can not rely on the police to protect your rights. The opinions expressed by politicians, religious groups, traditional groups and individuals in the national press and at provincial meetings give testament to the pervasiveness of this problem for queer individuals. Representation of the country nationally and internationally as liberated and accepting towards queer groups through the granting of sexual citizenship rights does not bear much relation to the actual lives of many queers in the country.

It might be easy therefore to argue that the needs and opinions of those queer individuals who continue to face homophobia within their communities have simply been made invisible by the same-sex marriage campaign and by other organisations or events that are meant cater for queers in the new South Africa. Yet to adopt this view would be to belittle the continued attempts by groups such as Triangle Project and Cape Town Pride who endeavour to service the needs of all groups in the city. Triangle has attempted to access and service black African queer men by re-imagining a very Western model of service provision for new settings. By so doing it has also been able to engage more fully with queer men from this community around the marriage campaign, helping give them a political voice with which to speak. Pride in Cape Town has continually made efforts to represent those who would otherwise remain partially invisible at events aimed at a very different community of queer men.

Yet there remains the constant problem of queer invisibility. Indeed, what has come to define Triangle Project and Cape Town Pride are their continued attempts not to let those who, within popular representations of queer social space, appear less visible stay less visible. While by no means always successful, there have been growing attempts to re-evaluate the needs and wishes of different identities. Unilateral ideas of service provision or celebration or politics need not to wholly and completely subsume difference. The increasing coming together of communities may therefore also offer groups the possibility of self-reflection and self-reflexivity. As such, the hope remains that what is made queerly visible in the political realm can have a positive outcome on those with the greatest abilities to organise and co-ordinate events, as difference itself becomes further understood.

The same-sex marriage campaign therefore highlights not only a real achievement in furthering the rights of queer individuals in the country but also an achievement which is yet to occur, or which will perhaps always remain in the process of becoming. This will be the continued need to foster awareness of the day-to-day needs of queers in environments where recourse to the law remains fragile or elusive. For their own benefit, these groups will have to be kept politically and socially visible not just among wider society but also among other groups of queers so that no one group is able to dictate the needs of any other. The same-sex marriage campaign's real achievement may therefore be yet to fully emerge.

Chapter Seven

The Costs of Invisibility

Introduction

This book has focused itself around the concept of queer visibility as a way of exploring the connections between queer identities and particular spaces. Queer visibility is therefore a lens through which it becomes possible to see the opportunities available to diverse groups of queer men to express difference. As a concept it therefore is more than simply concerned with the public performance of sexuality; it is also concerned with understanding how different groups were shaped by factors that then led to different opportunities to become visible. In that sense, it is as much interested with what goes on 'behind' the public performance as it is with the public performance itself. It consequently allows for a broader unpacking of the factors that go to shape variants of a heterosexual/homosexual binary than is normally allowed in explorations that can remain tied knowingly or inadvertently to 'the closet'. As such it is hoped that it will also further develop cross-community research. As discussed in chapter 1, 'the closet' can be criticised for its inapplicability in spaces not traditionally explored in sexuality studies. For example, 'the closet' as a linguistic and spatial metaphor may end up being seen as less relevant for individuals and communities where a linear 'coming out' does not form the most pivotal moment(s) in a queer life; where a particular manifestation of the heterosexual/homosexual binary tied to a particular historically regulated gendered binary does not play such a central role in a society; where the pressing needs of daily survival result in social configurations between queer and heterosexual somewhat removed from particular binary ideals associated with 'the closet'; or where unilateral methods deployed towards sexual equality may not actually be beneficial to large numbers of queers due to the liberationist binaries created around openness/equality and secretiveness/inequality. Nevertheless, while this book has not disagreed with the stance that 'the closet' need not be the defining element of queer life in many communities (see also Hayes 2000 and Ross 2005), it has argued still that what it does teach us about how heteronormative regulation more broadly can function is vital when exploring any community where some form of heterosexual/homosexual binary prevails. (As pointed out earlier, the 'heterosexual/homosexual binary' refers to a naming and compartmentalisation of difference, not to the necessary existence of 'homosexuality' as it related to a medicalised and anachronistic condition found initially in the West.) What this book has therefore tried to uncover is the spatiality of other sexual configurations at the margins of or beyond that offered by some readings of an elite white Western European 'closet', tied, often inadvertently, to a particular, by no means universal, queer subject. It has been hoped that this has highlighted other, sometimes invisible, queer social, cultural and political concerns.

This book therefore set about exploring how different queer visibilities among different groups have been simultaneously possible in one city. By so doing, it has tried to explore how visibility within particular urban communities depends on the history and the geography of those different communities and, crucially, the relationships between them. Concurrently, it has explored how the heterosexual/homosexual binary itself varies within each community, how heteronormative regulation varies, and hence the different opportunities that exist for queer men to become visible in urban space. As such it has also offered a way of breaking down distinctions between 'gay space' and spaces that are not. Different urban spaces are infused with different forms of heteronormative regulation that allow different forms of queer visibility to occur.

This book has also explored how groups remain visible or at times become socially and politically invisible when they interact with queer men from other communities. It asked the question: what happens if people want to become visible, if they want the community to see them, but for various reasons are unable to? How might this be the result of the way different visibilities interact with each other? How might a particular visibility, tied to a particular spatial logic, and political, social and cultural history be able to obscure other visibilities? And further, what efforts have been made to make these men visible again? How might knowledge of different visibilities lead to anxiety and some form of critical reflexivity about a particular identity? The second part of this book has therefore examined the problems of group invisibility in urban space and also the possibilities of renewed visibility in political discourse.

These are the issues that have concerned the majority of this book. The city of Cape Town in many ways has provided fertile ground to explore how the naming and living of race, gender, class and sexuality have combined to offer different queer men diverse opportunities to lead open and free lives.

But it is impossible to talk about queer men leading open and free lives without also examining the impact of HIV and AIDS. It therefore also important to examine how queer men have sometimes remained partially invisible in HIV discourses within and about the region. Because of this, it is also imperative to see how a study of the methods queer men have used to become visible may help focus understanding about the specific factors that may place specific groups at particular risk of HIV infection. As the following two sections will explore, a study of the historical factors that have resulted in different visibilities, together with an appreciation as to how queer visibilities help reflect contemporary queer interactions, could greatly enhance understanding as to the diversity and divergent needs of various queer groups. This is primarily because to focus on visibility is to focus on many of the factors that limit or give opportunity to queer groups to interact sexually and socially in different ways.

While organisations such as Triangle Project in Cape Town, the Durban Lesbian and Gay Community & Health Centre in KwaZulu-Natal, OUT in Pretoria (and more recently the Desmond Tutu Foundation in Cape Town) offer information and health support to queer men and women within their respective cities, very large numbers of queer individuals in rural areas and in other towns and cities remain neglected in HIV prevention programmes. Indeed, large numbers of queer individuals in the afore-mentioned cities also remain in part neglected due to the lack of a co-ordinated response that fully understands the diverse needs of diverse groups of queer men across the country. It is therefore hoped that the information provided in the following section will both assist in focusing attention on queer individuals and offer a useful lens through which to understand their social worlds.

HIV and the Cost of Invisibility

The reason that the sub-Saharan African epidemic has such a potential for changing the whole of society is that it is the world's only almost exclusively heterosexual epidemic. While homosexuality, bisexuality and intravenous drug use are estimated to be the cause of 87 percent of HIV infection in the United States, 80 percent in Europe and 65 percent in Latin America, they account for no more than one per cent of the sub-Saharan African epidemic . . . In sub-Saharan Africa anal sexual intercourse is suppressed as being associated with witchcraft . . . (Caldwell 1997: 173)

It is true that heterosexual sexual transmission – primarily through vaginal sexual intercourse – remains the central issue driving the sub-Saharan

Africa HIV epidemic. It does nonetheless present a specific problem to assume that infection and prevalence rates in the region represent an almost 'exclusively heterosexual epidemic'. It further remains problematic to dismiss anal sexual intercourse as something only associated with witch-craft. Having explored the communities described in this book, such a statement would at best be perceived as a gross generalisation. Indeed, such an epidemiological argument would rely heavily on the belief that there are very few queer men in sub-Saharan Africa, hardly any of whom are having sex. The evidence presented in this book hopefully adds to the growing weight of fact that shows that same-sex desire and same-sex sexual activity have been going on under the noses of epidemiologists in southern Africa for a very long time.[1]

Many early epidemiological studies of HIV infection in South Africa showed that initial infections were taking place almost exclusively among the white queer male population of cities such as Cape Town (Whiteside and Sunter 2000) (see below). While, by the early 1990s, focus had shifted to heterosexual spread and infection among women, it would a mistake to assume that queer men either stopped getting infected or stopped infecting each other. Indeed, the opening up of cities such as Cape Town post-apartheid would surely indicate increased social and sexual interaction between men than might have occurred previously.

By just focusing on the last twenty years, this book has shown that *across the entire city* there have been groups of queer men interacting socially and sexually with each other. These groups have not simply been consistently clandestine. Even the group most at risk of violent homophobia, those black African queer men in the Cape Town townships, had by the early 1990s started to become overtly visible to the wider community. Coloured cross-dressing queer men have a long history of a very visible queer identity dating back to the middle of the twentieth century. White queer men, while always at risk of state censure, were able by the 1970s, to develop emergent gay neighbourhoods. Just because these men failed to register in significant numbers in later epidemiological studies, does not mean they did not suffer from HIV infection. And yet, for many epidemiologists, there has continued to be a sidelining of the study of same-sex sexual activity in southern Africa. For example, the Nelson Mandela/HSRC Household Survey (Shisana and Simbayi 2002), generally viewed as one of the most comprehensive studies on sexual practices and knowledge of HIV and AIDS in South Africa, does not attempt to examine same-sex sexual activity. While acknowledging the importance of men who engage in this activity for HIV planning and aware-ness, it then goes on to sidestep the issue. As mentioned in the report itself, this was in part also due to the structure of the questionnaire administered to respondents:

The design of this household survey has been conceived in order to allow for detailed analyses of the major sub-populations in South Africa, including over-sampling when necessary to guarantee meaningful comparisons (for example, between the different races in the South African population). However, this design and the goal of ensuring national representativeness implies that some groups *that may be of particular interest for the understanding of the epidemic* could not be captured in sufficient numbers in this survey [including] *individuals with homosexual and bisexual practices.* (Shisana and Simbayi 2002: 31, emphasis added)

The report attempts to justify this position as follows:

It must however be acknowledged that similar limitations are encountered by all surveys about sexual and HIV-related risk behaviours based on general population samples in other countries. (Shisana and Simbayi 2002: 31)

Yet this latter clause fails to acknowledge the success of various well regarded surveys such as the National Surveys of Sexual Attitudes and Lifestyles of 1990 and 2000 on sexual behaviours in Britain (National Centre for Social Research et al. 2005; Wellings et al. 1994) and, more recently, Mosher et al. (2005) on sexual behaviours in the US. Each of these studies attempted to explore sexual activities among the general population, further examining factors such as gender, age, ethnicity and the sex of sexual partners.

It is only very recently that medical and health-related studies have given any serious acknowledgement to the existence of same-sex sexual activity among sub-Saharan African communities at all. Epidemiological studies as late as Brody and Potterat (2003) state with a rather worrying degree of surprise that there exists a far higher prevalence of anal intercourse within African communities than previously reported:

Our inquiry into the available, admittedly sparse, published literature suggests that anal intercourse is much more common in the populations living in sub-Saharan Africa than customarily suspected or reported by clinicians or researchers. Africans, like people from the rest of the world, apparently have significant experience with homosexual and heterosexual anal intercourse. (ibid., 434)

Studies in other parts of Africa such as the excellent Horizons studies in Senegal (Niang et al. 2002) and Kenya (Onyango-Ouma et al. 2005) are slowly opening a window into the sexual lives of men who for the majority of the HIV epidemic in Africa have been totally and utterly invisible. Yet as groundbreaking as these new studies are, there still remains overwhelming ignorance about the lives of the majority of queer individuals in the region.

As a recent International Gay and Lesbian Human Rights Commission report points out, it remains the case that researchers into sexual behaviours in Africa are greatly hindered in their ability to conduct meaningful research. Be it through a general unwillingness among otherwise rigorous scientists to assess same-sex HIV transmission or more generalised problems of homophobic stigma faced by researchers themselves, such barriers make understanding and reporting the lives of others a particularly problematic endeavour (Johnson 2007).

The failure to examine queer and broader Men who have Sex with Men (MSM) groups has also naturally led to an inability to understand the diversity that exists among these populations. A failure to understand these diversities means a failure to understand the specific issues that might affect the likelihood of HIV infection. Such a failure limits the ability of those involved in studying or attempting HIV prevention to engineer possible behavioural change. As has been shown elsewhere in South Africa, it is vital to understand not only identities but also the social and place-specific contexts that surround those identities if prevention efforts are going to be successful (Campbell 1997 and 2003).

As this book has highlighted, the processes by which queer communities become visible are themselves directly related to the social worlds that they inhabit. To understand queer visibilities in different communities is therefore also to understand many of the forces that may place particular groups at risk of HIV infection. The next section will therefore set out some key examples of specific issues related to HIV that affect different communities of queer men within South Africa. Drawing on discussions centred on queer visibilities in Cape Town, this section's aim is to highlight the sheer diversity of needs for each community.[2] As was highlighted in the introduction to this book, a key reason for conducting a cross-community study of the city was precisely to expose the incredible diversity of queer groups that live there. It must however be remembered that these examples are not meant to be exhaustive in their range, nor are they just meant to represent the problems of only specific communities.[3] Instead, they are discussed here to exemplify just how multifarious these social worlds are both in the city of Cape Town and also in the wider country.

Queer Visibilities, Queer Diversities and HIV

As previous chapters in this book have discussed, queer visibilities in the former townships are strongly mediated by the continued belief among some that 'homosexuality is unAfrican', or at the very least, socially stig-matised. Both at a state and a community level, this has helped foster denial as to the existence of same-sex desire and limited the opportunities of queer groups to lead open and free lives. It perhaps is therefore hardly surprising that queer men, when already confronted with limited acceptance by the wider community, choose not to compound that experience by disclosing a possible HIV-positive status. Indubitably, stigma, blame and denial associated with HIV more generally also need to be seen to have a direct effect on queer men within environments such as the former townships. As this respondent explains, once associated with HIV (for example, if a lover has died of an AIDS-related illness) an individual not only faces ostracisation from the wider community because of his sexual identity, but also ostracisation by fellow queer men because of his possible HIV-positive status:

> If you tell other people it's going to cause a lot of trouble to you. They are going to [be] isolated from [you] because they are going to think a lot of things about you – about you going to take the disease to them . . . you are going to lose your friends because of that . . . For example you go to [see other queer men] when you enter the place the gay people . . . are going to make some gossip about you. You are going to see they are talking about you. Even sometimes they are going to warn other people 'don't sleep with that guy' . . . because if you have a lover before who had HIV or AIDS or something like that so they are going to think that you are HIV-positive or have AIDS too. Because they didn't know that. They are not doctors. They just judge you have HIV or AIDS or something like that. But they didn't have your result to them. Ja. I think that is totally wrong.   THABO/23

Stigma and blame are further of issue within black African township queer communities especially, due to the specific ways in which queer men have become visible to the wider heteronormative community. In particular, the high importance placed on social nodal support groupings can present specific challenges for successful HIV prevention interventions. As explained in chapter 4, these groupings offer both social support and validation for black African queer men in otherwise often hostile environments. Yet their tight cohesiveness can also result in partner sharing. Such tightly connected groupings – and the solidarity they help engineer – can act as a barrier for individuals wanting to get tested for fear of what it would mean to the wider group.

> If it's five of us [in the group] and [you] came to me as my lover, they're all going to try to sleep with you. You see? Which is, if you've got something or if I have got something, we're going to spread that thing to the whole group. You see? That's what they do, which is really one of the things that I don't like. And that's why gay people, if there's someone, if they heard someone he's got some of friends, he's got HIV-positive, they get scared, because they share people. You see?   BULELANI/32

> People in township, they go, merry-go-round. Whenever you get a man, and then you have to pass it to me, and then I have to pass it to him.   KEVIN/32

A very well known gay person, that people knew, you know, he died of HIV and AIDS and people has never spoken about it . . . people that has slept with him, they are all silent, you know, uhm, they would always come to me, I know they slept with him, [X] has passed away, I said yes I know about that, and that's it.   JAMES/52

The risk for such men, should they test HIV-positive, centres on a fear that they would become socially ostracised from their social node grouping. But even before a test result is known, an individual, should they 'break ranks' and go for a test would end up calling into question the safety of all members of the group. While issues of broader community HIV stigma and its relationship to testing have been well documented in places such as Cape Town (Kalichman and Simbayi 2003; Simbayi et al. 2007), the issue of HIV stigma for many township queer men is doubly problematic due to the huge importance placed on social nodes. These nodes are a lifeline that helps give justification and validation to lifestyles that otherwise, at an extreme, remain negated and vilified. To lose belonging to such a node – to lose acceptance, friendship and support – is a loss many, understandably, wish not to bring upon themselves.

Issues of stigma and blame are also evident among the queer visibilities of coloured cross-dressing queer men in the city. While their social groups need not always be as strongly enforced as social nodes within the former black African townships, there remains evidence that these men (and their heterosexually-identified partners) are afraid not only of HIV infection but also social ostracisation:

There was panic after [a coloured queer man] died . . . So a lot of guys tend to sleep with each other and whatever, so all the heterosexual guys tend to jump from one gay guy to another. And there was panic, because, look – 'Who do we now know who has the virus?' You know what I'm saying? So there was panic amongst a few of them, because of the way they go about having sex.   PAUL/27

Because, at the end of the day, if I'm going to come out [as being HIV-positive], if I'm forcing people [that] I'm HIV [positive], and everybody [else] is saying [they are] negative, negative, negative, I'm not going to say, 'Yes, I am [positive]' . . . Of course the others, they're going to ostracise me subconsciously . . . So I'm not going to allow myself to be put in that situation where the possibility exists that I might, and I might be ostracised at a later stage by my friends who were supposed to be going to be [my] support group.   SIMON/32

Both these issues are also highly relevant to those men who consider themselves to be heterosexual (in possession of a 'straight' sexual identity) and yet engage sexually with queer men. Epidemiologically grouped, rather nebulously with queer-identified men, under the term 'Men who have Sex with Men' (MSM) or 'Same-Sex Practising' (SSP), this group present a specific problem in certain black African and coloured communities studied here. As documented in earlier chapters, this group can often function on the fringes of visible queer groupings, moving in and out of different queer social networks. In some instances, such 'straight' men help give validation and complement effeminate queer visibilities. Yet the comparative invisibility of such heterosexually-identified men in relation to, for example, coloured queer cross-dressers places them in danger of being overlooked by HIV safer-sex messaging and services directed specifically at queer groups. Simultaneously they may feel threatened in reporting same-sex sexual behaviour to health workers or those engaged in the study of sexual behaviours.

Great care must therefore be taken in making visible the existence of these men and the way they interact with both queer and heterosexual communities. Yet such men also should not simply be collected together as one uniform group. While the term MSM has its benefits in removing the primacy of a public sexual identity in the categorisation of men who should be targeted, it can also result in the homogenisation of such men. Just as the diversity of queer groups needs exploration for more effective safer-sex programmes, so too must the diversity of heterosexually-identified men who have sex with queer men be explored. As this book has shown, men who identify with some form of queer identity relate differently to heterosexually-identified men they have sex with in different communities. This is due to the different ways in which the two elements of the heterosexual/homosexual binary play out against each other, the diverse ways that heteronormativity is regulated and hence the diverse ways in which queer visibility is able to manifest. In many black African townships, any form of same-sex sexual desire is still severely stigmatised. While many queer men in the former townships acknowledge sexual activity with 'straight' men, such activity remains poorly acknowledged by the wider community. Yet in several working-class coloured areas, where cross-dressing is a very visible and well accepted form of queer public display, direct and sustained homophobia is less prevalent. In these communities a certain knowledge (although not necessarily widespread acceptance) of sex between heterosexually-identified and queer men is more common. Different strategies should therefore be deployed to make sure that these men's sexual health needs are recognised and catered for. Unlike studies elsewhere that focus on the clandestine nature of same-sex sexual activity, in a city such as Cape Town some queer communities relate to heteronormative society through the acknowledgement of sexual activity between queer and heterosexually-identified men. It therefore also needs to be remembered that it is quite simply insufficient to assume that MSM without a public queer identity will relate to queer sexuality or the HIV risks associated with unsafe sex in uniform ways.

It is subsequently hardly surprising that among many of the queer men studied in black African townships and coloured queer communities (and those heterosexually-identified men that may have sex with them) there remain distinct reasons not to admit to the threats posed by HIV. While knowledge of the virus itself and its modes of transmission was generally very high among those studied (an observation that is also reflected in the wider population of South Africa) issues of denial and blame remain prominent. As many researchers have previously explored, blame and denial are common emotive responses when groups are confronted with the social and psychological stresses associated with HIV and AIDS. Amongst several groups of black African and coloured queer men explored in this book, blame and denial work in ways that are directly related to the way they have tried to become visible within their own communities. Their quests to become visible in heteronormative space present them with distinct anxieties as to how an HIV-positive diagnosis would threaten that visibility – and the varying degrees of social safety they have attained. The impact of such stresses and fears also needs to be factored into the concerns that may emerge among heterosexually-identified men who have sex with queer men in these different communities. Specifically, their varying degrees of willingness to self-acknowledge as having sex with queer men will be a vital factor that determines how best to access these men.

By comparison, groups of men who have been able to associate with a type of queer visibility located traditionally around those identities discussed in chapter 2, in historically far more affluent areas, have by and large a far different relationship to knowledges of HIV and HIV prevention initiatives. While this is in no way to argue that issues of stigma, blame and community homophobia are unimportant, it also seems unlikely that the quotation at the beginning of this chapter was referring to these men as living in a community where 'anal sexual intercourse is suppressed as being associated with witchcraft'. As discussed in chapter 2, many of these men have associated strongly with elements of a lifestyle influenced by awareness of communities overseas after the end of apartheid. However, they were also the first community to be 'blamed' for AIDS in South Africa in the early 1980s. As briefly mentioned above, the very first AIDS cases in Cape Town were reported among white queer men, many of whom had recently returned from overseas (Gevisser 1995; Pegge 1995). Early newspaper representations of HIV in South Africa therefore showed similar concerns to those in the US and Western Europe. AIDS was a 'homosexual disease' that might 'contaminate' the wider (heterosexual) community (see also Raimondo 2003). As the *Sunday Times* reported on 9 January 1983:

> Seven months before he became the first South African to die of the newly
> discovered disease, a Pretoria airline steward – Ralf Kretzen, a self-confessed

homosexual – still handled food on overseas flights, even though he had open sores on his body. (*Sunday Times* 1983)

And as the *Cape Times* reported, as the lead front page story, on 30 May 1983 about the first confirmed AIDS case in Cape Town, AIDS as an outside threat closely associated to homosexuality was a powerful early trope in the city:

> When taken together with a history of homosexuality and visits to overseas centres where outbreaks of the disease have occurred, doctors suspected AIDS. (Molloy 1983)

Not only was the white queer community in South Africa successful at associating with particular Western renderings of a newly forming social and cultural identity, they also experienced similar public heteronormative fears as to the association between that identity and AIDS as were found in the US and Western Europe (Isaacs 1992). Organisations such as Triangle Project therefore become heavily involved in assisting these men, and also made important nascent attempts to help queer men in other communities as well. Yet it is the predominantly white queer community, the one which has most strongly associated with forms of queer visibility that draw inspiration from particular elements of Western metropolitan environments, which also has the strongest and longest cultural legacy around HIV and AIDS. Indeed, as commentators such as Paula Treichler (1999) and Larry Kramer (1991) in the US and Simon Watney (1994 and 2000) in the UK have discussed, the development of sexual identities in such sites in the West are intrinsically bound up with the AIDS epidemic.

At the same time however, this community now faces specific contemporary issues which are also closely related to similar phenomena in certain sites in the West. As several reports now acknowledge, HIV fatigue, whereby men become overburdened with targeted safer-sex messaging, is starting to become a noticeable issue that can affect the efficacy of HIV education and preventative campaigns (AIDS Committee of Toronto 2001; Ostow 2000). This can also be observed as a growing issue in Cape Town among certain groups of queer men. Further, while substance abuse is evident to varying degrees among all social groupings, a small but growing number of men within this community are engaging in increasingly creative methods of drug taking. While methamphetamine (often smoked in a crystalline from and termed Crystal Meth or Tik), MDMA (Ecstasy) or methcathinone (colloquially referred to as Kitty or Kat[4]) have long been used due to the belief that they promote sexual libido, other newer activities are now also taking place. For example, a relatively recent development in South

Africa is the intravenous injection of methamphetamine. This activity, commonly referred to as 'slamming', heightens libido, reduces inhibitions and therefore increases the possibility of unsafe sexual behavior. This activity can also present a risk if intravenous needles are shared. Such activities evidently need to be highlighted when targeting messaging and devising interventions for the sector of this community who abuse substances.

All these activities are however merely examples. They are not meant in any way to imply that all or even large numbers of each community take part in them. Neither should they be seen as exclusive to any one of the communities discussed. By no means all black African queer men in the former townships freely share partners. Neither, as explored in chapter 4, do large numbers of coloured queer men cross-dress. Equally drug taking obviously does not occur among all or necessarily even the majority of white queer men in the city. The social dynamics discussed in relation to any one community here could and do play out in other communities as well. To argue otherwise would be to associate too strongly with the concept of 'risk groups', where group affinity rather than actual behavior becomes a marker of HIV risk.[5] Particularly in a South African context (although clearly relevant anywhere), it would also be to transplant or neatly map 'risk group' to 'race group' – a dangerous and indeed highly unreasonable proposition (Farmer 1992).[6] Instead, this discussion has aimed to highlight how different social and economic power dynamics within each community that directly relate to and reflect different queer visibilities can help augment certain risk factors. For example, the fear of losing a group of close friends and confidants after an HIV-positive diagnosis could easily be seen as a possible concern for any individual, irrespective of social, cultural, economic or political background. Yet the forcefulness with which this fear might manifest and the outcome of such a loss are of specific concern to men for whom social support and validation groups are so vital.

The point of this discussion is therefore to show the *diversity* of dangers that have and will continue to threaten different groups of queer men in Cape Town – and indeed in wider South Africa. Yet it seems very easy for this diversity to be missed, if state officials, health officials and researchers fail to make visible the huge differences that exist among different queer communities, relying instead on a history of generalized and ill-suited epidemiological assumptions about sexuality and race (Kearns 2007). It is quite simply not good enough for epidemiologists or governments or researchers to ignore the existence and the multiplicity of queer identities and their associated visibilities in the region. Using the lens of queer visibility as a way to examine these communities can therefore help expose many of these differences and also help explore the specific factors that may contribute to particular risk activities.

Each of these communities has faced unique problems in being able to lead open lives. Each has in their own way tried to become visible to the wider community and reach a position of safety. These struggles, as highlighted in this book, have taken many different forms and have in innumerable ways been shaped by the racial history of South Africa. Having, to varying degrees, survived some of the most callous and longstanding policies ever instigated by a state against its own people, it therefore seems doubly immoral that the diversity of their needs in relation to HIV should now be kept invisible by homophobia, simplistic homogenisation or blind ignorance.

Rainbow Homophobia, Rainbow Lives

This book has set itself the task of exploring the strategies groups of queer men have deployed to lead open and free lives within their own communities. This book has then gone on to explore how such groups interact with each other, both socially and politically. This book has therefore explored in what ways affinity with a queer visibility requires overcoming pre-existing and entrenched barriers that keep groups invisible. The most powerful of such barriers remains, of course, heteronormativity – the regulative power to normalize a specific formation of (hetero)sexuality over and above of all others through the use of specific renderings of the heterosexual/homosexual binary. At an extreme, when directed and knowing discrimination take prominence, heteronormativity can manifest as homophobia. With such an interpretation, homophobia runs the risk of becoming a violent and sometimes deadly outcome of fear and prejudice. But this need not always be the case. As chapters 2, 3, and 4 have shown, queer groups have been remarkably resourceful, inventive, strategic and pragmatic in being able to engage different formations of heteronormative regulation and in some cases overcome homophobia in their respective communities. South African racial history and apartheid have acted as important settings for these different communities, allowing different groups different opportunities to become visible.

Yet at the beginning of the twenty-first century it is also clear that some communities have been more successful than others. South Africa's history of arbitrary and artificial categorisation of 'white', 'coloured' and 'black African' during apartheid and today the development of its 'Rainbow Nation' have resulted in specific cultural, social and political power dynamics playing themselves out within and between these groups. To explore sexual identity difference along racial lines therefore allows for an understanding of how colonial and apartheid racial classification affected and continue to affect different communities' perceptions of sexuality. Chapters 2, 3 and 4 have each examined the unique ways in which queer visibility was able to develop, in large part as a direct result of the way the apartheid state and earlier colonial racial controls were able to regulate different communities.

Yet this book has also highlighted how factors other than racial classification have been important. Similarities between coloured cross-dressing moffies and black African township men who cross-dress would seem to indicate that the different racial classifications and methods of apartheid regulation imposed on these two groups interface with other considerations as well. As another example, difference between men who associate strongly with Gat parties as a form of social entertainment and those who do not are in part strongly enforced by class differences. So too are the variations between different groups of coloured queer men, only a specific section of which cross-dress.

As discussed in chapter 1, race should therefore never be seen simply to holistically dictate the options queer groups have to become visible. All categories used in this book, be it definitions of sexuality, class, race or gender are quite clearly strategic concepts that help us to explore and understand how difference is itself comprehended. And therefore equally clearly, race should not simply be used to collapse down other strategic markers. But equally, in a South African context, issues of racism and racial classification can not simply be ignored. As the second part of this book has explored, racial classification during apartheid has continued to structure the way different queer groups are able to become visible and how different queer groups are able to interact with each other.

And in a South African (and indeed, southern African) context, the concept of race cannot be disregarded when discussing homophobia. This works two ways. First, racial classification during apartheid helped channel specific homophobic discourses within particular communities. For example, white queer men during apartheid have been shown to have suffered greatly due to their racial position in the country coming into conflict with their sexual identity. Homophobia emerged from the white state, as a 'logical' way of protecting itself – while also perhaps serving as a convenient way of promoting an insidious nationalistic conspiracy rhetoric. Among some coloured communities during apartheid, disassociation from, and scorn of, cross-dressing moffies was in part a result of the middle classes attempting to achieve a less ambivalent racialised class identity. Among black African township men, homophobia emerged most strongly as a result of a sudden visibility of queer sexuality, not possible during apartheid. In these instances then, homophobic manifestations are themselves in part shaped by the particular racialised histories of different groups.

Second, homophobia from many within South Africa today stems from an argument that vigilance needs to occur to protect against queer 'contamination' of different racially-defined communities. In other words, 'homosexuality is unAfrican'. While in part associated with the sudden visibility of queer sexuality post-apartheid among some black African communities, this argument has also developed from deeper nationalistic ideological concerns. Indeed, as the Human Rights Watch (2003) has discussed, homophobia in sub-Saharan African can be viewed as a way of diverting attention away from state failings elsewhere. It is interesting then that several current black African leaders in the region have ended up deploying a very similar argument to that of white nationalistic leaders in South Africa during apartheid. Contemporary leaders in countries as far ranging as Kenya, Tanzania, Namibia, Zimbabwe, Zambia, Malawi, Botswana and Uganda have sometimes used arguments that are eerily reminiscent of those from apartheid leaders who wished only to 'protect' their nation. It is also worth noting that both do so for perhaps more nefarious reasons.

Homophobia therefore, like queer visibility, must be seen to relate closely to different racialised discourses in South Africa. The intertwining of racial and sexuality-based beliefs and forms of discrimination therefore become more apparent. In other words, to discriminate against a group on the basis of that group's sexual desires is also to do so from a particular racialised position. The construction of homophobia within each community explored here is subsequently in part directly related to the way that community was structured by racialised discourses in the country. Equally, as chapter 5 has explored, to be seen to discriminate on the basis of a groups' racialised position is also to do so from a particular interpretation of sexuality. Here, different queer visibilities associated with different racialised histories come into conflict with each other and end up being associated with different forms of racism. Issues of gender identity and different spatial appropriations help to keep groups separate. Whether outright racism is a fair description of the type of social invisibilities that have been evident in the gay village over the past few years is perhaps less important than the fact that the space continues to be perceived as one based on a racist past.

Here therefore, the problems faced by various organisations and events in chapter 6 also become central again. Visible sexualised communities, whose differences from each other were defined by state-imposed racialised guidelines, are now trying to find ways to work with each other for greater success. Race, again, becomes a marker of how groups are willing to perceive each other and how they are able (or not) to work well with each other. The multitude of different strategies deployed by these different organisations and events gives testimony not only to the continued and deeply felt need to find solutions to these problems, but also to the huge problems that persist. Again, it is also possible here to see how 'race' as a category need not be the only way of understanding or of conceptualising the differences between different groups of queer individuals. After all, many of the problems that Triangle Project and Cape Town Pride have had to overcome stem also from economic concerns. Yet the legacy of apartheid means that it huge disparity continues to exist between different racialised communities.

And so it becomes compulsory also to see how the end result of this continued intertwining of race and sexuality, along with race-based and sexuality-based discrimination, played itself out during the heated same-sex marriage campaign. This event deftly underlines two concerns at once. First, it highlights the successes groups have had at attempting to create a broad solidarity among and between different racialised queer communities. As this book as repeatedly shown, groups within each community have had historically different needs along with different perceptions of themselves and/or others. Socially, this can easily result in group invisibilities and subsequent calls of racism. And yet, through the actions of groups such as Triangle Project in Cape Town, a broad consensus was created around the same-sex marriage campaign that helped different communities to see the similarities between themselves, rather than merely the differences. Whether this consensus holds and whether it has any lasting effects on broader perceptions between communities is clearly debatable. But such a concern should not take away from fact that, for a brief moment, communities that historically have viewed each other with varying amounts of mistrust were brought together in ways previously rarely, if ever, possible.

Second, the marriage campaign was able to raise the level of debate about queer issues more generally in the city and in the country. As chapter 6 illustrated, the marriage campaign proved to be such a contentious issue that widespread and heated debate continued throughout the South African winter of 2006. This had the effect not only of helping raise awareness of queer issues, it also had the effect of highlighting and in some instances even galvanising homophobic responses towards queer communities. These responses also perhaps illustrate the result of a country still coming to terms with its new constitution. After all, the sexuality clause in the new South African constitution was only written a decade before the same-sex marriage debate, and then with minimal public participation. It is therefore hardly surprising that groups would take it upon themselves to voice their uncertainty and displeasure at queer equality more generally at public meetings held to discuss the Civil Union Bill. Same-sex marriage, it appeared, was not the only issue on the agenda at these meetings. Rather, what was being debated, and in some instances contested, was the very legitimacy of the South African constitution for its own citizens. At an extreme, this debate was able to manifest around concern as to the possible 'unAfricanness' of the constitution. For some queer men in the former townships, this whole process has gone to solidify opposition to their rights.

The same-sex marriage campaign therefore neatly exemplifies many of the debates that have emerged throughout this book. Race and sexuality work through each other and play out in different ways to allow different men in different communities different opportunities to become visible in urban space. Yet these visibilities are marked by different forms of discrimination, both historical and contemporary. These discriminations are in many ways strongly structured by perceptions of race. Despite nationalist ANC claims and queer activist claims of liberation from oppression and the granting of sexual citizenship rights, the very visibility of queer men post-apartheid is again calling into question where exactly the majority of its citizens stand on issues of racism and issues of homophobia.

Into this mix comes the threat of HIV. For successful education programmes, for successful interventions of any kind, it will be necessary to understand the complex and varied social worlds of queer individuals in the country. It will therefore be necessary for epidemiological studies to pay greater attention to queer groups and the way each has become visible in heteronormative space so as to better understand the health needs of different communities. Concurrently, it will be necessary to see how fear, blame and denial feed into these concerns. Yet also, issues of homophobia can continue to shape the wider fortunes of queer men as well as their relationship to the HIV virus. To fully grapple with the complexity of the HIV epidemic among queer groups, and among those heterosexually-identified men with whom some have sex, will require an appreciation of the true complexity that goes to mark out their lives. Such an attempt is yet to truly begin.

Concluding the Case for Queer Visibility

This book began with a discussion detailing how some fundamental tenets of what might be termed the 'Western queer academy' come up against some epistemological hurdles in the new locations that queer studies and queer geographies are now travelling to. It examined how an inadvertent focus on 'the closet' can end up unintentionally giving primacy to particular sexual identities, cultural practices and political projects to the detriment of others. This can not only lead to the disadvantaging of other groups, it can also forestall appreciation of some of the complexities of cross-community interaction.

Nevertheless, such a re-evaluation should not be seen as a wholesale rejection of 'the closet' either. As discussed in chapter 1, any community where same-sex desire is seen as 'other' means that some form of the heterosexual/homosexual binary must exist. 'The closet' emerges from one particular heterosexual/homosexual binary relationship. Studies that consciously, implicitly or inadvertently focus on elements of 'the closet' therefore help illuminate for us how the regulation of same-sex desire and queer identities occur in particular places. However, such regulation is not universal. Other communities will experience differently other, sometimes vastly different heterosexual/homosexual binary relationships that relate to and are informed by urban space, national space, colonial histories, race-based identities, class-based identities, gendered identities, 'identity congruence', gay villages, global cultural flows, homophobia, rights-based claims, HIV/AIDS and each other in very divergent ways.

As such, this study focused instead on queer visibilities. As stressed in the beginning of this book, both 'queer' and 'visibilities'/'visible' are used here in very specific ways and draw on very particular elements of both terms. This study has not simply tried to transplant the wholesale use of the term 'queer' onto communities in Cape Town. It has instead attempted to draw inspiration from some of its particular uses. Amongst the inequalities, social exclusions and social injustices of the post-apartheid city, queer visibilities emerge as ways of appreciating the remarkably different ways in which queer groups have appropriated heteronormative spaces. In relation to each other, queer visibilities also highlight instances where group interaction creates new invisibilities and visibilities. The very visibility of some groups post-apartheid also offers the possibility of critical reflection on their own identities, possibly 'queering' what they know of themselves in relation to what is now emerging around them. The struggles some organisations and events have had at keeping marginalised groups visible are perhaps a good indication of this. So too, although in a diametrically opposite way, are the lengths some have gone to 'justify' exclusion in a space such as the gay village.

This however, has not been a study that has tried to assume any one visibility can be uniformly mapped onto any one 'race-based' community. It is also not a study that has tried to suggest these visibilities are fixed. Instead, the visibilities described have been presented to illustrate how race interfaces with issues such as place, community, class, gender and sexuality in different heteronormative spaces, to offer different groups different opportunities. The first part of this book went to great effort to show how difference within communities can be represented. Yet, for example, it would be foolish and indeed reductionist to assume cross-dressing forms the only distinction between groups of coloured queer men. Or that issues of representation of the gay village in Cape Town will always occupy much time in the minds of those who do not go there. The factors represented here are meant to show how difference itself can be constructed and actively produced due to many different factors in different spaces.

This study has therefore also adopted an approach that tries to err away from assuming monolithic categories of 'the West' and 'the rest'. As has been shown, there are no universally applicable 'Western gay identities' and neither are there wholly 'indigenous' queer communities in Cape Town. Instead there is complexity and an understanding of difference by different communities. Some of these communities associate strongly with a Western notion of 'the closet' and associated political and social liberation methods, others do not. Yet be it through direct antagonism, resistance or simple awareness of difference, they often rely on each other for their very existence and their very visibility.

The schema involved in a study of queer visibility therefore places what it is hoped will be an important slant on the study of queer communities on different parts of the globe. Being at its core a spatial approach, it is interested in how groups are able to become known about, accepted and visible within their own communities with varying forms of heteronormativity in space. As described in chapter 1, it is concerned first with understanding a particular element of sexual identities: the initial 'whys' and 'hows' that go to inform them. Yet also, it relates such an approach to the way different identities and their visibilities in space interface with each other. Social and political visibilities are therefore inherently relational. To be visible quite often, it would seem, implies letting other queer groups become partially invisible.

Queer men in Cape Town have been shown to exist in worlds where numerous shifting social, political, cultural and economic relationships continue to affect (and in some cases, define) their lives. In a country such as South Africa, issues specifically related to racism and homophobia (and the relationships between the two) remain in many ways deeply important in understanding the way queer men in any community view themselves and other groups. Such diversity therefore requires exploration in a way that respects these men's very difference and the way that difference is reproduced or challenged. That respect will help keep all who wish to conduct such research aware not only of the similarities between men in different parts of the community, the city or the world, but also aware of the changing ways in which these groups relate to each other. Such an approach will help keep people conscious of the needs and wishes of these groups, so that no one remains sidelined, 'closeted', or indeed, invisible.

Notes

CHAPTER 1   QUEER VISIBILITIES IN CAPE TOWN

1 For example, Sheikh Yusouf Al-Qaradhawi on Al-Jazeera TV stated in 2004:
   'But there are strong tendencies in the West to destroy the family. An example
   of this is the marriage of men with men and women with women . . . In addition, several Western parliaments have permitted this and issued laws about it
   so it has won legal recognition. This stands in contrast to Christianity, Judaism
   and all religions.' Quoted in *The Middle East Media Research Institute TV
   Monitor Project* Clip No. 392 28 November 2004. Available from www.memritv.
   org/Transcript.asp?P1=392. Meanwhile in Nigeria in 2006, Minister of Justice
   Bayo Ojo presented to the Federal Executive Council legislation that would
   make it illegal to take part in, witness or aid a same-sex marriage (Amnesty
   International 2006a). In December 2005, Latvia had also made it illegal for
   same-sex couples to marry (Amnesty International 2006b).
2 Speech by President George W. Bush, 24 February 2004. 'President Calls
   for Constitutional Amendment Protecting Marriage.' Available from www.
   whitehouse.gov/news/releases/2004/02/20040224-2.html
3 The decision to focus on male queer sexuality is discussed at the end of this
   chapter.
4 Such a view can succumb to the sometimes dangerous position of supposing
   overt visibility (and at an extreme, 'outing') is always the preferred position for
   queer individuals in society. Such a view is myopic for two reasons. First, it
   can end up assuming that only a particular manifestation of visibility is the
   desired outcome (for example, through the exportation of Westerncentric
   ideas of liberation elsewhere without any concern as to how they may interface
   with local cultures). Second, it can then become decidedly easy to ignore
   or sideline the at times life-threatening dangers of assuming a unilateral and
   one-dimensional 'one-size-fits-all' queer visibility in hostile and homophobic
   environments. See, for example, chapter 4 in this book.

5   It appears that Oswin remains constrained by her choice at first not to explore black African and coloured communities in Cape Town and then to claim that there is no simple resistance to globalised identities in the representational space of 'gay Cape Town'. This is problematic, first, since it forecloses much discussion on how these identities rely on each other to exist, and, second, is therefore unable to see how representations of globalisation affect township inhabitants and coloured individuals on outlying Cape Flat suburbs. This in turn limits an understanding of how representations of globalisations of queer identities by black African and coloured groups will also directly affect the way those in the more formalised city perceive themselves and wish to be perceived. This point is explored in more detail below.

6   As Foucault (1978, 1986 and 1987) and Halperin (1990) have pointed out, sexual activities between men and boys during the Classical Period, while known about by others, had more to do with power status and social position than with *sexual identity* determined by sexual object choice (which today is placed often in opposition to what can be termed 'heterosexuality' through the creation of a heterosexual/homosexual binary). In the pre-modern and early modern periods also, sexual behaviour was not a marker of a person's sexual identity. Instead 'sodomy', while a 'sinful' act, was not a marker of an individual's personality or 'identity'; rather the individual was the 'author' of a morally objectionable act (see for example Boswell 1980). This is, of course, not to say that there were no 'sexual identities' in the early-modern period, but rather that there was a distinct difference between pre- and early-modern legal definitions of sodomy and nineteenth-century psychiatric constructions of homosexuality.

7   Marlon B. Ross (2005) provides a very interesting reading of Eve Sedgwick's (1990) *Epistemology of the Closet*, describing how such a text ends up depending on a particular raced history tied to modernity to justify the alleged importance placed on 'the closet' (either as minoritising or universalising). Hence it obscures all others with different racialised, gendered or geographical histories.

8   Indeed, 'the closet' is also increasingly being called into question in sites of supposed greater relevance. See for example Seidman (2002) and Manalansan IV (1995).

9   As Marlon B. Ross (2005) explains, this is also not to suggest that 'the closet' has absolutely no purchase whatsoever with these different queer groups. (Such a view would be to create an artificial boundary between the West and elsewhere). Rather it is to suggest it is a mistake to assume that an explicit or (perhaps more troubling) implicit one-dimensional elite European–American reading of 'the closet' tied to a rigid heterosexual/homosexual binary and a narrow reading of 'the homosexual' *onto* diverse queer groups with diverse racial and class-based histories is in any way sufficient in exploring their identities and interfaces with each other.

10 A debate well covered elsewhere in geography. See for example Philo (2000).

11 See also Constantine-Simms (2001).

12 As chapter 4 will explore in more detail, there are also distinct problems in assuming a modernist progression away from overtly effeminate gendered

queer performances towards more 'modern' masculine performances. Sexual identity performance therefore is in danger of being read as a marker of modernity. This is clearly decidedly problematic – and doubly so when exploring queer visibilities in Cape Town.

13   See for example, Gregson and Rose (2000) for more on this point in relation to performativity.

14   Both to create 'desegregated' and 'deracialised' spaces. The former referring to spaces where middle-class white groups mix with middle-class black African groups. The latter referring to spaces where black African informal settlements have encroached into 'white areas' but where no social interaction occurs between groups (Saff 1998).

15   See also Statistics South Africa (http://www.statssa.gov.za) for a clear indication along many divergent dimensions of the materiality of contemporary spatial exclusion.

16   As Gillian Hart (2007) has explored through a reading of Stuart Hall's work (see discussion in this chapter) such apprehension can also manifest around perversely contradictory positions as to who is being represented and how their position is understood in relation to articulations of race, class and nation – issues that are reflected in other ways throughout this book.

17   Although in comparison to other cities in South Africa, Cape Town was relatively un-segregated at the beginning of National Party rule (Western 1981).

18   There was, nevertheless, resistance from some Cape Town authorities. In particular the Cape Town City Council refused, during the 1950s, to help the Land Tenure Advisory Board in providing proposals for racial land designation. This was in stark contrast to areas of the city strongly associated with Afrikaner nationalism such as the Northern Suburbs (chapter 3), which cooperated fully with the Board (Bickford-Smith et al. 1999).

19   Although they are also labels that have been strongly resisted by some. See, for example, Western (1981). See also chapter 3.

20   Archive research primarily took place at the Gay and Lesbian Archives of South Africa (GALA), an independent project of the South African History Archive (SAHA) housed at the University of Witswatersrand, Johannesburg. Additional research took place at the South Africa National Library in Cape Town.

CHAPTER 2   LEGACIES AND VISIBILITIES AMONG WHITE QUEER MEN

1   This is not to argue the space is solely populated by white queer men. Chapters 5, 6 and 7 address the issue of community interaction, both within this space and beyond.

2   Father Trevor Huddleston was a member of the Anglican Church and considered one of the strongest opponents of apartheid. Writing in 1956, he describes a view held by some within the Dutch Reformed Church that those who were seen as culturally and spiritually 'advanced' had a mission to 'lead' and 'protect' the 'less advanced' (Western 1981).

3   The idea of giving assistance to groups in need is a theme that continued with the South African Defence Force (SADF) 'offering' 'sexual adjustment' to

queer men during their national service. A harrowing account, based on actual experience, of life as a queer man within the SADF is given by van der Merwe (2006).

4   See for example the work of Bogle (2002) and Gray (1995).

5   These nationalistic fears also manifested themselves throughout the apartheid years in mining compounds, where white families lived in relative proximity to large numbers of black African males (Elder 1995 and 2003). Again, the need to protect white women from these men was crucial if the white nation was going to be protected against the black African 'threat' (Retief 1995). See also chapter 4.

6   Employers would freely fire women if they became pregnant. Further, Bozzoli (1983) has argued that this concern also stemmed from a paradoxical need to maintain support for a racialised capitalist hegemony by placing white housewives in a position to benefit from black African domestic help. This engineering served not only to release middle-class women from domestic labour but also to help preclude the possibility of a politicised and organised feminist consciousness developing, as was occurring in other advanced capitalist countries at the time. This, Bozzoli argues, helped to maintain a patriarchal system of control in apartheid South Africa for far longer and without nearly as much contestation as for countries in the West.

7   As discussed in the previous chapter, 'homosexuality' and 'homosexual' are used here to describe the 'affliction' and 'medicalisation' of same-sex activity and those who identify with it. This is distinct from the broader and more emancipatory use of 'queer' in this book.

8   Initial information concerning South African newspaper articles from the 1960s accessed in GALA file AM 2580. Additional research undertaken at the South African National Library.

9   As would perhaps be expected no mention whatsoever is given to the possibility of a similar 'problem' among black African men (see chapter 4).

10 The most famous example of this law being put into practice – and then abysmally failing – occurred when two men were arrested in a well known gay sauna in Johannesburg. As Cameron (1995) explains, in 1987 two judges of the Supreme Court decided that 'a party' had not occurred when a police major, visiting a sauna to entrap queer men, barged into a cubicle where a couple were having sex, and turned on the light. The two men in question jumped up and ran out as soon as the major appeared. The Court decided that because the two men had jumped apart as soon as the major switched on the light it was impossible to argue that a 'party' (under the *three* men at a party rule) had come about. The accused were acquitted.

11 Similarities can also be found with police harassment in New York during the early part of the twentieth century. As Chauncey (1994) explains, harassment was more important than prosecution for those who were considered undesirable by the state. Further similarity can also be found with the recent activity of one newspaper in Uganda which has taken it upon itself to 'out' lesbians and gay men to the country (Ngubane 2006).

12 For a satirical take on police ideology linked to fears of communism and fears of homosexuality see Sharpe (1977).

13   Simon Nkoli is today rightly viewed as a pivotal figure in the development of queer rights in South Africa. As an openly queer black African man within the anti-apartheid movement he was able to bring together issues of sexuality-based and race-based discrimination in South Africa in ways previously not possible. His arrest and bringing to trial during the famous Delmas Treason Trial together with his honesty about his sexuality helped raise his profile internationally. He remained involved in queer politics, being a key organiser of the 1990 Johannesburg Pride march (the first of its kind – chapter 6) and helped campaign for the inclusion of the sexual equality clause in the constitution. He died of AIDS in Johannesburg in 1998.

14   This is of course not to suggest there were no activists in Cape Town engaged in drawing attention to the similarities between anti-homophobic and anti-racist programmes. The work of groups such as the Organisation of Lesbian and Gay Activists (OLGA) point to this. However, even then there were distinct problems in being able to access and support black African queer groups (Nicol 2005). See also chapter 6.

15   Cape Town tourism website, accessed January 2006, www.cape-town.org/directory.asp?McatId=5

16   The post-colonial imposition of which appears to go somewhat unnoticed.

17   In 2001 the Mayor of Durban, on the east coast of South Africa, came under fire for telling Cape Town it could 'stay with its moffies and its gays'. While the incident proved an embarrassment for Durban, the mayor of Cape Town, Peter Marais, was able to use the incident to highlight the unique success of Cape Town in attracting queer tourists.

18   Perhaps a strong indication of just how powerful this rebranding has been for Cape Town comes from exploring the small number within the city who took it upon themselves to keep the city 'safe' from 'threats' for a short period in the late 1990s. An Islamic vigilante organisation calling itself PAGAD (People Against Gangsterism and Drugs), set up initially to fight crime in coloured areas of the Cape Flats (see chapter 3), started bombing individuals and groups it saw representing 'threats' to the city. The list of targets included moderate Muslims, the *Planet Hollywood* restaurant in the city and a gay nightclub called the *Blah Bar*. The organisation was also accused of an attack on a Jewish bookshop owner.

19   A factor that must also be seen to apply to other communities studied in this book.

20   While De Waterkant remains the focal point and most visible space of queer Cape Town, there are numerous other 'gay friendly' and gay run businesses located near to the CBD and in Green Point, Sea Point and Bantry Bay. These include shops and guesthouses.

21   At a most basic level, the names of some of the establishments in this space show affinity with particular Western urban locations.

22   Links between white South Africans and Europe can clearly be traced back to the first colonialists to arrive on the Cape in the seventeenth century. More recently considerations as to the place of South Africans within Europe came to the fore during the Second World War, when Afrikaners and British debated which side of the conflict they should support. For Afrikaners and (what would

later be termed) the National Party, apartheid ideology was reinforced by refer-ence to German National Socialism. In many ways this ideology proved an important ideological blueprint for later apartheid controls (Dubow 1995; Furlong 1991).

23 An internal report for Cape Town Tourism in 2002 expressly pointed out the importance of attracting gay and lesbian travellers to Cape Town. This report makes mention of the fact that the new Constitution in South Africa, which has prohibited discrimination on the basis of sexuality, has helped further the development of this 'niche' sector. The report goes on to recommend active targeting of gay and lesbian visitors with attractions that have been popular overseas. Cities such as San Francisco and Sydney are mentioned as possible blueprints. (Cape Town Tourism 2002, *Pink Tourism Case Study: Cape Town.*)

24 See also Oswin (2004) for a very interesting exploration and successful decon-struction of these arguments.

25 More generally as well, Afrikaner culture in South Africa is perceived by many as holding largely negative views of homosexuality, especially due to the influ-ence of the Dutch Reformed Church (Crous 2006).

26 Much has been written about these two competing histories. In addition to those titles cited elsewhere, see also Thompson (1971).

27 Neither of course, does one have to be 'ethnically' Afrikaans or English to assume only one particular view. As we will see below, 'GARATH/38', while holding strongly negative views about a particular Afrikaner culture and Gat parties, still self-identifies as Afrikaans.

28 Further, in contrast to the predominantly male space of the gay village, Gat parties attract equal numbers of lesbians as gay men.

29 While it would be wrong to categorise all members of these early movements as opposed to the idea of homosexuality as a distinct political or social identity, it must be remembered that the majority of these groups' members *were* opposed to any form of political action. As Morgan (1996) explains, most individuals were terrified that membership of a political organisation would publicly expose their sexual identities.

CHAPTER 3   COLOURED VISIBILITIES AND THE RACED NATURE OF HETERONORMATIVE SPACE

1 This is not however to say there were no hierarchies based on skin colour. As Bickford-Smith (1990) explains: 'One can say that there was something of a hierarchy of pigmentation, by no means complete, in terms of occupation and wages [within District Six] – where the lighter, in very general terms, tended to be better off than the darker' (p. 37).

2 Black African groups were removed from the District in 1901 (Saunders 1984).

3 Various organisations were set up to confront the forced removals – and later redevelopments. These included the District Six Association, the Friends of District Six and Hands Off District Six Campaign (Soudien 1990).

4 It is also of note that Cape Town City Council was itself averse to the idea of creating exclusively white areas within the District. This lack of will on the part

of city planners (and associated tensions with central government) no doubt go some way to explaining why the removals took so long to complete (Hart 1990).

5 In 1671, 75 per cent of children born to slave women owned by the Dutch East India Company in Cape Town had a European father (Martin 1999).

6 Data taken from Statistics South Africa. Available from: www.statssa.gov.za

7 Data taken from Statistics South Africa. Available from: www.statssa.gov.za

8 Similar issues were raised in the US during the early twentieth century with scientific accounts of the 'Mulatto' population, such as Byron Reuter's *The Mulatto in the United States*. Scientific rationality was used here to show how the biracial body was a very 'peculiar' manifestation, caused by the mixing of two distinct and 'pure' races (referenced in Somerville 1996).

9 For those interested in coming to terms with understanding the forced segregation that was the result of apartheid policies, I highly recommend the District Six Museum in Cape Town and the Apartheid Museum in Johannesburg.

10 As one interviewee explained in conversation about what he viewed as the 'logic' of apartheid control: it was viewed by some white individuals as 'better' to have groceries packed by a coloured individual than a black African individual.

11 A continued fear of miscegenation was also important in these considerations. For example, in 1949 the Prohibition of Mixed Marriages Act was passed which forbid interracial marriages. Then, in 1950, under the Immorality Act, it became a criminal offence for any white person to have any sexual relations with a person of a different race group.

12 As Western (1981) hypothesises, an 'ideal' apartheid planned city in Cape Town would have had coloureds groups flanking black Africans groups – literally acting as a 'buffer' between white and black African communities. However, several factors including the pre-existing location of white groups (who could not be relocated) and economic need hindered this perfected geometry from developing in the city.

13 A better comparison between coloured groups in South Africa and a US community would be that of some Latino communities. These communities acknowledge their mixed heritage but their members may view their community culture as more important in defining their identity than their 'biological' ethnicity (Garcia Bedolla 2005).

14 This chapter is indebted to the collections of GALA South Africa held at the University of Witswatersrand. A special thank you to GALA archivist Anthony Manion, who helped immeasurably.

15 GALA file AM 2709 Oral Histories Collection.

16 As discussed in the chapter 1, 'homosexuality' and 'homosexual' are used here to describe the 'affliction' and 'medicalisation' of same-sex activity and those who identify with it. This is in distinction with the broader and more emancipatory use of 'queer' in this book.

17 Similar justifications and similar outcomes were also evident in Sophia Town, Johannesburg during the period.

18 Criminal gangs were more a form of internal policing within the District than an actual fear for residents (Hart 1990).

19   As Chetty (1995) explains, mocking and subverting the conventions of gender and sexuality were very much part of the ritual of events such as the Coon Carnival. The Carnival was an opportunity to perform and act out personas that were not otherwise acceptable to the rest of society – in this case, white society.

20   Historically, the Carnival took place at New Year since this was one of the traditional slave holidays. The carnival emerged out of Christmas and New Year celebrations in the latter part of the nineteenth century and was in part influenced by visiting American minstrel groups (Bickford-Smith 1995b).

21   The stereotypical image white groups had of coloured groups as drunkards also furthered such an attempt on the part of some middle-class coloured groups. This image, which can be traced back to the colonial period when the Khoikoi traded livestock with the Dutch for brandy, has continued to the present. As Western (1981) notes, it has also commonly been internalised by some middle-class coloured communities themselves.

22   Newspaper records researched at the GALA file AM 2860 Matthew Krouse collection and the South African National Library.

23   However, as Robinson (2004) points out, the removal of economic apartheid in Johannesburg is starting to take place spatially in the built environment (see also Parnell and Robinson 2006). However, even in Johannesburg it is noted that 'Despite the best efforts of the authorities and communities, some elements of the segregated apartheid city are unlikely to disappear, and may well be entrenched through new political and economic dynamics' (2004: 171).

24   The term 'dragging 24/7' is used to denote men who cross-dress continually.

25   Cross-dressing as a visible display of queer sexuality has also been noted amongst less affluent coloured communities in KwaZulu-Natal (Potgieter 2006).

26   By comparison and in contrast, lesbian sexualities can remain heavily stigmatised in some less affluent coloured areas in Cape Town. Research on Mitchell's Plane in Cape Town points to the fact that unlike male queer sexuality, female queer sexuality has not been successful in relating to, challenging or subverting heteronormativity in ways that grant much acceptance or validation (Sanger and Clowes 2006).

27   An individual connected to the gangs informed me that if I wanted to have someone 'taken care of', I could pay an intermediary R2000 (£180). My nominated victim would then be murdered in such a way as to look like they were caught in 'unrelated' gang gun crossfire.

28   The basis for the names of these gangs is today hard to ascertain for certain. However, some evidence shows that the 28s or *Ninevites* developed from a group of men headed by an individual called Nongoloza Mathebula. Nongoloza gave testimony for an inquiry in 1912 into the perceived widespread practice of same-sex sexual activity both in mining compounds and prisons. (At the time, an issue of grave concern for white rulers in Britain – see chapter 5). He notes that sex with other men was common among this gang before they first entered the prison system. The 27s are today believed to have come into existence as an offshoot of the 28s. It is thought that sometime in the early

years of the twentieth century, one of Nongoloza's deputies, Kikilijan, formed the 'Scotland Gang' or 27s to distance himself from the homosexuality of Nongoloza (Epprecht 2005; van Onselen 1985). The 26s meanwhile came about due to interaction between the 27s and the 28s in Point Prison, Durban. Today, it is assumed by some that the old rituals and beliefs of the three prison gangs are being subsumed within modern contemporary gangs such as 'The Firm' or 'The Americans'. Within Cape Town, these gangs have remained largely coloured in composition and draw inspiration from inmates at Pollsmoor Prison in the city (Steinberg 2004).

29   While evidence shows these gangs have been in existence since the end of the nineteenth century, the ending of apartheid has led to increased crime activity on their part. This has in part been due to the sudden influx and competition of crime organisations from Nigeria, Russia and Peru after 1990. It is also associated with the problems of a state (and its law enforcement divisions) going through a period of radical transformation (Redpath 2001a and 2001b).

30   A tattoo associated with the 28s is 'MUMDAD'. For the uninitiated, MUMDAD can be mistaken for a shortened version of 'Mum and Dad'. In reality, 'MUM' stands for 'Men Use Men' and 'DAD' stands for 'Day After Day'. It was also noted that one gang in Lavender Hill associated with the 28s, called the 'Mongrels', have a rite of initiation whereby a prospective member is anally penetrated by an existing gang member.

31   It should also be remembered that just because the popular perception of the 28s gang may be based on sexual activity with another man this does not automatically mean that members of other gangs will not engage in such activities while existing within the prison system.

32   There is also a higher rate of unemployment in these poorer communities, resulting in men remaining in or near their homes. In 2001 Lavender Hill unemployment of economically active individuals was 30.8%, while in Grassy Park it was 12.8%. (Statistics South Africa, http://www.statssa.gov.za, and City of Cape Town website, http://www.capetown.gov.za/censusInfo/Census2001-new/Census%202001.htm)

33   Such representations of masculinity and aversion to visible displays of femininity have also been noted in Afrikaner literature on queer sexuality (Crous 2006).

34   The same can be said for some scholars within sexuality studies who see cross-dressing not as an empowering act, but as a form of false consciousness. Such a view, as described in chapter 1, stems from an inability to see beyond 'the closet'.

CHAPTER 4   HOW TO BE A QUEER XHOSA MAN IN THE CAPE TOWN TOWNSHIPS

1   For example, the 'Black Peril' became associated with miscegenation (chapter 3) and the fear of whites' corruption in unsegregated cities (see also chapter 2). Similar concerns had also been raised in the United States. For example,

Somerville (1996) notes that a southern physician in 1903 argued that African-Americans were particularly inclined towards sexual relationships with white women, something that was 'unique' to their 'race'.

2   The 1865 census found that there were less than 300 black African individuals compared to over 13,000 coloured and Asian individuals and 15,000 white individuals in the city.

3   The Xhosa today are the second-largest black African group in South Africa behind the Zulu. In Cape Town however 2001 official statistics show that over 800,000 individuals list isiXhosa as their first language, while only 7,000 list isiZulu as their first language. (http://www.statssa.gov.za)

4   A small number of 'free blacks' had been in the Cape from the seventeenth century, distinct from the Khoisan. In 1821, they numbered 1789 individuals. This group were subsumed within the coloured community early on (Martin 1999).

5   This area is now located in the central Southern Suburbs of the city, near the affluent historically white Pinelands suburb.

6   This apartheid policy was meant to remove the appearance of political repression and also to reduce financial costs incurred by the state regulating the lives of black African groups. One example of how futile and ill-conceived this policy was: homelands were up to one hundred miles away from where some black African workers had employment. Because wages were kept artificially low for black African groups there was no way they could afford to pay for a 200 mile round trip to work. As Lelyveld (1985) notes, by the late 1970s the state was having to subsidise black African bus passengers to the rate of US$1000 per person per year. This sometimes meant homeland bus subsidies higher than the gross domestic product of the entire homeland.

7   In reality, these lands were all that was left over after the conquests in the late nineteenth century – land that was unfavourable for white settlement.

8   This was especially of concern for apartheid planners in Cape Town, since the Cape itself, with its Mediterranean style climate and diverse scenery, was viewed as particularly favourable for white inhabitants.

9   Although, admittedly, the accuracy of numbers of black African individuals in the city remains questionable.

10   From Statistics South Africa (http://www.statssa.gov.za) and the City of Cape Town website (http://www.capetown.gov.za/censusInfo/Census2001-new/Suburbs/Khayelitsha.htm).

11   Although such history has also been critiqued for its tendency towards the romantic. See chapter 3.

12   Earlier evidence is also apparent. For example, Murray and Roscoe (1998) have documented how same-sex relations among peers and among men of different ages were commonly recorded in many southern African societies during the early colonial period. As they have shown, authors such as Kolb (1719) on men in the Kalahari Desert (today occupying parts of Botswana, Zimbabwe, Namibia and South Africa) indicate same-sex sexual practices were common. These practices themselves ranged from adolescent isolated sexual encounters to sexual acts between youths and older men, to long-term deep friendships and partnerships. In 1883, the Basotho chief Moshesh in South

Africa testified that there were no punishments under customary law for what the European courts would have termed 'unnatural crimes' (Botha and Cameron 1997).

13 While Moodie's work has at times been criticised (see for example Spurlin 2001) for allegedly trying to 'explain away' mine marriages as nothing but an outlet for heterosexual male desire, Epprecht (2004) suggests that some relationships must also have functioned so as to benefit those men with same-sex desire.

14 It has been noted by Sibuyi (1993) that these gender roles were also in effect during sex. For example, wives were never allowed to ejaculate into the boss boy. This may be different to coloured cross-dressing moffie culture, where it was noted informally that the cross-dressing moffie may well sexually penetrate the more overtly masculine male. Clearly however, there was no way to actually corroborate this piece of evidence.

15 See also Foucault (1986) and Halperin (2002) for a discussion of how age produces masculinity, through for example a deeper voice.

16 Linda is not necessarily a female name in Zulu or Xhosa and hence should not be seen to imply transgenderism.

17 As Louw (2001) has pointed out, the term skesana may well be a derivative of zenana, a Hindu term for cross-dressing male prostitute. This suggestion is given added credence when it is realised KwaZulu-Natal province has the largest population of Indians in South Africa. 12.3 per cent of inhabitants in the province are classified as Indian/Asian, compared to 2.5 per cent nationally.

18 Evidence from Johannesburg points to the violence of Pantsulas as well, especially in relation to skesanas (McLean and Ngcobo 1995).

19 Anecdotal evidence suggested that Pantsulas were also having sex with Ivys in Cape Town – although this identity was not related solely to sexual activity with other men. Indeed, it was not an identity presupposed on such activity.

20 Donham (1998) has conducted a groundbreaking analysis of the key factors that led to such a shift in Soweto, Johannesburg in the early 1990s among queer groups with a very different history of visibility and acceptance to those in Cape Town.

21 Sylvester Charles Rankhotha (2005) has provided an eloquent discussion as to why some Zulu queer men in Pietermaritzburg have chosen to cross-dress as a way of expressing their sexuality. An appreciation of heteronormative and patriarchal gender roles clearly plays a part in these visibilities, as it does in visibilities in Cape Town.

22 There had also, obviously, been contact between white and black African queers throughout the apartheid period. There is, for example, anecdotal evidence of black African men forming relationships with white queer men during apartheid and presenting themselves as 'live in' servants in white areas (Krouse and Berman 1993). There is also an excellent account in an article by Lewis and Loots (1995) about the problems and possibilities of a coloured and white same-sex relationship in Cape Town during the 1980s – along with problems of racist and class-based perception from different communities.

23 It should be pointed out that violent crime generally in black African townships and the coloured areas of the Cape Flats is higher than in predominantly white areas. While exact figures that break down coloured and black African groupings in South Africa are hard to ascertain, it has been noted that when coloured and black African groups are grouped together, they account for 93% of all homicides reported in the country, while only comprising 89% of the total population (Masuku 2002). Further, it has also been noted that the top four police zones in Cape Town with the highest homicide rate are the black African townships of Nyanga (135 murders per 100,000 people), Langa (131murders per 100,000 people), Guguletu (127 murders per 100,000 people) and Philippi (95 murders per 100,000 people) (Khayelitsha is not counted as one police zone, but spread between the above areas and other townships). This compares with an area such as Sea Point, discussed in chapter 3, which has a homicide rate of 59 murders per 100,000 people (Schönteich and Louw 2001).

24 Statistics South Africa. Data taken from the 2001 Census on the City of Cape Town Municipality. Data based on those classified as 'employed' and 'unemployed' between the ages of 15 and 65 years old and excluding those classified as 'not economically active' (http://www.statssa.gov.za).

25 It should also be noted that in addition to the factors outlined here, homophobic violence has been seen to result from widespread male disempowerment coupled with unemployment (Wells and Polders 2006). This is also an issue that strongly affects broader gender dynamics in heterosexual relationships (Campbell 2003).

26 While not the explicit focus of this book, lesbians in the former townships have also continued to experience extreme homophobia from certain elements of the wider community. During my time in South Africa numerous women were abused, raped and murdered due to their decision to publicly and courageously express their sexual desires to the wider community. See www.mask.org.za for a list of recent incidents in South Africa.

27 This is obviously not a wholly comprehensive list. Other nodes may well exist elsewhere, most notably in Langa township where anecdotal evidence suggests there are a few queer friendly shebeens.

CHAPTER 5   SOCIAL INVISIBILITIES

1 The 2001 Census shows that nearly 75 per cent of residents in Green Point self-identify as white. Only 11 per cent identify as black African. Just under 12 per cent identify as coloured. Statistics South Africa (http://www.statssa.gov.za).

2 By way of comparison, the total cost of all mini-bus taxi rides necessary to travel from Khayelitsha to Green Point, where the gay village is located, would be approximately R10.

3 See discussion in chapter 3, p. 77.

4 One notable exception to this is the Cape Malay Bo-Kaap area next to the gay village.

CHAPTER 6   POLITICAL INVISIBILITIES (AND VISIBILITIES)

1   The 6010 Supper Club was a social organisation arranged around restaurant dinners. By 1982 it was formalised as a social support organisation and then later that year joined with the Gay Association of South Africa (GASA) to form GASA 6010 (Gevisser 1995).
2   For the problems discussed in this section, the focus will remain with black African men. Clearly some of the problems mentioned in this section would equally apply to some within the coloured community. However the problems discussed here relate far more forcefully to black African queers, which as the previous chapters have argued remain overwhelmingly the most economically and socially disadvantaged group in the city.
3   It was noted that stigma attached to HIV/AIDS often became associated with those who visited the Guguletu office (see also chapter 7).
4   As recorded by The International Association of Lesbian, Gay, Bisexual and Transgender Pride Coordinators. Available from: www.interpride.org
5   Recent events at the turn of the new millennium in these countries have seen at times violent and confrontational moments between queer activists and homophobic groups. Although of course, such endeavours on the part of queer activists also call into questions issues of national politics, transnational citizenship and the influence of intra-national bodies (Stychin 2000).
6   In reference to the South African use of this southern African dance during the apartheid era, that became synonymous with anti-government protest. The term can now refer simply to anti-government protest generally.
7   The PMG provides records of South African Parliamentary Committees. These are available from: www.pmg.org.za
8   Meetings were held in Soweto, Gauteng; Polokwane, Limpopo; Welkom, Free State; Nelspruit, Mpumalanga; New Hanover, KwaZulu-Natal; Mthatha, Eastern Cape; Moses Kotana Municipality, North West; Galeshewe, Northern Cape Polokwane, Limpopo; and Woodstock, Western Cape.

CHAPTER 7   THE COSTS OF INVISIBILITY

1   See Epprecht (1998) for a powerful and damning account of this problem specifically in relation to Zimbabwe.
2   The following section has been immeasurably enriched by discussions with Triangle Project in Cape Town. Their work, along with the work of organisations such as the Durban Lesbian and Gay Community and Health Centre in KwaZulu-Natal has helped open a window into the health needs of communities historically marginalised in the country.
3   It should also be remembered that while these examples will have bearing on queer communities across the country – most notably perhaps around issues of blame, stigma and homophobia – they remain most relevant to men in urban areas.

4   Not to be confused with Ket or K, common names in Cape Town for the dissociative anaesthetic ketamine which is also used recreationally among certain groups.

5   Although as Simon Watney (1996) has also explained, to totally disband the concept of 'risk group' can also have negative effects. As Watney points out, HIV infection is not an 'equal opportunities' disease but does affect some 'groups' more than others.

6   Although this was attempted in the US during the early years of the HIV epidemic with Haitians being singled out as a particular 'risk group' (Farmer 1992).

Bibliography

Achmat, M. and Raizenberg, T., 2006. 'Cape Town Pride was a blast!' in S. De Waal and A. Manion (eds.) *Pride: protest and celebration*. Johannesburg: Fanele.

Adhikari, M., 1994. 'Coloured identity and the politics of coloured education: the origin of the Teachers' League of South Africa' *International Journal of African Historical Studies* 27(1), 101–126.

Adler, S. and Brenner, J., 1992. 'Gender and space: lesbians and gay men in the city' *International Journal of Urban and Regional Research* 16(1), 24–34.

Ahluwalia, P. and Zegeye, A., 2003. 'Between black and white: rethinking coloured identity' *African Identities* 1(2), 253–280.

AIDS Committee of Toronto, 2001. *Research Report: Drug use and HIV risk among gay men in the dance/club scene in Toronto: how should AIDS prevention programmes respond?* AIDS committee of Toronto. Available from: http://cbr.cbrc.net/files/1053799856/gaymen_druguse.pdf

Aldrich, R., 2004. 'Homosexuality and the city: an historical overview' *Urban Studies* 41(9), 1719–1737.

Altman, D., 1972. *Homosexual: oppression and liberation*. Sydney: Angus and Robertson.

Altman, D., 1996. 'On global queering' *Australian Humanities Review*. Available from: http://www.lib.latrobe.edu.au/AHR/archive/Issue-July-1996/altman.html

Altman, D., 2001. *Global sex*. Chicago: University of Chicago Press.

Amnesty International, 2006a. 'Nigeria: same sex bill negates Nigeria's obligations to fundamental human rights' *Amnesty International* AFR 44/013/2006.

Amnesty International, 2006b. 'Latvian authorities fail to protect LGBT community' *Amnesty International* EUR 52/003/2006.

Anderson, K., 1987. 'The idea of Chinatown: the power of place and institutional practices in the making of a racial category' *Annals of the Association of American Geographers* 77(4), 580–598.

Anderson, K., 1991. *Vancouver's Chinatown: racial discourses in Canada 1875–1980*. Montreal: McGill-Queen's University Press.

Anderson, K., 1998. 'Sites of difference: beyond a cultural politics of race polarity' in R. Fincher and J.M. Jacobs (eds.) *Cities of difference*. New York: Guilford.

Appiah, K., 1995. 'African identity' in L. Nicholson and S. Seidman (eds.) *Social postmodernism*. Cambridge: Cambridge University Press.

Armstrong, E.A., 2002. *Forging gay identities: organising sexuality in San Francisco 1950–1994*. Chicago and London: University of Chicago Press.

Ashforth, A., 1997. 'Lineaments of the political geography of state formation in twentieth-century South Africa' *Journal of Historical Sociology* 10(2), 101–126.

Bacchetta, P., 2002. 'Rescaling transnational "queerdom": lesbian and "lesbian" identitary-positionalities in Delhi in the 1980s' *Antipode* 34(5), 937–973.

Barlett, R., 1994. *The making of Europe: conquest, colonisation and cultural change 950–1350*. London: Penguin.

Bath, G., 2004. '"Pink" travel to the Mother City' iafrica.com. Available from: travel.iafrica.com/searchsa/westerncape/324105.htm

Beffon, J., 1995. 'Wearing the pants: butch/femme roleplaying in lesbian relationships' in M. Gevisser and E. Cameron (eds.) *Defiant desire*. London: Routledge.

Bell, D., 1994. 'In bed with the state: political geography and sexual politics' *Geoforum* 25(4), 445–454.

Bell, D. and Binnie, J., 2000. *The sexual citizen: queer politics and beyond*. Cambridge: Polity.

Bell, D. and Binnie, J., 2004. 'Authenticating queer space: citizenship, urbanism and governance' *Urban Studies* 41(9), 1807–1820.

Bell, D. and Binnie, J., 2006. 'Editorial: geographies of sexual citizenship' *Political Geography* 25(8), 869–873.

Bell, D. and Valentine, G. (eds.), 1995a. *Mapping desire: geographies of sexualities*. London: Routledge.

Bell, D. and Valentine, G., 1995b. 'Queer country: rural lesbian and gay lives' *Journal of Rural Studies* 11(2), 113–122.

Bell, D., Binnie, J., Cream, J. and Valentine, G., 1994. 'All hyped up and no place to go' *Gender, Place and Culture* 1(1), 143–157.

Berry, I., 1959. ' "Oh, so this is what they call a Cape Moffie Drag" ' *Drum*, January, 60–61.

Bickford-Smith, V., 1990. 'The origins and early history of District Six to 1910' in S. Jeppie and C. Soudien (eds.) *The struggle for District Six: past and present*. Cape Town: Buchu.

Bickford-Smith, V., 1995a. *Ethnic pride and racial prejudice in Victorian Cape Town*. Cambridge: Cambridge University Press.

Bickford-Smith, V., 1995b. 'Black ethnicities, communities and political expression in late Victorian Cape Town' *Journal of African History* 36, 443–465.

Bickford-Smith, V., van Heyningen, E. and Worden, N., 1999. *Cape Town in the twentieth century*. Cape Town: David Philip.

Binnie, J., 1995. 'Trading places: consumption, sexuality and the production of queer space' in D. Bell and G. Valentine (eds.) *Mapping desire: geographies of sexualities*. London: Routledge.

Binnie, J., 2004. *The globalization of sexuality*. London: Sage.

Binnie, J. and Skeggs, B., 2004. 'Cosmopolitan knowledge and the production and consumption of sexualised space: Manchester's gay village' *Sociological Review* 52(1), 39–61.

Binnie, J. and Valentine, G., 1999. 'Geographies of sexuality – a review in progress' *Progress in Human Geography* 23(2), 175–187.

Blum, V.L., 2002. 'Introduction: the liberation of intimacy: consumer–object relations and (hetero)patriarchy' *Antipode* 34(5), 845–863.

Bogle, D., 2002. *Toms, coons, mulattoes, mammies and bucks: an interpretative history of blacks in American films.* London: Continuum.

Bollens, S.A., 1998a. 'Ethnic stability and urban reconstruction – policy dilemmas in polarized cities' *Comparative Political Studies* 31(6), 683–713.

Bollens, S.A., 1998b. 'Urban planning amongst ethnic conflict: Jerusalem and Johannesburg' *Urban Studies* 35(4), 729–750.

Bonnett, A. and Nayak, A., 2003. 'Cultural geographies of racialization – the territory of race' in K. Anderson, M. Domosh, S. Pile and N. Thrift (eds.) *Handbook of cultural geography.* London: Sage.

Boraine, A., Crankshaw, O., Engelbrecht, C., Gotz, G., Mbanga, S., Narsoo, M. and Parnell, S., 2006. 'The state of South African cities a decade after democracy' *Urban Studies* 43(2), 259–284.

Boswell, J., 1980. *Christianity, social tolerance, and homosexuality: gay people in Western Europe from the beginning of the Christian Era to the fourteenth century.* Chicago: University of Chicago Press.

Botha, K. and Cameron, E., 1997. 'South Africa' in D. West and R. Green (eds.) *Sociolegal control of homosexuality: a multi-national comparison.* New York: Plenum.

Bozzoli, B., 1983. 'Marxism, feminism and South African studies' *Journal of Southern African Studies* 9(2), 137–171.

Brickell, C., 2000. 'Heroes and invaders: gay and lesbian pride parades and the public/private distinction in New Zealand media accounts' *Gender, Place and Culture* 7(2), 163–178.

Brody, S. and Potterat, J.J., 2003. 'Assessing the role of anal intercourse in the epidemiology of AIDS in Africa' *International Journal of STD and AIDS* 14(7), 431–436.

Brown, G., Browne, K. and Lim, J., 2007. 'Introduction, or why have a book on geographies of sexualities?' in G. Brown, K. Browne and J. Lim (eds.) *Geographies of sexualities: theory, practice and politics.* Aldershot: Ashgate.

Brown, M., 1997. *Replacing citizenship: AIDS activism and radical democracy.* New York and London: Guilford.

Brown, M., 2000. *Closet space: geographies of metaphor from the body to the globe.* London: Routledge.

Brown, M. and Staeheli, L.A., 2003. 'Are we there yet? Feminist political geographies' *Gender, Place and Culture* 10(3), 247–255.

Burgess, S., 2002. *SA Tribes: who we are, how we live, what we want from life.* Cape Town: David Philip.

Burrows, A., 2004. *Magical thinking.* New York: St. Martin's.

Butler, J., 1993. *Bodies that matter: on the discursive limits of 'sex'.* London: Routledge.

Byrne, D., 2005. 'Excavating desire: queer heritage in the Asia-Pacific region' Centre for Transforming Cultures, University of Technology, Sydney. Available from: http://bangkok2005.anu.edu.au/papers/Byrne.pdf

Cage, K., 2003. *Gayle: the language of Kinks and Queens – a history and dictionary of gay language in South Africa*. Cape Town: Jacana Media.

Caldwell, J.C., 1997. 'The impact of the African AIDS epidemic' *Health Transmission Review* 7(supplement 2), 169–188.

Cameron, E., 1995. 'Unapprehended felons: gays and lesbians and the law in South Africa' in M. Gevisser and E. Cameron (eds.) *Defiant desire*. London: Routledge.

Campbell, C., 1997. 'Migrancy, masculine identities and AIDS: the psychosocial context of HIV transmission on the South African gold mines' *Social Science and Medicine* 45(2), 273–281.

Campbell, C., 2003. *'Letting them die': why HIV prevention programmes fail*. Oxford: James Currey.

Cape Town Tourism, 2002. *Pink tourism case study: Cape Town*. Cape Town Tourism. Internal Report.

Castells, M., 1983. *The city and the grass roots: a cross-cultural theory of urban social movements*. London: Edward Arnold.

Castells, M., 2004. *The power of identity*. 2nd edition. Oxford: Blackwell.

Charney, C., 1995. 'Between ignorance and tolerance: South African public attitudes on issues concerning gays, lesbians and AIDS' Unpublished report. Johannesburg: AIDS Law Project.

Chauncey, G., 1994. *Gay New York: the making of the gay male world, 1890–1940*. New York: Basic.

Chetty, D., 1995. 'A drag at Madame Costello's' in M. Gevisser and E. Cameron (eds.) *Defiant desire*. London: Routledge.

Chisholm, D., 2005. *Queer constellations: subcultural space in the wake of the city*. Minneapolis: University of Minnesota Press.

Christopher, A.J., 1994. *Atlas of Apartheid*. London: Routledge.

Christopher, A.J., 1995. 'Regionalization and ethnicity in South Africa 1990–1994' *Area* 27(1), 1–11.

Christopher, A.J., 2001. *The atlas of changing South Africa*. London: Routledge.

Clark, P. and Crous, W., 2002. 'Public transport in metropolitan Cape Town: past, present and future' *Transport Reviews* 22(1), 77–101.

Clarke, E.O., 2000. *Virtuous vice: homoeroticism and the public sphere*. Durham, NC: Duke University Press.

Clarke, N.L. and Worger, W.H., 2004. *South Africa: the rise and fall of apartheid*. London: Pearson Longman.

Cock, J., 2005. 'Engendering gay and lesbian rights: the Equality Clause in the South African Constitution' in N. Hoad, K. Martin and G. Reid (eds.) *Sex and politics in South Africa*. Cape Town: Double Storey.

Cohen, C., 1999. *The boundaries of blackness: AIDS and the breakdown of black politics*. London: University of Chicago Press.

Cohen, C., 2005. 'Punks, bulldaggers, and welfare queens: the radical potential of queer politics?' in E.P. Johnson and M.G. Henderson (eds.) *Black queer studies: a critical anthology*. Durham, NC and London: Duke University Press.

Cohen, P., 1993. *Home rules: some reflections on racism and nationalism in everyday life*. London: University of East London.

Constantine-Simms, D. (ed.), 2001. *The greatest taboo: homosexuality in black communities*. London: Alyson.

Constitutional Court, 2005. *In the Constitutional Court of South Africa: Minister of Home Affairs and Another v Fourie and Another, with Doctors for Life International (first amicus curiae), John Jackson Smyth (second amicus curiae) and Marriage Alliance of South Africa/Lesbian and Gay Equality Project and Eighteen Others v Minister of Home Affairs and Others – Media Summary.* Pretoria: Constitutional Court of South Africa. Available from: http://www.constitutionalcourt.org.za/Archimages/5261.pdf

CONTRALESA, 2006. *Submission delivered by Nkosi Mwelo Nonkonyana (Zanemvula!), M.P. General Secretary – CONTRALESA – South Africa at Public Headings of Parliament Port Folio Committee on Home Affairs.* Available from the Parliamentary Monitoring Group: www.pmg.org.za/docs/2006/061024contralesa.pdf

Conway, D., 2004. ' "All these long-haired fairies should be forced to do their military training. Maybe they will become men." The End Conscription Campaign, sexuality, citizenship and military conscription in Apartheid South Africa' *South African Journal of Human Rights* (20)2, 207–229.

Coombes, A.E., 2004. *History after apartheid: visual culture and public memory in a democratic South Africa.* Durham, NC: Duke University Press.

Cope, R.L., 1986. 'Strategic and socio-economic explanations for Carnarvon's South African confederation policy: the historiography and the evidence' *History of Africa* 13, 13–34.

Cope, R.L., 1989. 'C.W. de Kiewiet, the imperial factor and South African "Native Policy" ' *Journal of Southern African Studies* 15(3), 486–505.

Croucher, S., 2002. 'South Africa's democratisation and the politics of gay liberation' *Journal of South African Studies* 28(2), 315–330.

Crous, M., 2006. ' "En eks' dis 'n trassie" – perspectives on Afrikaner homosexual identity' *Agenda* 67, 48–56.

Crush, J., 1994. 'Scripting the compound – power and space in the South African mining industry' *Environment and Planning D: Society and Space* 12(3), 301–324.

Cruz-Malavé, A. and Manalansan, M.F. (eds.), 2002. *Queer globalizations: citizenship and the afterlife of colonialism.* New York: New York University Press.

Currier, J., 2000. *Where the rainbow ends.* New York: Overlook.

Da Costa, W.J., 2006. 'Gays to protest against tone of debate on same-sex hearings' *Cape Times* 16 October, 9.

Davies, R., 1976. 'Mining capital, the state and unskilled white workers in South Africa, 1901–1913' *Journal of Southern African Studies* 3(1), 41–69.

Davis, M., 1990. *City of quartz: excavating the future in Los Angeles.* London: Verso.

Davis, T., 1995. 'The diversity of queer politics and the redefinition of sexual identity and community in urban spaces' in D. Bell and G. Valentine (eds.) *Mapping desire: geographies of sexualities.* London: Routledge.

D'Emilo, J., 1983. *Sexual politics, sexual communities: the making of a homosexual minority in the United States, 1940–1970.* Chicago: University of Chicago Press.

D'Emilio, J., 2002. *The world turned: essays on gay history, politics, and culture.* Durham, NC and London: Duke University Press.

de Villiers, R., 1971. 'Afrikaner nationalism' in M. Wilson and L. Thompson (eds.) *The Oxford history of South Africa, Vol. II 1870–1966.* Oxford: Oxford University Press.

De Waal, S., 1995. 'Etymological note: on "moffie"' in M. Gevisser and E. Cameron (eds.) *Defiant desire*. London: Routledge.

De Waal, S., 1999. 'Marching from fear to fun' *Mail and Guardian* 17 September, 27.

De Waal, S. and Manion, A. (eds.), 2006. *Pride: protest and celebration*. Johannesburg: Fanele.

Deegan, H., 1999. *South Africa reborn: building a new democracy*. London: UCL Press.

Delanty, G., 1995. *Inventing Europe: idea, identity, reality*. Basingstoke: Macmillan.

Derrida, J., 1982. *The margins of philosophy*. Brighton: Harvester Press.

Dirsuweit, T., 1999. 'Carceral spaces in South Africa: a case study of institutional power, sexuality and transgression in women's prison' *Geoforum* 30(1), 71–83.

Donham, D.L., 1998. 'Freeing South Africa: The "modernisation" of male–male sexuality in Soweto' *Cultural Anthropology* 13(1), 3–21.

Douwes-Dekker, L., Majola, A., Visser, P. and Brember, D., 1995. *Community conflict: the challenge facing South Africa*. Ndabeni: Juta & Co.

Dubow, S., 1992. 'Afrikaner nationalism, apartheid and the conceptualization of "race"' *The Journal of African History* 33(2), 209–237.

Dubow, S., 1995. *Scientific racism in modern South Africa*. Cambridge: Cambridge University Press.

Duggan, L., 2002. 'The new homonormativity: the sexual politics of neoliberalism' in R. Castronovo and D.D. Nelson (eds.) *Materializing democracy: towards a revitalized cultural politics*. Durham, NC and London: Duke University Press.

Dunkle, K.L., Jewkes, R.K., Brown, H.C., Gray, G.E., McIntyre, J.A. and Harlow, S.D., 2004. 'Gender-based violence, relationship power, and risk of HIV infection in women attending antenatal clinics in South Africa' *The Lancet* 363(9419), 1415–1421.

Durrheim, K. and Dixon, J., 2001. 'The role of place and metaphor in racial exclusion: South Africa's beaches as sites of shifting racialization' *Ethnic and Racial Studies* 24(3), 433–450.

Elder, G., 1995. 'Of moffies, kaffirs and perverts: male homosexuality and the discourse of moral order in the apartheid state' in D. Bell and G. Valentine (eds.) *Mapping desire: geographies of sexualities*. London: Routledge.

Elder, G., 2002. 'Response to "Queer patriarchies, queer racisms, international"' *Antipode* 34(5), 988–991.

Elder, G., 2003. *Hostels, sexuality, and the apartheid legacy: malevolent geographies*. Athens: Ohio University Press.

Elder, G., 2005. 'Love for sale: marketing gay male p/leisure in contemporary Cape Town, South Africa' in L. Nelson and J. Seager (eds.) *Companion to feminist geography*. Oxford: Blackwell.

Elphick, R. and Giliomee, H., 1989. 'The origins and entrenchment of European dominance at the Cape, 1652–c.1840' in R. Elphick and H. Giliomee (eds.) *The shaping of South African society, 1652–1840*. Cape Town: Maskew Miller Longman.

Epprecht, M., 1998. '"Good God almighty, what's this!": homosexual "crime" in early colonial Zimbabwe' in S. Murray and W. Roscoe (eds.) *Boy-wives and female husbands: studies of African homosexualities*. London: Macmillan.

Epprecht, M., 2001. '"Unnatural vice" in South Africa: The 1907 Commission of Enquiry' *International Journal of African Historical Studies* 34(4), 121–140.

Epprecht, M., 2004. *Hungochani: the history of dissident sexuality in southern Africa*. London: Ithaca.

Equality Project, 2004. 'Press Release: Lesbian and gay people demand the right to marry! Anything else is not equal' Equality Project. 9 July. Previously available from: www.equality.org.za

Etherington, N., 1979. 'Labour supply and the genesis of South African confederation in the 1870s' *Journal of African History* 20(2), 235–253.

Farmer, P., 1992. *AIDS and accusation: Haiti and the geography of blame*. Berkeley and Los Angeles: University of California Press.

Forest, B., 1995. 'West Hollywood as symbol – the significance of place in the consideration of a gay identity' *Environment and Planning D: Society and Space* 13(2), 133–157.

Foucault, M., 1978. *The history of sexuality volume 1: an introduction*. London: Allen Lane.

Foucault, M., 1986. *The history of sexuality volume 2: the use of pleasure*. London: Viking.

Foucault, M., 1987. *The history of sexuality volume 3: care of the self*. London: Allen Lane.

Furlong, P.J., 1991. *Between crown and swastika: the impact of the radical right on the Afrikaner Nationalist Movement in the fascist era*. Hanover, NH: Wesleyan University Press.

Gaitskell, D. and Unterhalter, E., 1989. 'Mothers of the nation: a comparative analysis of nation, race and motherhood in Afrikaner nationalism and the African National Congress' in N. Yuval-Davis and F. Anthias (eds.) *Women–Nation–State*. London: Macmillan.

Garcia Bedolla, L., 2005. *Fluid borders: Latino power, identity and politics in Los Angeles*. Berkeley: University of California Press.

Gear, S., 2001. 'Sex, sexual violence and coercion in men's prisons'. Paper presented at *AIDS in Context* International Conference, 4–7 April, University of Witswatersrand, South Africa. Available from: http://www.wits.ac.za/csvr/papers/papgear1.htm

George, R., 2003. 'Tourists' fear of crime while on holiday in Cape Town' *Crime Prevention and Community Safety: An International Journal* 5(1), 13–25.

Gevisser, M., 1995. 'A different fight for freedom: a history of South African lesbian and gay organisation from the 1950s to the 1990s' in M. Gevisser and E. Cameron (eds.) *Defiant desire*. London: Routledge.

Gevisser, M., 2000. 'Love will tear us apart' *Sunday Times* 2 January. Available from: http://www.suntimes.co.za/2000/01/02/millennium/mil34.htm

Gevisser, M. and Cameron, E. (eds.), 1995. *Defiant desire*. London: Routledge.

Giliomee, H., 1987. 'Western Cape farmers and the beginnings of Afrikaner nationalism, 1870–1915' *Journal of Southern African Studies* 14(1), 38–64.

Giliomee, H., 1995. 'The non-racial franchise and Afrikaner and coloured identities' *African Affairs* 94, 199–225.

Giliomee, H., 2003. *The Afrikaners: biography of a people*. Charlottesville: University of Virginia Press.

Gilroy, P., 1987. *There ain't no black in the Union Jack*. London: Unwin Hyman.

Golden City Post, 1968. 'Screaming "Doris Day" sent to jail' *Golden City Post*, 4 August, 8.

Gorna, R., 1996. *Vamps, virgins and victims: how can women fight AIDS?* London: Cassell.

Gray, H., 1995. 'Black masculinity and visual culture' *Callaloo* 18(2), 401–405.

Gregson, N. and Rose, G., 2000. 'Taking Butler elsewhere: performativities, spatialities and subjectivities' *Environment and Planning D: Society and Space* 18(4), 433–452.

Haefele, B.W., 1998. 'Gangsterism in the Western Cape – who are the role players?' *Crime and Conflict* 14, Summer, 19–22.

Hall, D.E., 2003. *Queer theories*. New York: Palgrave Macmillan.

Hall, S., 1993. 'New ethnicities' in J. Donald and A. Rattansi (eds.) *'Race', culture and difference*. London: Sage.

Halperin, D.M., 1990. *One hundred years of homosexuality: the new ancient world*. London: Routledge.

Halperin, D.M., 2002. *How to do the history of homosexuality*. London: University of Chicago Press.

Harding, L., 2007. 'Gay activists beaten and arrested in Russia' *The Guardian Online* 28 May. Available from: www.guardian.co.uk/frontpage/story/0,,2089687,00.html

Harrison, D., 2006. 'Glenn de Swardt and Randal Serfon of the Triangle Project protest against the Civil Union Bill outside Parliament in Cape Town' Photograph in *Mail and Guardian* 20 October, 38.

Hart, D.M., 1990. 'Political manipulation of urban space: the razing of District Six, Cape Town' in S. Jeppie and C. Soudien (eds.) *The struggle for District Six: past and present*. Cape Town: Buchu.

Hart, G., 2007. 'Changing concepts of articulation' *Africanus: Journal of Development Studies* 37(2), 46–65.

Hartwick, E., 1998. 'Geographies of consumption: a commodity-chain approach' *Environment and Planning D: Society and Space* 16(4), 423–437.

Harvey, D., 1973. *Social justice and the city*. London: Edward Arnold.

Harvey, D., 1989. *The condition of postmodernity: an enquiry into the origins of cultural change*. Oxford: Blackwell.

Harvey, D., 1992. 'Social justice, postmodernism and the city' *International Journal of Urban and Regional Research* 16(4), 588–601.

Hayes, J., 2000. *Queer nations: marginal sexualities in the Maghreb*. Chicago: University of Chicago Press.

Hemmings, C., 1995. 'Locating bisexual identities: discourses of bisexuality and contemporary feminist theory' in D. Bell and G. Valentine (eds.) *Mapping desire: geographies of sexualities*. London: Routledge.

Hemmings, C., 2000. *Bisexual spaces: a geography of sexuality and gender*. London: Routledge.

Hendricks, C., 2001. 'Ominous liaisons: tracing the interface of "race" and sex at the Cape' in Z. Erasmus (ed.) *Coloured by history, shaped by place*. Cape Town: Kweal Books.

Herdt, G. (ed.), 1994. *Third sex, third gender*. New York: Zone.

Herdt, G., 1999. *Sambia sexual culture: essays from the field*. London: University of Chicago Press.

Hoad, N., Martin, K. and Reid, G. (eds.), 2005. *Sex and politics in South Africa*. Cape Town: Double Storey.

Hoad, N., 1999. 'Between a white man's burden and a white man's disease: tracking lesbian and gay human rights in Southern Africa' *GLQ: A Journal of Lesbian and Gay Studies* 5(4), 559–584.

Hoad, N., 2000. 'Arrested development and the queerness of savages: resisting evolutionary narratives of difference' *Postcolonial Studies* 3(2), 133–158.

Hollinghurst, A., 2004. *The line of beauty*. London: Picador.

Holmes, R., 1995. 'White rapists made coloureds (and homosexuals): the Winnie Mandela trial and the politics of race and sexuality' in M. Gevisser and E. Cameron (eds.) *Defiant desire*. London: Routledge.

Holmes, R., 1997. 'Queer comrades: Winnie Mandela and the moffies' *Social Texts* 15(3/4), 161–180.

Howell, P., 2007. 'Foucault, sexuality, geography' in J.W. Crampton and S. Elden (eds.) *Space, knowledge, power: Foucault and geography*. Aldershot: Ashgate.

Houlbrook, M., 2005. *Queer London: perils and pleasures in the sexual metropolis, 1918–1957*. Chicago: University of Chicago Press.

Huddleston, T., 1956. *Naught for your comfort*. London: Collins.

Human Rights Campaign, 2004. *Resource guide to coming out for African Americans*. Human Rights Campaign, Washington.

Human Rights Commission, 2006. 'Submission to Home Affairs portfolio committee, National Assembly on Civil Union Bill [B26-2006]' Available from: http://www.pmg.org.za/docs/2006/061010sahrc.doc

Human Rights Watch, 2003. 'More than a name: state-sponsored homophobia and its consequences in southern Africa' Human Rights Watch. Available from: http://hrw.org/reports/2003/safrica/

Human Rights Watch, 2007. 'Russia: gay rights under attack' Human Rights Watch. 14 June. Available from: http://hrw.org/english/docs/2007/06/13/russia16174.htm

Ingram, G.B., Bouthillette, A. and Retter, Y. (eds.), 1997. *Queers in space: communities, public spaces, sites of resistance*. Seattle: Bay.

Inness, S.A., 1997. *The lesbian menace: ideology, identity and the representation of lesbian life*. Amherst: University of Massachusetts Press.

Isaacs, G., 1992. *Male homosexuality in South Africa: identity formation, culture and crisis*. Cape Town: Oxford University Press.

Jackson, P., 1988. 'Street life: the politics of carnival' *Environment and Planning D: Society and Space* 6(2), 213–227.

Jackson, P.A., 2001. 'Pre-gay, post-queer: Thai perspectives on proliferating gender/sex diversity in Asia' *Journal of Homosexuality* 40(3/4), 1–25.

Jackson, P. and Sullivan, G., 1999. *Lady boys, tom boys, rent boys: male and female homosexualities in contemporary Thailand*. New York: Haworth Press.

Jackson, S.M., 2003. 'Being and belonging: space and identity in Cape Town' *Anthropology and Humanism* 28(1), 61–84.

Jacobs, J., 1996. *Edge of empire: postcolonialism and the city*. London: Routledge.

James, C., 1996. 'Denying complexity: the dismissal and appropriation of bisexuality in queer, lesbian, and gay theory' in B. Beemyn and M. Eliason (eds.) *Queer studies: a lesbian, gay, bisexual and transgender anthology.* New York: New York University Press.

Jeppie, S., 1990. 'Popular culture and carnival in Cape Town: the 1940s and 1950s' in S. Jeppie and C. Soudien (eds.) *The struggle for District Six: past and present.* Cape Town: Buchu.

Jeppie, S., 2001. 'Reclassifications: Coloureds, Malay, Muslim' in Z. Erasmus (ed.) *Coloured by history, shaped by place.* Cape Town: Kweal Books.

Johnson, C.A., 2007. *Off the map: how HIV/AIDS programming is failing same-sex practicing people in Africa.* New York: International Gay and Lesbian Human Rights Commission.

Johnston, L., 2005. *Queering tourism: paradoxical performances of gay pride parades.* London: Routledge.

Joint Working Group, 2006. *Parliamentary Submission: Civil Union Bill.* Available from: www.pmg.org.za/docs/2006/061010jwg.pdf

Jones, J., 1996. 'The new ghetto aesthetic' in V. Berry and C. Manning-Miller (eds.) *Mediated messages and African American culture.* London: Sage.

Kalichmam, S.C. and Simbayi, L.C., 2003. 'HIV testing attitudes, AIDS stigma, and voluntary HIV counselling and testing in a black township in Cape Town, South Africa' *Sexually Transmitted Infections* 79(6), 442–447.

Kassiem, A., 2004. 'Gay nightclub admits to racial discrimination' *Cape Argus* 11 February, 1.

Kates, S.M. and Belk, R.W., 2001. 'The meaning of lesbian and gay pride day: resistance through consumption and resistance to consumption' *Journal of Contemporary Ethnography* 30(4), 392–429.

Katzen, B. and Baker, S., 1972. *Looking at Cape Town.* Cape Town: H. Timmins.

Kearns, G., 2007. 'The history of medical geography after Foucault' in J.W. Crampton and S. Elden (eds.) *Space, knowledge and power: Foucault and geography.* Aldershot: Ashgate.

Kelley, P., Pebody, R. and Scott, P., 1996. *How far will you go? A survey of London gay men's migration and mobility.* London: GMFA.

Kinnes, I., 1995. 'Reclaiming the Cape Flats: a community challenge to crime and gangsterism' *Crime and Conflict* 2, 5–8.

Knopp, L., 1992. 'Sexuality and the spatial dynamics of capitalism' *Environment and Planning D: Society and Space* 10(6), 651–669.

Knopp, L., 1994. 'Social justice, sexuality and the city' *Urban Geography* 15, 644–660.

Knopp, L., 1997. 'Gentrification and gay neighbourhood formation in New Orleans: a case study' in A. Gluckman and B. Reed (eds.) *Homo economics: capitalism, community, and lesbian and gay life.* London: Routledge.

Knopp, L., 1998. 'Sexuality and urban space: gay male identities, communities and cultures in the U.S., U.K. and Australia' in R. Fincher and J. Jacobs (eds.) *Cities of difference.* New York: Guilford.

Kobayashi, A., 2004. 'Critical "race" approaches' in J.S. Duncan, N.C. Johnson and R.H. Schein (eds.) *A companion to cultural geography.* Oxford: Blackwell.

Kolb, P., 1719. *The present state of the Cape of Good-Hope.* London: Innys and Manby.

Kramer, L., 1991. *Reports from the holocaust: the making of an AIDS activist.* Harmondsworth: Penguin.

Kramer, J.L., 1995. 'Bachelor farmers and spinsters: gay and lesbian identities and communities in rural North Dakota' in D. Bell and G. Valentine (eds.) *Mapping desire: geographies of sexualities.* London: Routledge.

Kristeva, J., 1982. *Powers of horror: an essay on abjection.* New York: Columbia University Press.

Krouse, M. and Berman, K. (eds.), 1993. *The invisible ghetto.* Johannesburg: Gay Men's Press.

Lane, P., 2005. 'South Africa's equality courts: an early assessment' Centre for the Study of Violence and Reconciliation. Available from: http://www.csvr.org.za/wits/papers/paprctp5.htm

Latimer, T.T., 2004. 'The closet' in C.J. Summers (ed.) *glbtq: an encyclopaedia of gay, lesbian, bisexual, transgender, and queer culture.* Available from: http://www.glbtq.com/social-sciences/closet.html

Le Grange, L., 1996. 'The urbanisation of District Six' in J. Greshoff (ed.) *The last days of District Six.* Cape Town: The District Six Museum.

Le May, G.H.L., 1995. *The Afrikaners: an historical perspective.* Oxford: Blackwell.

Leap, W., 2003. 'Language, belonging and (homo)sexual citizenship in Cape Town, South Africa' in W. Leap and T. Boellstorff (eds.) *Speaking in queer tongues: globalization and gay language.* Urbana: University of Illinois Press.

Leap, W., 2005. 'Finding the centre: claiming gay space in Cape Town' in M. van Zyl and M. Steyn (eds.) *Performing queer: shaping sexualities 1994–2004, volume one.* Paarl: Kwela.

Lelyveld, J., 1985. *Move your shadow: South Africa black and white.* London: Abacus.

Lester, A., 2003. 'Introduction: historical geographies of Southern Africa' *Journal of Southern African Studies* 29(3), 595–613.

Lewis, J. and Loots, F., 1995. '"Moffies en manvroue": gay and lesbian life histories in contemporary Cape Town' in M. Gevisser and E. Cameron (eds.) *Defiant desire.* London: Routledge.

Lind, C., 2005. 'Importing law, politics and sexuality' in M. van Zyl and M. Steyn (eds.) *Performing queer: shaping sexualities 1994–2004, volume one.* Paarl: Kwela.

Livingston, D., 1992. *The geographical tradition.* Oxford: Blackwell.

Livingston, J., 1990. *Paris is burning.* [Film]. Burnaby: Off White Productions Inc.

Lodge, T., 1999. *South African politics since 1994.* Cape Town: David Philip.

Lodge, T., 2002. *Politics in South Africa: from Mandela to Mbeki.* Cape Town: David Philip.

Louw, R., 2001. 'Mkhumbane and new traditions of (un)African same-sex weddings' in R. Morrell (ed.) *Changing men in Southern Africa.* London: Zed Books.

Luirink, B., 2000. *Moffies: gay life in Southern Africa.* Cape Town: Rustica Press.

Luirink, B., 2006. 'The first Pride was for men an early expression of how promising things were going to be for change in South Africa' in S. De Waal and A. Manion (eds.) *Pride: protest and celebration.* Johannesburg: Fanele.

Luongo, M., 2002. 'Rome's world Pride: making the Eternal City an international gay tourism destination' *GLQ: A Journal of Lesbian and Gay Studies* 8(1–2), 167–181.

McClintock, A., 1990. ' "No longer in a future heaven": women and nationalism in South Africa' *Transition* 51, 104–123.

McClintock, A., 1995. *Imperial leather: race, gender and sexuality in colonial contest.* London: Routledge.

McEwan, C., 2000. 'Engendering citizenship: gendered spaces of democracy in South Africa' *Political Geography* 19(5), 627–651.

McEwan, C., 2005. 'New spaces of citizenship? Rethinking gendered participation and empowerment in South Africa' *Political Geography* 24(8), 969–991.

McLean, H. and Ngcobo, L., 1995. ' "Abangibhamayo bathi ngimnandi (Those who fuck me say I'm tasty)": gay sexuality in Reef townships' in M. Gevisser and E. Cameron (eds.) *Defiant desire.* London: Routledge.

Mail and Guardian Online, 2006. 'Muslim council condemns gay-marriage judgement' Available from: http://www.mg.co.za/articlePage.aspx?articleid=258422&area=/breaking_news/breaking_news__national/

Manalansan IV, M.F., 1995. 'In the shadows of Stonewall: examining gay transnational politics and the diasporic dilemma' *GLQ: A Journal of Lesbian and Gay Studies* 2(4), 178–198.

Mapisa-Nqakula, N., 2006. 'Civil Union Bill is about equality for all in our country' *Cape Times* October 20, 9.

Martin, D., 1999. *Coon carnival: new year in Cape Town, past and present.* Cape Town: David Philip.

Massey, D., 1995. *Spatial divisons of labour: social structures and the geography of production.* 2nd edition. London: Macmillan.

Masuku, S., 2002. 'Prevention is better than cure: addressing violent crime in South Africa' *South African Crime Quarterly* (2), 5–12.

Mathabane, M., 1986. *Kaffir boy: the true story of a black youth's coming of age in Apartheid South Africa.* New York: Macmillan.

Maupin, A., 1980. *Tales of the city.* London: Corgi.

Meredith, M., 2005. *The State of Africa: a history of fifty years of independence.* London: Free Press.

Minty, Z., 2006. 'Post-apartheid public art in Cape Town: symbolic reparations and public space' *Urban Studies* 43(2), 421–440.

Mitchell, D., 2000. *Cultural geography: a critical introduction.* Oxford: Blackwell.

Mock, C.T. and Rattan, W.R., 2006. 'Gay in Cape Town, South Africa' PinkAgenda.com. Available from: http://www.glbtevents.com/travel/capetown.html

Molloy, B., 1983. 'First AIDS diagnosed in city' *Cape Times* 30 May, 1.

Moodie, T.D., 1988. 'Migrancy and male sexuality in the South African gold mines' *Journal of Southern African Studies* 14(2), 228–256.

Moodie, T.D., 2001. 'South African mine migration and the vicissitudes of male desire' in R. Morrell (ed.) *Changing men in South Africa.* Pietermaritzburg: University of Natal Press.

Moodley, K. and Adam, H., 2000. 'Race and nation in post-apartheid South Africa' *Current Sociology* 48(3), 51–69.

Morgan, T.D., 1996. 'Pages of whiteness: race, physique magazines, and the emergence of public gay culture' in B. Beemyn and M. Eliason (eds.) *Queer studies: a lesbian, gay, bisexual and transgender anthology*. London: New York University Press.

Morse, S.J. and Peele, S., 1974. '"Coloured power" or "Coloured bourgeoisie"? Political attitudes among South African Coloureds' *Public Opinion Quarterly* 38(3), 317–334.

Mosher, W.D., Chandra, A. and Jones, J., 2005. 'Sexual behaviour and selected health measures: men and women 15–44 years of age, United States, 2002. Centre for Disease Control *Advance data from vital and health statistics* 362. Available from: http://www.cdc.gov/nchs/data/ad/ad362.pdf

Mudimbe, V., 1988. *The invention of Africa: gnosis, philosophy, and the order of knowledge*. Bloomington: Indiana University Press.

Murray, S.O., 2000. *Homosexualities*. Chicago: University of Chicago Press.

Murray, S.O. and Roscoe, W. (eds.), 1997. *Islamic homosexualities: culture, history and literature*. New York: New York University Press.

Murray, S.O. and Roscoe, W., 1998. 'Southern Africa: overview' in S.O. Murray and W. Roscoe (eds.) *Boy-wives and female husbands: studies of African homosexualities*. Basingstoke: Macmillan.

Muthien, B., 2005. 'Playing on the pavement of identities' in M. van Zyl and M. Steyn (eds.) *Performing queer: shaping sexualities 1994–2004, volume one*. Paarl: Kwela.

Nast, H.J, 2002. '"Queer patriarchies, queer racisms, international" *Antipode* 34(5), 874–909.

National Centre for Social Research [Johnson, A., Fenton, K., Copas, A., McCadden, A., Carder, C., Ridgeway, G.], Royal Free and University College Medical School [Mercer, C.], University College London, Department of Primary Care and Population Sciences, Centre for Sexual Health and HIV Research [Wellings, K., Macdowall, W., Manchahal, K.], London School of Hygiene and Tropical Medicine, 2005. *National Survey of Sexual Attitudes and Lifestyles II, 2000–2001* [computer file]. Colchester: UK Data Archive.

Nero, C.I., 2005. 'Why are gay ghettos white?' in E.P. Johnson and M.G. Henderson (eds.) *Black queer studies: a critical anthology*. London: Duke University Press.

Ngubane, M., 2006. 'Redpepper shifts focus to lesbians now' *Behind the Mask* website 6 September. Available from: http://www.mask.org.za/article.php?cat=uganda&id=1315

Niang, C.I., Diagne, M., Niang, Y., Moreau, A.M., Gomis, D., Diouf, M., Seck, K., Wade, A.S., Tapsoba, P. and Castle, C., 2002. 'Meeting the sexual health needs of men who have sex with men in Senegal', *Horizons Program*. The Population Council. Available from: http://www.popcouncil.org/pdfs/horizons/msmsenegal.pdf

Nicol, J., 2005. 'Interview: "if we can't dance to it, it's not our revolution"' in N. Hoad, K. Martin and G. Reid (eds.) *Sex and politics in South Africa* Cape Town: Double Storey.

Nkoli, S., 1993. 'This strange feeling' in M. Krouse and K. Berman (eds.) *The invisible ghetto*. Johannesburg: Gay Men's Press.

Nkoli, S., 1995. 'Wardrobes: coming out as a black gay activist in South Africa' in M. Gevisser and E. Cameron (eds.) *Defiant desire*. London: Routledge.
Nkoli, S., 2006. 'Opening address at the 1990 Johannesburg Pride march' reproduced in S. De Waal and A. Manion (eds.) *Pride: protest and celebration*. Johannesburg: Fanele.
Norval, A., 1996. *Deconstructing apartheid discourse*. London: Verso.
Ntshingila, F., 2006. 'Marriage Bill flares up all and sundry' *Sunday Times* 1 October, 15.
Nuttall, S. and Coetzee, C. (eds.), 1998. *Negotiating the past: the making of memory in South Africa*. Oxford: Oxford University Press.
O'Toole, J., 1973. *Watts and Woodstock: identity and culture in the United States and South Africa*. London: Holt, Rinehart and Winston.
Onyango-Ouma, W., Birungi, H. and Geibel, S., 2005. 'Understanding the HIV/STI risks and prevention meeds of men who have sex with men in Nairobi, Kenya', *Horizons Program*. The Population Council. Available from: http://www.popcouncil.org/pdfs/horizons/msmkenya.pdf
Ostow, D.G., 2000. 'The role of drugs in the sexual lives of men who have sex with men: continuing barriers to researching this question' *AIDS and Behaviour* 4(2), 205–219.
Oswin, N., 2004. 'Towards radical geographies of complicit queer futures' *Acme: An International E-journal for Critical Geographies* 3(2), 79–86.
Oswin, N., 2005. 'Researching "gay Cape Town" finding value-added queerness' *Social and Cultural Geography* 6(4), 567–586.
Oswin, N., 2006. 'Decentering queer globalization: diffusion and the "global gay"' *Environment and Planning D: Society and Space* 24(5), 777–790.
Parker, R., 1999. *Beneath the equator: cultures of desire, male homosexuality, and emerging gay communities in Brazil*. London: Routledge.
Parnell, S. and Robinson, J., 2006. 'Development and urban policy: Johannesburg's City Development Strategy' *Urban Studies* 43(2), 337–355.
Patton, C., 1994. *Last served?: Gendering the HIV pandemic*. London: Taylor & Francis.
Patton, C. and Sánchez-Eppler, B., 2000. *Queer diasporas*. Durham, NC: Duke University Press.
Pegge, J.V., 1995. 'Living with loss in the best way we know how: AIDS and gay men in Cape Town' in M. Gevisser and E. Cameron (eds.) *Defiant desire*. London: Routledge.
Peniston, W.A., 2004. *Pederasts and others: urban culture and sexual identity in nineteenth-century Paris*. New York: Harrington Park.
Phillips, O., 2005. 'Ten white men thirteen years later: the changing constitution of masculinities in South Africa, 1987–2000' in M. van Zyl and M. Steyn (eds.) *Performing queer: shaping sexualities 1994–2004, volume one*. Paarl: Kwela.
Phillips, R., 2004. 'Sexuality' in J.S. Duncan, N.C. Johnson and R.H. Schein (eds.) *A companion to cultural geography*. Oxford: Blackwell.
Phillips, R., West, D. and Shuttleton, D. (eds.), 2000. *De-centring sexualities: politics and representations beyond the metropolis*. London: Routledge.
Philo, C., 2000. 'More words, more worlds: reflections on the "cultural turn" and social geography' in I. Cook, D. Crouch, S. Naylor and J. Ryan (eds.) *Cultural turns/geographical turns: perspectives on cultural geography*. Harlow: Prentice Hall.

Pinnock, D., 1997. *Gangs, rituals and rites of passage*. Cape Town: Sun Press and Institute of Criminology.

Platzky, L. and Walker, C., 1985. *The surplus people: forced removals in South Africa*. Johannesburg: Ravan.

Popke, E.J., 2000. 'Violence and memory in the reconstruction of South Africa's Cato Manor' *Growth and Change* 31(2), 235–254.

Potgieter, C., 2006. 'Masculine bodies, feminine symbols: challenging gendered identities or compulsory femininity' *Agenda* 67, 116–127.

Pourtavaf, L., 2004. 'The pirates leave the village: queering new spaces' *Journal for the Arts, Sciences, and Technology* 2(2), 91–96.

Power, L., 1996. 'Forbidden fruit' in M. Simpson (ed.) *Anti-gay*. London: Freedom Editions.

Prieur, A., 1998. *Mema's house, Mexico City: on transvestites, queens and machos*. Chicago: University of Chicago Press.

Puar, J., 2002. 'A transnational feminist critique of queer tourism' *Antipode* 34(5), 935–946.

Quilley, S., 1997. 'Constructing Manchester's "new urban village": gay space in the entrepreneurial city' in G.B. Ingram, A. Bouthillette and Y. Retter (eds.) *Queers in space: communities, public spaces, sites of resistance*. Seattle: Bay.

Quintal, A., 2006. 'Parliament tiptoes around issue of same-sex marriage as court deadline approaches' *Cape Times* 2 August, 3.

Quiroga, J., 2000. *Tropics of desire: interventions from queer Latin America*. New York: New York University Press.

Raimondo, M., 2003. ' "Corralling the virus": migratory sexualities and the "spread of AIDS" in the US media' *Environment and Planning D: Society and Space* 21(4), 389–407.

Rand Daily Mail, 1966. 'Five pay "men only" party fines' *Rand Daily Mail* 24 January, 1.

Rankhotha, S.C., 2005. 'How black men involved in same-sex relationships construct their masculinities' in M. van Zyl and M. Steyn (eds.) *Performing queer: shaping sexualities 1994–2004, volume one* Paarl: Kwela.

Reddy, T., 2001. 'The politics of naming: the constitution of coloured subjects in South Africa' in Z. Erasmus (ed.) *Coloured by history, shaped by place*. Cape Town: Kweal Books.

Reddy, V., 2002. 'Black and gay: perceptions and interventions around HIV in Durban' *Agenda: Empowering Women for Gender Equality* 53, 89–95.

Reddy, V. and Louw, R., 2002. 'Black and gay: perceptions and interventions around HIV in Durban' *Agenda* 53, 89–95.

Redpath, J., 2001a. 'The Hydra phenomenon, rural sitting ducks, and other recent trends around organised crime in the Western Cape: including a brief comparison with trends in Gauteng' Institute for Human Rights and Criminal Justice Studies, Technikon South Africa. Presented at the 2nd World Conference: Modern Criminal Investigation, Organised Crime and Human Rights, International Convention Centre, Durban, South Africa, 3–7 December 2001. Available from: http://www.tsa.ac.za/corp/research/papers/redpath2001hydra.doc

Redpath, J., 2001b. 'The bigger picture: the gang landscape in the Western Cape' *Indicator South Africa* 18(1), 34–40.

Reid, G., 2006. 'How to become a "real gay": identity and terminology in Ermelo, Mpumalanga' *Agenda: Empowering Women for Gender Equality* 67, 137–145.

Reid-Pharr, R., 2002. 'Extending queer theory to race and ethnicity' *Chronicle of Higher Education* 48, B7–B9.

Retief, G., 1995. 'Keeping Sodom out of the Laager: state repression of homosexuality in apartheid South Africa' in M. Gevisser and E. Cameron (eds.) *Defiant desire*. London: Routledge.

Rive, R., 1986. *Buckingham Palace: District Six*. Cape Town: David Philip.

Rive, R., 1990. 'District Six: fact and fiction' in S. Jeppie and C. Soudien (eds.) *The struggle for District Six: past and present*. Cape Town: Buchu.

Robinson, J., 1990. 'A perfect system of control? State power and "Native Locations" in South Africa' *Environment and Planning D: Society and Space* 8(2), 135–162.

Robinson, J., 1996. *The power of apartheid: state, power and space in South African cities*. Oxford: Butterworth-Heinemann.

Robinson, J., 2004. 'The urban basis for emancipation: spatial theory and the city in South African politics' in L. Lees (ed.) *The emancipatory city? Paradoxes and possibilities*. London: Sage.

Robinson, J., 2006. *Ordinary cities: between modernity and development*. London: Routledge.

Ross, M.B., 2005. 'Beyond the closet as a raceless paradigm' in E.P. Johnson and M.G. Henderson (eds.) *Black queer studies: a critical anthology*. London: Duke University Press.

Ross, R., 1999. *The concise history of South Africa*. Cambridge: Cambridge University Press.

Rothenberg, T., 1995. ' "And she told two friends": lesbians creating urban social space' in D. Bell and G. Valentine (eds.) *Mapping desire: geographies of sexualities*. London: Routledge.

Rundle, D., 2006. 'Our biggest concern was that there would only be twenty or fifty people . . .' in S. De Waal and A. Manion (eds.) *Pride: protest and celebration*. Johannesburg: Fanele.

Rydström, J., 2005. 'Solidarity – with whom?' in N. Hoad, K. Martin and G. Reid (eds.) *Sex and politics in South Africa*. Cape Town: Double Storey.

Saad, T. and Carter, P., 2005. 'The entwined spaces of "race", sex and gender' *Gender, Place and Culture* 12(1), 49–51.

Saff, G., 1994. 'The changing face of the South African city: from urban apartheid to the deracialisation of space' *International Journal of Urban and Regional Restructuring* 18(3), 337–391.

Saff, G., 1998. *Changing Cape Town: urban dynamics, policy and planning during the political transition in South Africa*. Lanham: University Press of America.

Saff, G., 2001. 'Exclusionary discourses towards squatters in suburban Cape Town' *Ecumene* 8(1), 87–101.

Sam, T.C., 1995. 'Five women: black lesbian life on the Reef' in M. Gevisser and E. Cameron (eds.) *Defiant desire*. London: Routledge.

Sanger, N. and Clowes, L., 2006. 'Marginalised and demonised: lesbians and equality? Perceptions of people in a local Western Cape community' *Agenda* 67, 36–47.

Saunders, C., 1984. 'The creation of Ndabeni: urban segregation and African resistance in Cape Town' *Studies in the History of Cape Town* 1, 165–176.

Schönteich, M. and Louw, A., 2001. 'Crime in South Africa: a country and cities profile' Crime and Justice Programme, Institute for Security Studies. Occasional Paper 49. Available from: http://www.iss.co.za/Pubs/Papers/49/Paper49.html

Schreiner, O., 1923. *Thoughts on South Africa*. London: T. Fisher Unwin.

Schulmann, S., 1998. *Stagestruck: theatre, AIDS and the marketing of gay America*. Durham, NC: Duke University Press.

Sedgwick, E.K., 1990. *Epistemology of the closet*. Berkeley: University of California Press.

Seekings, J. and Nattrass, N., 2005. *Class, race and inequality in South Africa*. New Haven, CT: Yale University Press.

Seidman, S., 1993. 'Identity and politics in a "postmodern" gay culture: some historical and conceptual notes' in M. Warner (ed.) *Fear of a queer planet: queer politics and social theory*. Minneapolis: University of Minnesota Press.

Seidman, S., 1998. 'Are we all in the closet? Notes towards a sociological and cultural turn in queer theory' *European Journal of Cultural Studies* 1(2), 177–192.

Seidman, S., 2002. *Beyond the closet: the transformation of gay and lesbian life*. London: Routledge.

Seymour, J., 2003. 'Energising the KwaZulu-Natal gay and lesbian tourism market: Tourism KwaZulu-Natal's initial gay and lesbian tourism strategy', Zulu Kingdom. Available from: http://www.kzn.org.za/kzn/investors/186.xml

Sharpe, T., 1977. *Indecent exposure*. London: Secker and Warburg.

Shisana, O. and Simbayi, L., 2002. *Nelson Mandela/HSRC study of HIV/AIDS: South African national HIV prevalence, behaviour risks and mass media*. Cape Town: Human Sciences Research Council.

Sibuyi, M., 1993. 'Tinoncana etimayinini: the wives of the mine' in M. Krouse and K. Berman (eds.) *The invisible ghetto*. Johannesburg: Gay Men's Press.

Simbayi, L.C., Kalichman, S.C., Strebel, A., Cloete, A., Henda, N. and Mqeketo, A., 2007. 'Disclosure of HIV status to sex partners and sexual risk behaviours among HIV-positive men and women, Cape Town, South Africa' *Sexually Transmitted Infections* 83(1), 29–34.

Simpson, M., 1996. 'Preface' in M. Simpson (ed.) *Anti-gay*. London: Freedom Press.

Sinfield, A., 1998. *Gay and after*. London: Serpent's Tail.

Smith, A., 2005. 'Where was I in the eighties?' in N. Hoad, K. Martin and G. Reid (eds.) *Sex and politics in South Africa*. Cape Town: Double Storey.

Smith, S., 1989. 'Race and racism' *Urban Geography* 10(6), 593–606.

Somerville, S., 1996. 'Scientific racism and the homosexual body' in B. Beemyn and M. Eliason (eds.) *Queer studies: a lesbian, gay, bisexual and transgender anthology*. New York: New York University Press.

Somerville, S., 2000. *Queering the color line: race and the invention of homosexuality in American culture*. Durham, NC: Duke University Press.

Sonn, J., 1996. 'Breaking down borders' in W. James, D. Caliguire and K. Cullinan (eds.) *Now that we are free: coloured communities in a democratic South Africa*. London: Lynne Rienner.

Sontag, S., 1967. 'Notes on camp' in *Against interpretation*. London: Eyre and Spottiswoode.

Soudien, C., 1990. "District Six: from protest to protest", in S. Jeppie and C. Soudien (eds.) *The struggle for District Six: past and present*. Cape Town: Buchu.

Soudien, C., 2001. 'District Six and its uses in the discussion about non-racialism' in Z. Erasmus (ed.) *Coloured by history, shaped by place*. Cape Town: Kweal Books.

Southall, R., 2004. 'The ANC and black capitalism in South Africa' *Review of African Political Economy* 100, 313–328.

Spinks, C., 2001. 'A new apartheid? Urban spatiality, (fear of) crime, and segregation in Cape Town, South Africa' Development Studies Institute Working Paper Series No. 01–20. Available from: www.lse.ac.uk/collections/DESTIN/pdf/WP20.pdf

Spivak, G., 1990. *The post-colonial critics: interviews, strategies, dialogues*. London: Routledge.

Spruill, J., 2004. 'Ad/dressing the nation: drag and authenticity in post-apartheid South Africa' *Journal of Homosexuality* 46(3), 91–111.

Spurlin, W.J., 2001. 'Broadening postcolonial studies/decolonising queer studies: emerging "queer" identities and cultures in Southern Africa' in J.C. Hawley (ed.) *Postcolonial, queer*. New York: State University of New York.

Steinberg, J., 2004. *The number: one man's search for identity in the Cape underworld and prison gangs*. Johannesburg: Jonathan Ball.

Stoler, A.L., 1995. *Race and the education of desire: Foucault's History of Sexuality and the colonial order of things*. Durham, NC: Duke University Press.

Stychin, C.F., 2000. 'A stranger to its laws: sovereign bodies, global sexualities, and transnational citizens' *Journal of Law and Society* 27(4), 601–625.

Stychin, C.F., 2006. '"Las Vegas is now where we are": queer readings of the Civil Partnership Act' *Political Geography* 25(8), 899–920.

Sunday Express, 1967. 'They often meet in bars' *Sunday Express* 12 March, 23.

Sunday Times, 1983. 'Gay plague: more victims?' *Sunday Times* 9 January, 3.

Swarr, A.L., 2004. 'Moffies, artists and queens: race and the production of South African gay male drag' *Journal of Homosexuality* 46(3/4), 73–89.

Swarr, A.L. and Nagar, R., 2003. 'Dismantling assumptions: interrogating "lesbian" struggles for identity and survival in India and South Africa' *Signs: Journal of Women in Culture and Society* 29(2), 491–516.

Tan, C.K., 2001. 'Transcending sexual nationalism and colonialism: cultural hybridisation or process of sexual politics in '90s Taiwan' in J.C. Hawley (ed.) *Postcolonial, queer*. New York: State University of New York.

Tatchell, P., 2005. 'The moment the ANC embraced gay rights' in N. Hoad, K. Martin and G. Reid (eds.) *Sex and politics in South Africa*. Cape Town: Double Storey.

The Star, 1966. 'Vice squad find 350 men in one house' *The Star* 22 January, 1.

Thomasson, E., 1998. 'Cape Town woos pink rand' *Q-Online* December 28. Available from: http://www.q.co.za/news/1998/9812/981230-gaycape.htm

Thompson, L., 1971. 'Great Britain and the Afrikaner republics' in M. Wilson and L. Thompson (eds.) *The Oxford history of South Africa, Vol. II: 1870–1966*. Oxford: Oxford University Press.

Thompson, L., 2001. *A history of South Africa*, 3rd edition. New Haven, CT: Yale University Press.

Till, K.E., 2004. 'Political landscapes' in J.S. Duncan, N.C. Johnson and R.H. Schein (eds.) *A companion to cultural geography*. Oxford: Blackwell.

Toms, I., 1995. 'Ivan Toms is a fairy?' in M. Gevisser and E. Cameron (eds.) *Defiant desire*. London: Routledge.

Treichler, P.A., 1999. *How to have theory in an epidemic: cultural chronicles of AIDS*. Durham, NC: Duke University Press.

Trengove Jones, T., 2000. 'A matter of Pride and prejudice' *Sunday Times* 5 November, 21.

Triangle Project, 2007. 'History of the organisation', Triangle Project website. Accessed 21 August 2007. Available from http://www.triangle.org.za/index.php?pageno=22

Tucker, S., 1997. *The Queer Question: Essays on Desire and Democracy*. Boston, MA: South End Press.

Turok, I., 2001. 'Persistent polarisation post-apartheid? Process towards urban integration in Cape Town' *Urban Studies* 38(13), 2349–2377.

Urquhart, C., 2006. 'Protests fail to stop Jerusalem gay pride event' *The Guardian Online*. 11 November. Avalable from: http://www.guardian.co.uk/israel/Story/0,,1945420,00.html

Valentine, G., 1993. '(Hetero)sexing space: lesbian perceptions and experiences of everyday space' *Environment and Planning D: Society and Space* 11(4), 395–413.

Valentine, G., 1995. 'Out and about – geographies of lesbian landscapes' *International Journal of Urban and Regional Research* 19(1), 96–112.

Valentine, G., 2005. 'Tell me about . . .: using interviews as a research methodology' in R. Flowerdew and D. Martin (eds.) *Methods in human geography: a guide for students doing research projects*, 2nd edition. London: Pearson.

Valocchi, S., 1999. 'The class-inflected nature of gay identity' *Social Problems* 46(2), 207–224.

van der Merwe, A.C., 2006. *Moffie: a novel*. Hermanus: Penstock.

van Onselen, C., 1985. 'Crime and total institutions in the making of modern South Africa – The life of Mathebula Nongoloza' *History Workshop Journal* 19, 62–81.

van Zyl, M., 2005. 'Cape Town activists remember sexuality struggle' in N. Hoad, K. Martin and G. Reid (eds.) *Sex and Politics in South Africa*. Cape Town: Double Storey.

van Zyl, M. and Steyn, M. (eds.), 2005. *Performing queer: shaping sexualities 1994–2004, volume one*. Paarl: Kwela.

Verlang, B.G. and Bedford, B., 2006. *Spartacus international gay guide*, 35th edition. Berlin: Bruno Gmünder Verlag.

Vetten, L. and Bhana, K., 2001. *Violence, vengeance and gender: a preliminary investigation into the links between violence against women and HIV/AIDS in South Africa*. Johannesburg: Centre for the Study of Violence and Reconciliation.

Viljoen, J., 1994. 'A covenant is written out of the history books' in P.W. Romero (ed.) *Profiles in diversity – women in the New South Africa*. East Lansing: Michigan State University Press.

Vimbela, V. and Olivier, M., 1995. 'Climbing on her shoulders: an interview with Umtata's "first lesbian"' in M. Gevisser and E. Cameron (eds.) *Defiant desire*. London: Routledge.

Visser, G., 2001. 'Social justice, integrated development planning and post-apartheid urban reconstruction' *Urban Studies* 38(10), 1673–1699.

Visser, G., 2002. 'Gay tourism in South Africa: issues from the Cape Town experience' *Urban Forum* 13(1), 85–94.

Visser, G., 2003a. 'Gay men, tourism and urban space: reflections on Africa's "gay capital"' *Tourism Geographies* 5(2), 168–189.

Visser, G., 2003b. 'Gay men, leisure space and South African cities: the case of Cape Town' *Geoforum* 34(1), 123–137.

Visser, G., 2004. 'Second homes and local development: issues arising from Cape Town's De Waterkant' *GeoJournal* 60(3), 259–271.

Waitt, G., 2005. 'Sexual citizenship in Latvia: geographies of the Latvian closet' *Social and Cultural Geography* 6(2), 161–181.

Wallace, K., 1967. 'Spotlight on S.A.'s growing social problem: one in ten may be deviant' *Sunday Express* 12 March, 23.

Wallace, M.O., 2002. *Constructing the black masculine: identity and ideality in African American men's literature and culture*. Durham, NC: Duke University Press.

Warner, M. (ed.), 1993. *Fear of a queer planet: queer politics and social theory*. Minneapolis: University of Minnesota Press.

Warner, M., 2000. *The trouble with normal: sex, politics and the ethics of queer life*. Cambridge, MA: Harvard University Press.

Watney, S., 1994. *Practices of freedom: selected writings on HIV/AIDS*. London: Rivers Oram.

Watney, S., 1996. ' "Risk groups" or "risk behaviours"' in J. Mann and D. Tarantola (eds.) *AIDS in the world II*. Oxford: Oxford University Press.

Watney, S., 2000. *Imagining hope: AIDS and gay identity*. London: Routledge.

Waxa, C., 2006. 'Unequal before the law' Photograph. *Cape Times* 17 October, 4.

Weeks, J., 1990. *Coming out: homosexual politics in Britain, from the nineteenth century to the present*, revised edition. London: Quartet Books.

Weir, J., 1996. 'Going in' in M. Simpson (ed.) *Anti-Gay*. London: Freedom Press.

Wellings, K., Field, J., Johnson, A.M., Wadsworth, J. and Bradshaw, S., 1994. *Sexual behaviour in Britain: the National Survey of Sexual Attitudes and Lifestyles*. Harmondsworth: Penguin.

Wells, H. and Polders, L., 2006. 'Anti-gay hate crimes in South Africa: prevalence, reporting practices and experiences of the police' *Agenda* 67, 20–28.

Welsh, F., 1998. *A history of South Africa*. London: HarperCollins.

Western, J., 1981. *Outcast Cape Town*. Minneapolis: University of Minnesota Press.

Western, J., 2001. 'Africa is coming to the Cape' *The Geographical Review* 91(4), 615–640.

Weston, K., 1995. 'Get thee to the big city: sexual imaginary and the great gay migration' *GLQ: A Journal of Lesbian and Gay Studies* 2(2), 253–277.

White, E., 1980. *States of desire: travels in gay America*. New York: Dutton.

White, E., 1997. *The farewell symphony*. London: Chatto & Windus.

Whiteside, A. and Sunter, C., 2000. *AIDS: The challenge for South Africa*. Cape Town: Human and Rousseau.

Wilchins, R., 2004. *Queer theory, gender theory: an instant primer*. London: Alyson.

Willoughby, G., 2002. *Archangels*. Howick: Brevitas.

Wolff, L., 1994. *Inventing Eastern Europe: the map of civilisation on the mind of the Enlightenment*. Stanford, CA: Stanford University Press.

Worden, N., 1985. *Slavery in Dutch South Africa*. Cambridge: Cambridge University Press.

Worden, N., 2000. *The making of modern South Africa: conquest, segregation and apartheid*, 3rd edition. Oxford: Blackwell.

Index

Printed and bound by CPI Group (UK) Ltd, Croydon, CR0 4YY

09/06/2025

14686114-0002